7ᵗʰ Oct

**26677  Isaac Clark** of ___
14/ —  Farmer, ———
         Wearing Apparel, printed
Mich 1814  Dwellinghouse only Situate as aforesaid Brick
Newman   tiled One hundred fifty pounds,                        150
         Stock & Utensils in all or any of his barns, Stables
17/6     Granaries other farm Offices and Rickyards
         or other parts of his farm only near five
         hundred & fifty pounds,                                 550
         NB. This Office to be free from loss on such           £700
         hay or Corn as shall be destroyed or dama
         ged by natural heat, ———
              C. Pole.   W. Moffat.    W C Shaw

                              Dᵒ

**26678  Alexander Canning** of Markᵗ
18/9     Lavington in Wilts plumber & Glazier.
         On his new dwellinghouse only Situate as
Mich 1814  aforesaid timber & tiled three hundred Pdˢ           300
Newman   Household goods, wearing Apparel, printed
         books and plate therein only Sixty Pds                  60
12/6     Stock & Utensils therein only One hundred
         & forty Pounds,                                         140
                                                               £500
              C. Pole   W. Moffat   W C Shaw
                              Dᵒ

**26679  Messrˢ Woods & Bradshaw**
5. 5. —  of the Town of Lancaster Ironmongers &
         Grocers           On their new Shop &
ᵗ 1814   Warehouse over on the East side of Sᵗ Nicholas
         Street in said Town Stone Slated One thousand Pdˢ     1000
Henderson Stock & Utensils hazardous Goods included
         therein only two thousand five hundred Pdˢ            2500
7/6                                                           £3,500
              C. Pole    W. Moffat    W C Shaw

# The historian and the business of insurance

OLIVER M. WESTALL
*editor*

# The historian and the business of insurance

MANCHESTER UNIVERSITY PRESS

Copyright © Manchester University Press 1984

Whilst copyright in the volume as a whole is vested in Manchester University Press, copyright in the individual papers rests with their respective authors, and no chapter may be reproduced in part or in whole without the express permission in writing of both author and publisher.

Published by
Manchester University Press
Oxford Road, Manchester M13 9PL, U.K.
51 Washington Street, Dover, N.H. 03820, U.S.A.

*British Library cataloguing in publication data*

The historian and the business of insurance.
1. Insurance—Great Britian—History
I. Westall, O.M.
368'.0941     HG8597
ISBN 0-7190-0998-7

*Library of Congress cataloging in publication data*
Main entry under title:
The historian and the business of insurance.
  Includes bibliographical references and index.
  1. Insurance—Great Britain—History—Addresses, essays, lectures. 2. Insurance, Fire—Great Britain—History—Addresses, essays, lectures. 3. Insurance, Life—Great Britain—History—Addresses, essays, lectures. 4. Insurance—History—Research—Addresses, essays, lectures. I. Westall, Oliver M.
HG8597.H57  1984      368'.941      83-19939
ISBN 0-7190-0998-7

Printed in Great Britain by
Butler & Tanner Ltd, Frome and London

# Contents

| | | |
|---|---|---|
| Foreword | *page* | vi |
| Insurance in British history<br>Barry Supple  *Christ's College, Cambridge* | | 1 |
| The practice of insurance against fire, 1750–1840, and historical research<br>D. T. Jenkins  *University of York* | | 9 |
| The Norwich Union and the British fire insurance market in the early nineteenth century<br>Roger Ryan  *Southport College of Arts and Technology* | | 39 |
| The Indemnity in the London marine insurance market, 1824–50<br>Sarah Palmer  *Queen Mary College, London* | | 74 |
| The record of the Standard Life Assurance Company in the life insurance market of the United Kingdom, 1850–64<br>J. H. Treble  *University of Strathclyde* | | 95 |
| Competition and structural change in the Buenos Aires fire insurance market: the local board of agents, 1875–1921<br>Charles A. Jones  *University of Warwick* | | 114 |
| David and Goliath: the Fire Offices Committee and non-tariff competition, 1898–1907<br>Oliver M. Westall  *University of Lancaster* | | 130 |
| Life assurance in war and depression: the Standard Life Assurance Company and its environment, 1914–39<br>John Butt  *University of Strathclyde* | | 155 |
| Hogg Robinson: the rise of a Lloyd's broker<br>Stanley D. Chapman  *University of Nottingham* | | 173 |
| Index | | 190 |

# Foreword

There can be little doubt of the significance of the history of insurance for the student of British economic development. The service it has provided has facilitated the management of risk in trade, industry and family life. While no serious attempt has been made to measure this, few would dispute that it has encouraged investment and initiative. Less directly, insurance institutions have stimulated saving and accumulated funds to an extent that has affected the level and direction of national investment. The efficiency of British insurers developed an enormous overseas business, earning underwriting revenues and income from large foreign investments. In all these ways, outlined in Professor Supple's introduction, insurance has played an important role in British economic development.

In another way, the involvement of insurance in so many aspects of the economy has meant that its history has reflected the evolution of business and social life in a most intimate and revealing way. To describe the main divisions of the business — marine, fire, life and accident insurance — is to emphasise how they interpenetrate the central themes of economic history. Foreign trade, capital formation, social security, transport systems, the consumer-durable industries; all these, and more, can be indirectly, yet often very precisely, traced and examined, through the growth in their associated insurance markets, and, above all, as Dr Jenkins illustrates, through the systematic and often comprehensive documentation insurance has generated.

These are both important themes, but they do not form the main focus of this collection, which is directed towards the business history of insurance. It is sometimes assumed that the special characteristics of the business are sufficiently esoteric to separate it from the main stream of business history. Of course, as with any industry, insurance has its own techniques that can be pursued for their own sake as an equivalent to the antiquarian approach to industrial technology which separates it from its environment. While an understanding of insurance methods is necessary, this collection of studies has been compiled on the assumption that it is their economic significance that is important, and that, once appreciated, they form a framework within which the central concerns of modern business history, of competition, cooperation and integration, can be pursued.

It will not be surprising if the editor of such a collection risks a larger claim: that insurance history provides an especially fruitful laboratory for exploring these concerns. The business was marked by the early development of relatively sophisticated forms of organisation. Professor Supple here, and in his other work, has emphasised the need to develop corporate and co-operative arrangements from the beginning of the eighteenth century in order to create sufficient confidence in policy contracts for a successful market to develop. Co-operation also took the shape of collusive arrangements of a precocious scope and sophistication from the late eighteenth century. Forward integration took place in the nineteenth century as the previously loosely organised agency system was tightened up, and eventually through the introduction of branch office organisations. This encouraged the horizontal integration of fire and life insurance to take advantage of joint marketing arrangements. Company organisation developed more slowly in marine insurance, yet in the years surrounding the First World War it was drawn, along with the new accident business, into large multi-market 'composite' companies. Integration and corporate growth increased market power and strengthened collusive tendencies, but this did not eliminate competition between the new large companies. It simply shifted its emphasis away from the price the consumer paid to such areas as the proliferation of branch offices, the introduction of new types of policy and the range of cover available.

Yet these organisational developments did not permeate the industry entirely. Unlike many of the industries where similar processes took place, albeit at a later date, all the non-market organisational forms were continually tested and challenged by competition from simpler, smaller, less integrated insurers. In the early nineteenth century the supremacy of the London fire corporations was eroded by small and often provincial offices. In the late nineteenth century the close co-operation between fire offices was always subjected to competitive discipline. The market control established by forward integration into branch office organisations was matched by the evolution of independent brokers. In the marine market corporate forms made slow progress in competition with the more individualistic approach of Lloyd's. Indeed, one of the more striking developments in twentieth-century insurance has been the progress of Lloyd's in non-marine markets.

This collection cannot cover all these themes. It was not designed as a systematic account for that would have ironed out the detail and variety of approach offered by each contributor. Yet most of them are touched on in some way. Though it is not the former's principal purpose, Dr Jenkins and Roger Ryan combine to provide a clear picture of the rise of the provincial offices. Ryan's account of the early years of the Norwich Union also penetrates the problems of the perennially vigorous mutual form of insurance, whereby policy-holders co-operated to spread insurable risk among themselves. Dr Palmer reproduces this theme in the context of marine insurance. Her account of the Indemnity, an early company operating in this market, shows its close links with the traditional hull clubs, mutual insurance associations of shipowners. Yet she shows how little the corporate form had to offer the marine market in competition with Lloyd's, at least in the first half of the nineteenth century.

Dr Chapman gives us a picture of the bustling energy which lay behind the success of that institution. Drawing strength from the easy entry and family connections which ensured a ready supply of entrepreneurial vigour, its brokers were eager to exploit market opportunities. In the nineteenth century they used their international connections to benefit in trade. In the twentieth, they diversified into most branches of insurance. Their flexibility and economy of operation gave them a powerful competitive position. This success in so many markets eventually necessitated a range of specialist skills that could only be supported by large concerns with more complex forms of organisation, and Dr Chapman traces their evolution and the strains this sometimes imposed.

The editor and Dr Jones, in separate contributions, compare formal collusion in the home and foreign fire insurance markets. While they outline the administrative means by which this was attempted, both are more concerned to understand the environment from which collusion emerged and which determined its success. The editor investigates the market power of the large fire offices and the competitive response it provoked through the growth of such new institutional arrangements as the large independent brokers and the entry of Lloyd's into the fire market. Dr Jones probes the difficulties of exploiting foreign markets. British companies' success led to discriminating legislation which made competition with local offices more difficult. Effective control was weakened by the local agency system. By the early twentieth century these problems were leading to a special form of integration: the direct control of indigenous companies.

The emphasis placed on marketing organisation in the fire market reflected the difficulty or ineffectiveness of relying entirely upon premium rate adjustments as a competitive device in an oligopolistic environment. Dr Treble and Professor Butt show that similar problems existed in life assurance. Their essays demonstrate the reliance that had to be placed on efficient sales organisations, policy development and innovation if corporate growth was to be achieved. In this they illustrate the micro-economic foundations of the continued expansion of life business. The increased participation of policy-holders in investment success, offered by successive policy improvements, transformed its service from that of simple protection to that of a major savings medium. Professor Butt follows this process into the inter-war years and is thus able to examine the origins of the major impetus provided by the growth of pensions business.

These essays illustrate the range and complexity of issues in the business development of the insurance industry. In doing so they contribute to a wider discussion than their own main focus, and bring the discussion back to our starting point. The expansion of insurance and the value of its social contribution have been based on its capacity to develop efficient forms of market organisation and to innovate creatively. While it is not the whole story, this capacity can be most satisfactorily understood in terms of the response of particular types of business institution to specific market structures — the theme which runs through the chapters of this book. The business history of insurance is central to the important role Professor Supple describes it playing in social and economic history.

Finally, the second wider concern, that of the use of insurance to illuminate other areas of history, is equally dependent on the business process, which has determined the availability and quality of material available. Dr Jenkins illustrates this by introducing the archives likely to interest the largest number of historians — the early policy registers of the Sun and the Royal Exchange Assurance. His critical appreciation of their nature and value is at once a practical guide and a contribution to the history of insurance practice and organisation.

O.M.W.

# Acknowledgements

The idea of publishing a collection of studies on insurance history originated in discussions between the editor and the Insurance History Committee of the Chartered Insurance Institute. I should like to thank its members, particularly the then Secretary, James Heaney, for their enthusiastic encouragement of the project. Their hope is that, by demonstrating the variety, interest and importance of the subject, the volume will encourage more work to be carried out on the many archives now available. Through the good offices of the Chartered Insurance Institute, publication has been facilitated by a generous grant from the British Insurance Association.

O.M.W.

BARRY SUPPLE

# Insurance in British history

Considered as an economic and social activity, insurance is an ambiguous phenomenon. It originated as a means of guarding against the most basic and individual of risks (the loss of a ship or its cargo, the outbreak of fire in domestic properties, premature death), and has matured into a set of complex arrangements facilitating economic transactions and harmonious social existence throughout sophisticated societies. It combines elements of gambling and of certainty — speculative hazard and the reduction or even elimination of chance by using the predictability of 'random' occurrences in large numbers of instances. Appealing above all to the desire for stability and predictability, the business of insurance has evolved through competition and the vigorous exploration of novelty, as well as by some of the most effective collusive devices in modern business history. The act of insurance is based on the mutual pooling of resources and hazards, but has flowered through proprietary profit-making as well as (occasionally) mutual organisations and even (over the last few decades) public provision. Moreover, the very word 'insurance' implies a unity, or at least consistency, between activities which, from an *economic* standpoint, are quite disparate in character. Admittedly, the principal types of insurance (marine, fire, life, accident and theft in their various forms, employer's liability) all involve the same basic principle: the provision against individual loss by the pooling of funds (premiums) by those at risk (the insured). Yet the fact remains that, from the perspective of the insurers or of the economic role of the act of insurance, such transactions have little more in common than, say, the respective purchase of clothing, furniture, gardening implements and food. Why, nevertheless, it is both customary and useful to consider 'insurance' as a single economic phenomenon is a pertinent point of departure in any general appraisal of its history.

The answer to the implicit question is, of course, that the variegated aspects of the business of insurance are united by their characteristics *as* business and as commercial techniques — by the accepting of sufficient risks to reduce the chance of concentrated loss; by the means of gathering business and profiting from the holding of funds; by the comparability of the administrative structures used for the marketing of most types of underwriting; by the frequent (although not invariable) efficiency derived from combining different sorts of insurance within a single 'composite' firm. In effect, the *economic* unity of insurance exists largely on the side of supply, and its coherence within economic history is defined by its institutional characteristics as a business. It is, therefore, no accident that the historical interest in insurance over the last two decades has coincided with the renewed concern with business history. For although (as Dr Jenkins indicates in his essay) the first extensive use of insurance records in the 1960s was as a source of information on other sorts of economic activity, and notably capital accumulation in the textile industry, insurance history itself has been primarily an adjunct of business, or frequently company, history.

Indeed, as most of the following chapters demonstrate, the basic structure of insurance history (and to some extent even the use of insurance archives to shed light on other aspects of the past) has been fashioned by its business records. And this is largely a direct and logical consequence of the historical nature of insurance itself. For, in contrast to the purchase of most other goods and services, 'payment' for insurance is prospective rather than instantaneous or retrospective. Whether the 'customer' envisages the premium as a form of investment, ultimately to be returned with interest (as is the case with most modern life insurance or pension contracts) or as a contribution to a pool from which he may draw a benefit if the need arises in the future, he is peculiarly dependent on the stability and longevity of the institution and funds providing the service. For insurance to flourish it was therefore necessary to ensure a degree of continuity and temporal stability beyond those which an isolated individual could guarantee. Even in the case of marine insurance, with a long tradition of individual or non-corporate underwriting, this was true. The need for long-run security was mitigated by the convention of insuring for specific journeys or relatively short periods, and the market was sustained by the early evolution of an elaborate system of formal and informal safeguards – by the network of confidence-inspiring institutional procedures and arrangements known as Lloyd's. And more generally, insurance contracts, other than those in marine underwriting, came quite early to depend on corporations rather than on individuals. Nor was this a matter of psychological reassurance alone. There were potential advantages in moderately large-scale operations in an area of business dealing in risks and probabilities and investment; in the importance of catering to and exciting demand; and in the necessity for complex record-keeping, effective routines and extensive organisational networks. These all helped ensure that the provision of insurance was a corporate business (whether profit-making or mutual), and that its activities were registered in well structured activities which were retained over decades and even centuries.

To this extent, therefore, companies were the building blocks of the progress of insurance. (Indeed, when commercial law made it difficult to create orthodox companies in the eighteenth and early nineteenth centuries, unorthodox but effective legal devices were used to satisfy the corporate prerequisites of insurance growth.) Nevertheless, as with all historical research, the contents and structures of archives may easily distort the study of insurance history. On the one hand, it can divert attention away from aspects of the business of insurance which were not directly embodied in corporate institutions or the relationships between them. This no doubt explains why so little is known about the highly individualistic business of marine underwriting, in spite of its supreme importance within the insurance 'industry' up to the late nineteenth century. By the same token, those aspects of economic organisation, such as insurance brokerage, which remained essentially private have also been relatively neglected — although, as Dr Chapman's essay suggests, that topic is now receiving more attention. On the other hand, and perhaps even more important, the corporate-business orientation of so much insurance history has led to an uneven emphasis as between supply and demand. We still know too little about the evolution of the insurance 'habit', the attitudes towards risk, the economic and social incentives to insurance, the extent to which the market for insurance had to be created or was itself a function of economic growth. Nevertheless, it is far too early in the history of the relatively new *genre* of systematic insurance history to begin to complain about the relative neglect of various themes. For the lively interest in the business of insurance and the archives that it generated has still much to teach about an extraordinarily important aspect of economic history.

The essays assembled in this book are virtually all concerned with British insurance in the nineteenth and twentieth centuries, and (with three exceptions) are devoted to fire and life underwriting. Such a specific pattern is in large part a reflection of the need to elaborate a limited number of important themes. But it also reflects the historiography of the subject matter. On the one hand, there has been so much more research on corporate underwriting in the fire and life branches that it is more appropriate to emphasise those fields. On the other, in spite of the ancient and cosmopolitan origins of indisputable insurance activities (mutual life insurance in the ancient world, marine insurance in medieval Italy), the elaborate evolution of the principal branches of insurance is directly associated with the modernisation of economic and social arrangements, and, therefore, with the growth of the British economy from the late eighteenth century.[1] Admittedly, marine insurance was very well developed in sixteenth-century England; there are instances of *ad hoc* life insurance contracts in the same period; and the intermittent threat of conflagration produced plans for extensive fire insurance in seventeenth-century London, which culminated, after the rebuilding that followed the Great Fire, in the successful flotation of various companies (the Fire Office, the Friendly Society and the Amicable Contributors or Hand in

4   *The business of insurance*

Hand) in the 1680s and 1690s. Nevertheless, the basis of effective modernisation lay in the late eighteenth and (more especially) the early nineteenth centuries — when economic expansion stimulated both supply and demand.

This was to some extent so even in marine insurance (which was already well established before the days of Britain's industrial greatness). It was, however, in the fields of fire and life insurance that the emergence of modern industrial society in Britain was most directly associated with a transformation of underwriting.

In the first instance, urbanisation and industrialisation — the increasing concentration and awareness of the value of residential, social, industrial and commercial property — produced a sustained boom in fire insurance: the sums assured almost quadrupled between the mid-1780s and the late 1820s, and virtually doubled in the next two decades. Given its character, fire underwriting was completely controlled by incorporated businesses. Indeed, during the eighteenth century London-based companies had been overwhelmingly dominant, and as late as the first decade of the nineteenth century were responsible for some 90% of sums assured in England and Wales (at mid-century they still handled about 75%). More than this, the advantages of security and size initially enabled a handful of pioneer companies to monopolise much of the market; and in 1806 the Sun Fire Office (1710), the Royal Exchange Assurance (which was empowered to issue fire policies in 1721) and the Phoenix Fire Office (1782) were still responsible for some 60% of English fire business. In the course of the eighteenth century the structure of fire insurance — agencies and branches, the inter-company co-ordination of premium rates, policy conditions and averaging — had assumed a modern form. As the inflationary stimulus of the Revolutionary and Napoleonic wars gave way to more sustained growth in the opening decades of the nineteenth century the obvious scope for competition led to a proliferation of companies in the provinces as well as in London. Premium rates were driven down, the leading firms struggled to co-ordinate their activities and systematise their risk-taking, and the familiar alternation of collusion and hectic competition began to assert itself.

A similar *lietmotif* of growth, instability and restructuring characterised the parallel expansion of life insurance — which began its modern development later than fire underwriting, but which experienced an even more expansive development in the nineteenth century. The *conceptual* basis for life underwriting — a knowledge of probability, annuity calculations, mortality statistics — was readily available in the seventeenth. But it was not until the last decades of the next century that scientific life insurance began. Prior to that there had been some corporate experiments. The Amicable Society for a Perpetual Assurance Office (founded in 1706 but limited to 2,000 policy-holders), the Royal Exchange Assurance and the London Assurance — chartered for marine insurance in 1720 — began to insure lives from 1721.[2] But both the extent and the character of these ventures were limited. Generally, the contracts were for a limited term (usually one year), written at a uniform premium irrespective of age, and not related to systematic information about actual mortality experience. Only with the creation of the Society for Equitable Assurances on Lives and Survivorships, a mutual company, in 1762, did the modern basis of life insurance — level premiums graded by age at entry and calculated on the basis of adequate mortality tables — appear. Even so, it took a further twenty years before the Royal Exchange Assurance followed suit. During that delay the Equitable had seized a further competitive advantage by issuing with-profits policies. The Equitable encountered only modestly effective rivals: only two new offices (the Westminster in 1792 and the Pelican in 1797) were formed before 1800.

In spite of this slow start, life insurance underwent a rapid and extensive growth in the first half of the nineteenth century as the knowledge of the requisite techniques, the appreciation of the low level of risks, and the growing business and middle-class markets converged. Fifteen offices had been promoted during the wars of 1793–1815; a further twenty-nine were successfully founded in 1815–30, and fifty-six in 1830–44. By the early 1850s there were almost 200 in existence. The sums assured by life policies increased some fifteenfold in the first half of the nineteenth century; and the extent of the practice of life insurance — like the proliferation of middle-class incomes and business and legal transactions in need of protection — was far greater in Britain than in any other country.

That the growth of life insurance was, indeed, an aspect of business development was demonstrated by the form and structure which characterised it. Even that important minority of life underwriting which was undertaken by specialist firms organised on a mutual basis was impelled by competition and the imperatives of salesmanship and active marketing. More generally, proprietary offices were shaped by the need to market their services, by the pressure towards innovation in their products, and (frequently) by the possibility of harnessing to their purposes existing networks of agencies and branches — devised by parent or sister companies to handle their fire insurance business. By mid-century, too, the investment aspects of life insurance had come to the fore: with-profits or bonus policies were the principal weapon of competition and appeal to potential policy-holders, endowment policies had begun, although they were not to become dominant for fifty years; and the funds of life assurance companies had emerged as a potent element in the nation's capital market.

There was, then, a close correspondence between the evolution of the economy in the initial stages of industrialisation and the rapid maturing of marine, fire and life insurance. Moreover, once firmly established, commercial underwriting kept pace with the extension and increasing sophistication of the economy. This was exemplified not simply in the growth in sums assured and the developing variety of policies, but also in the world-wide extension of the underwriting business of British companies. As international specialisation was facilitated by improvements in communications and transport, and by the enhanced flows of capital and labour, so a unified world economy evolved in the second half of the nineteenth century. In that context British insurance (like British investment, trade, people, and enterprise) penetrated overseas markets. This was particularly marked in the case of fire insurance and in relation to the Americas and the Empire. But it was also a more general phenomenon. And the superiority of British insurance practice (which was probably more marked than the superiority of British industrial technology) provided the basis of enormously successful multinational companies, whose profits helped bolster both the flow of invisible earnings and the international strength of the British economy in the generations before the first world war. By 1914 British fire insurance companies may have derived as much as two-thirds of their fire premium income of some £30 million abroad. By the early twentieth century, insurance was an integral part of Britain's role in the international economy — facilitating investment and commercial transactions, providing the means for private savings, playing an increasingly important role in the world's capital markets, and increasing the foreign exchange earnings which were used to strengthen Britain's overseas investments. Life office foreign investment abroad alone must have been of the order of £200 million on the eve of the first world war.

In contrast to the other main branches, accident insurance was a relatively late development: extensive underwriting of the risks of accidental damage to property or injury to persons, of sickness and legal liability, of burglary, and of other misfortunes or losses did not really occur until the second half of the nineteenth century; and some of the most active branches of twentieth-century insurance (motor, aircraft, giant industrial installations) were naturally conditioned by the history of the technological advances on which the risks were based. Of course, this had also been the case in the previous century (indeed, the emergence of modern accident insurance was particularly dependent on the development of the railways from the 1840s), and in any case, it took some time for new insurance habits to develop. Yet all this amounted to only a slight delay. Specialist accident companies grew very rapidly in the last decades of the nineteenth century, and by the early years of the twentieth a general accident business was firmly established, tariffs had been drawn up, and the Accident Offices Association formed (1906). At that time, too, the existing insurance companies (many of which had already combined fire and life insurance in a 'composite' business, although good practice and government regulation obliged them to present and manage their life funds separately) saw the advantages of further extending their operations, just as some of the accident companies began to extend into non-accident business. The resulting integration (which, however, still left some specialist life offices in positions of importance) marked an important structural change in the insurance industry. It had come to be increasingly dominated by multi-divisional big businesses, and assumed a pattern which was to endure, even though over the next sixty years acquisition and mergers greatly intensified the degree of corporate concentration. The power this generated was, however, checked to some extent by the growing importance of Lloyd's as a writer of non-marine insurance of all kinds.

Of course, our knowledge of the dynamics and structure of the insurance 'industry' as it has evolved over the last two centuries is still very uneven. Thus, in spite of their huge size in the twentieth century, there has been relatively little work on the growth of accident business or 'industrial' life assurance (the latter catering for wage-earning policy-holders who preferred regular visits from agents to collect premiums); the investment policies of life offices, although they have become dominant elements in the capital market, have not been adequately explored on a comparative basis; and, as has already been mentioned, non-corporate marine underwriting and the demand for insurance (in its social as well as economic aspects) have been unduly neglected. Many other important topics could be added to such a list.

And yet, considering the relatively short time in which insurance records have been available and historians' interest aroused, the achievements of insurance history are very considerable. In particular, as this sort of book makes manifest, a useful number of serious company histories is now available, and (given the corporate character of insurance business) that is perhaps the most fruitful point of entry to the general economic character of the industry. Deriving from this fact, too, as is also suggested by this collection, historians have concerned themselves to very good purpose with the structural aspects of the industry (especially in the critical period of growth in the nineteenth century and in terms not simply of the organisation of individual firms but also of the pattern and management of markets); with the balance between bureaucratisation and individual initiative in the formative period of growth; with the roots and consequences of the alternation between competition and collusion which has so sharply characterised insurance activity; with the thrust towards overseas expansion in the second half of the nineteenth century; with the persistence of corporate entities which adopt an almost independent existence in such a setting; with the evolution of life insurance policies and marketing; with the geographic diffusion of the industry; and with the vicissitudes that have attended the economic and social instability of the twentieth century.

Themes such as these — exemplified in the following chapters as well as in other substantial work currently in progress[3] — are indicative of the rich potential of the field in terms of social, economic and business history. Both as an object of research in its own right and as an avenue to explore broader and more variegated issues, insurance history has, in a very short time, assumed an important presence. It will undoubtedly evolve in range as well as growth in size. Meanwhile, however, this book suggests a few of the contributions that it has already made.

8  *The business of insurance*

*Notes*

1   For general treatments of the history of British insurance see G. Clayton, *British Insurance*, 1971, chapters 1–11; H. A. L. Cockerell and Edwin Green, *The British Insurance Business, 1547–1970. An Introduction and Guide to Historical Records in the United Kingdom*, 1976, chapters 1–5; H. E. Raynes, *A History of British Insurance*, 1964; Barry Supple, *The Royal Exchange Assurance. A History of British Insurance, 1720–1970*, 1970, chapters 3–6, 10, 12, 17–18.

2   In the second half of the eighteenth century there was also a minor boom in friendly societies (i.e. mutual insurance clubs) paying death as well as sickness benefits.

3   In his forthcoming history of the Phoenix Assurance Company, Clive Trebilcock will deal extensively with (*inter alia*) their overseas business, entrepreneurial initiative and structural evolution.

D. T. JENKINS

# The practice of insurance against fire, 1750–1840, and historical research

I *Fire insurance records and recent historical research*

During the 1960s the history of eighteenth and nineteenth-century fire insurance began to receive the attention of historians in two different ways. Firstly publication of substantial business histories for two of the major London fire offices permitted an insight into how fire insurance developed and began to cope with the increasing complexities of an industrialising economy. Also recognition emerged that the often voluminous records left behind by the fire offices potentially provide a source of information on the contemporary economy and society which in some respects is unrivalled.

The departure point for this new interest was the publication in 1960 of P. G. M. Dickson, *The Sun Insurance Office, 1710–1960*.[1] There had previously been no shortage of histories of individual fire offices but very few of these had succeeded in going beyond a brief outline of the main phases of development of the company concerned and the personalities involved. Some so-called 'company histories' amounted to little more than glossy publicity brochures, perhaps hardly surprising in an industry where firms have generally prided themselves on their history and have recognised that age suggests stability and security to the minds of the public.

At the end of the decade Barry Supple, *The Royal Exchange Assurance. A History of British Insurance, 1720–1970*, took knowledge of the history of the industry a considerable step further.[2] Thus the two major fire offices of the eighteenth century had received detailed historical attention, and such was their dominance of the business at that time that these studies effectively amounted to a history of the industry as a whole.

Documents relating to fire insurance were by no means new to historians. Many collections of personal, estate, legal and business records contain examples of fire policies and correspondence about various aspects of fire insurance. These records had, on many occasions, been used, as part of the more general collections, to provide evidence of property, its contents and value. However, to my knowledge, up to the 1960s no substantial use had been made of the records of fire offices for purposes other than research into the history of insurance.

Recognition that fire policies in particular were of potential value in other areas of historical enquiry developed as a result of the debate about the role of capital formation in industrialisation and the search for new sources of data to enable the construction of estimates of capital stock and formation for the British economy during its industrialisation period, and through the desire to test the varying views on the importance of capital which had recently been put forward by P. M. Deane, S. Pollard and, in particular, W. W. Rostow.[3]

S. D. Chapman and I, independently and unbeknown to each other, within the space of a few months in 1967 realised that for one major industrial sector of the economy in particular, namely textiles, fire insurance policies were conceivably an important source for the identification and valuation of fixed capital. In the textile industries there had long been a high fire risk through the nature of the processes and through some of the raw materials used. Moreover, unlike in some industries, it was clear that a very high proportion of plant, machinery and other fixed capital was susceptible to combustion. Again, coincidentally, the records of the Sun Fire Office had recently been deposited at the Guildhall Library in the City of London and were readily accessible. Chapman and I both found very quickly that textile mills were well represented in the policy registers from the 1780s.

Chapman's work was directed, in particular, to the cotton industry and to the textile mills in the Midland counties. The initial fruits of his searches were given as a conference paper entitled 'Fixed Capital Formation in the British Cotton Manufacturing Industry'.[4] The searches of the Sun Fire Office registers by Chapman and his two research assistants produced data which later significantly assisted him in the writing of a series of articles on textile history, including a study of the Peels, an examination of power costs, an analysis of capital assets in the domestic sector and articles on the hosiery industry, on factory development and on factory housing.[5]

My own interest in the fire policy registers of the Sun Fire Office and of the Royal Exchange Assurance Company related specifically to the textile industries in the West Riding of Yorkshire. I found that the registers of the Sun were amazingly comprehensive in their coverage of Yorkshire wool textile mills. Over 63% of the mills extant in 1800 were being insured by the office at that time. There was a similarly high coverage of other types of textile mills for the late eighteenth century. But by the early decades of the nineteenth competition from new London and local offices was met with such laxity by the Sun that it lost most of its Yorkshire textile business. The results of this work on Yorkshire were initially produced, in 1969, as a doctoral thesis and were subsequently published in D. T. Jenkins, *The West Riding Wool Textile Industry, 1770–1835. A Study of Fixed Capital*

*Formation*.[6] Information gleaned from insurance records has also contributed substantially to my articles on early factory development in Yorkshire and to a discussion of the Yorkshire cotton industry in the nineteenth century.[7] Various insurance archives were of value in my study, with K. G. Ponting, *The British Wool Textile Industry, 1770–1914*, and insurance valuations contribute to a forthcoming assessment of investment in the industry from 1750 to 1850.[8]

Much other research into the textile industries has benefited from evidence gleaned from the insurance policies. J. Butt has used those of the 1790s to help identify the progress of the Scottish cotton spinning industry.[9] Our knowledge of the Yorkshire textile industries in the eighteenth and nineteenth centuries has been substantially advanced by three recent theses, all of which have used the policies extensively.[10] Likewise a study of woollen mills in Wiltshire and Somerset was able to glean a great deal from them.[11]

Although research into the textile industries has so far predominated in the use of the fire policy registers, perhaps partly as a result of the transcripts, card indexes and finding lists that both Chapman and I have been able to make available to others, broader use has been, and is still being, made of the records.

An extension, beyond the textile industries, of the use of insurance valuations for research into capital formation in the British economy between 1750 and 1850 was undertaken in an S.S.R.C.-supported project by S. Pollard in the early 1970s. Pollard's researchers sampled the Sun Fire Office registers and coded the contents of about 50,000 policies. The results of this project are due to be published shortly.

M. W. Beresford has recognised the value of insurance records for building and urban history and has written of his 'love affair' with them.[12] His search through over half a million policies in the registers of the Sun and Royal Exchange before 1807 yielded 2,183 relating to Leeds property, and a study of those policies and the operation of the Sun Fire Office agency in Leeds has recently appeared under the title 'Prometheus insured. The Sun Fire Agency in Leeds during urbanisation, 1716–1826'. Beresford's notes on Leeds policies have also contributed to a series of other local studies.[13]

Some use of the records has been made in other work. J. Orbell's research on corn milling in the industrial revolution used the registers of the Sun Fire Office.[14] Elizabeth Adams has carried out extensive research in the registers in relation to her work on the British pottery and porcelain industries. Her article on the Bow insurances includes an index of fire policies of 'ceramic interest' for the period 1745–63.[15]

Members of the Furniture History Society are at present working in the Guildhall Library and are using the policy registers as part of their research towards a compilation of *A Dictionary of English Furniture Makers, 1660–1840*.[16]

## II  Record survival

Attention had been drawn to the existence and potential uses of the fire office policy registers in various other articles,[17] but it is fair to comment that since the realisation, some fifteen years ago, of the wealth and variety of information in those registers there has been surprisingly little and limited use of them.

Of the many fire insurance records that survive undoubtedly of most interest are those relating to the Sun Fire Office, both because of their comprehensiveness and because of the dominance of that company. Even in 1830, with all the new formations and competitive pressures, the Sun was still almost twice as large, measured by premium income, as any other office, although its share of the total business had fallen to about 17% from 28% in 1806.

The Sun Fire Office records consist of a wide variety of material, including the minute books of its various committees, journals, ranges of account books, endorsement books and loss registers, but perhaps of most significance are the registers of policies. These policies were issued in two ways, directly, through the London head office or the Craig's Court, Whitehall, office to callers, or through provincial agents. Agents also kept a record of the business they dealt with. A few agents' books survive and are invaluable for the areas they cover.

The head-office copy registers for the Sun Fire Office exist as one unindexed series up to 1793, containing 600,000 policies.[18] From 1793 separate registers were maintained, again unindexed, for London and provincial issues.[19] About 1⅓ million entries were made in these in the next seventy years. A few volumes are missing from the Guildhall Library holdings and some are in such a state of decay as to make their use difficult or impossible.

The policy registers of the Phoenix do not survive, except for some agency books. But a few records are still available for the Royal Exchange Assurance Company, including some registers for the period from 1753 to 1833.[20] During these eight decades the company issued almost half a million policies, and copies of somewhat over one-third of these are extant. Many of the early records were destroyed by a disastrous fire at the Royal Exchange in 1838. The company kept, from at least the 1790s, a separate series of registers for their larger, or 'special risks', mainly industrial property, but only one register from this series has been traced.[21]

Almost all types of combustible property were covered by insurance, the only exceptions being a few classes of industrial property which the offices considered far too hazardous for any premiums to be set. The Sun Fire Office had considerable business in domestic property of all sizes, including many of the major country houses and town mansions. It insured much agricultural property, including both buildings and farm stock, and a wide range of industrial and commercial businesses from small workshops to the largest of breweries, textile mills and dock warehouses. When it carried out a review of its industrial risks in the 1820s it found it had on its books property relating to such diverse trades as gingerbread bakers, bedstead upholders, oar makers, tallow melters and chandlers, lamp-black manufacturers and brush makers. Likewise it insured all types of shops and offices, theatres, churches, cloth halls, town halls, inns and brewhouses, schools and libraries.[22]

In 1716 about two-thirds of Sun Fire Office policies were issued for houses and shops; 10% related to inns, 9% to warehouses and only 5% to agricultural property. Only 1% of policies were for industrial risks. By 1790 the proportion of agricultural risks had increased to 10%. Houses and shops still formed two-thirds. Industrial risks had risen to 8% of policies issued.[23]

The geographical distribution of the Sun's business was determined by the existence and activity of local agents and the degree of local competition. In the eighteenth century the busiest agencies were those in the major country towns. Exeter, Canterbury, Winchester, York, Edinburgh and other similar towns stand out in the registers. Dickson sampled the policies for 1716 and found that 37% related to London property and that the best represented areas outside London were Berkshire, Gloucestershire and Lincolnshire.[24] By the 1790s provincial business was more widespread. A report prepared in 1797 showed that 55%, by value, of property insured by the Sun was in the home counties. Another 14% was in the adjacent southern counties.[25] Table 1 shows the distribution for the rest of the country. Table 2 shows the

Table 1. *Distribution of Sun Fire Office insurances, 1797 (£ million)*

| | | | |
|---|---|---|---|
| London, Essex, Kent, Middlesex and Surrey | 44·6 | Cheshire, Lancashire, Yorkshire | 5·8 |
| Berkshire, Hampshire, Sussex | 7·4 | Cumberland, Durham, Northumberland, Westmorland | 0·5 |
| Bedfordshire, Buckinghamshire, Hertfordshire, Oxfordshire | 4·1 | Scotland | 5·2 |
| East Anglia | 3·5 | | |
| Midland counties | 5·0 | Great Britain | 81·7 |

*Note.* There were very small amounts of business in Wales and Ireland.
*Source.* Public Record Office, Chatham Papers, 30/8/187, Hugh Watts to William Pitt, 22 June 1797.

relative importance of London and provincial business for the Sun and the Royal Exchange Assurance early in the nineteenth century, including sums insured and fire losses. By the 1840s the proportion of business in industrial districts had grown. In that year country business formed 60% of the Sun premium income. Dwellings and contents still formed 56% of policies issued. Farms made up 12%, warehouses 12% and shops 6%.[26]

Fire policies provide a vast amount of information about these different properties and their contents. Details of owners, tenants, mortgagees, partners and executors and their occupation and places of residence are normally

Table 2. *The fire insurance business of the Sun and the Royal Exchange, 1813–24 (£'000)*

|  | The Sun, 1813–23 | | The Royal Exchange, 1815–24 | |
| --- | --- | --- | --- | --- |
|  | London | Provincial | London | Provincial |
| Premiums received | 603·8 | 536·3 | 184·6 | 434·0 |
| Capital insured | 412,156 | 354,738 | 120,500 | 246,130 |
| Gross fire loss | 456·5 | 295·1 | 81·3 | 183·0 |

Source. G.L., MS., 14,116.

recorded. Contents of property, including animals, wine, furniture and clothing, works of art, libraries of books, business and industrial stock, and machinery, are generally specified in varying detail. Many policies contain physical details of buildings insured, including measurements, numbers of storeys, number and location of rooms and their uses, construction materials and information on fire prevention. Uses of property are recorded, as well as details of heating and lighting methods, types of processes, means of power and whether night work was carried out. And, of course, there are also the valuations of property and their contents for insurance purposes.

The practice of offices differed as regards the renewal and alteration of policies. Most offices allowed policies to be renewed annually for seven years. At the end of that period a new proposal had to be made. But by the early nineteenth century some policies appear to have been allowed to run indefinitely, with endorsements. Alterations in the detail of policies required, with some offices, the issue of a new policy, but with most a simple entry in an endorsement register was sufficient. For the larger policies of industrial concerns it was more common for new policies to be issued more regularly, sometimes annually or even more frequently, to allow for changes in description and valuation. When property was being built it was not uncommon for policies to be issued every few weeks to allow for the increasing value of the property. The same applied when buildings were gradually being stocked with raw materials or machinery.

Even though the scanning of the registers to find policies relating to a particular locality can be speeded up through a knowledge of the names of local agents, the process is still tedious.[27] Moreover this is by no means a foolproof method, as it was not uncommon for property to be insured through distant agencies. Country property of London residents was often insured through the London head office in the case of the Sun and the Royal Exchange.

The registers of the main companies were not indexed originally but some progress is being made in the development of indexes for them. Besides the unpublished finding lists of Beresford, Chapman and myself, and the list of potteries mentioned above, there are some partial indexes available. Deposited at the Guildhall Library is an index of forty drawers of cards, compiled by the late Alan Redstone.[28] The cards cover the Sun registers from 1714 to 1731 and are organised county by county for England. London, Scottish and Welsh policies are excluded. There are separate series for Bristol and Berwick on Tweed. The cards give details of names, occupations, titles and ranks by county, parish and village and occasionally by street or house name. A few later registers are also covered by the index; those for the Sun Fire Office for 1793–94 and for the Royal Exchange Assurance Company for 1773–75.

Parts of Chapman's personal index have also been published. Details of policies relating to the Devon cloth industry between 1726 and 1770 have recently been listed and K. G. Ponting has published, from Chapman's lists, similar information for the textile industries of Dorset and Somerset.[29]

A more comprehensive index is nearing completion. At the instigation of the S.S.R.C., B. Supple and R. Floud have supervised a computerised listing of some 350,000 policies from the Sun and Royal Exchange registers for the period from 1776 to 1792. When the retrieval system for the index is finally in operation it will enable policies to be identified and located by individual names, through location and through occupation.

Perhaps the knowledge that this index, for the crucial early years of the industrial revolution, is being prepared has persuaded potential researchers to bide their time. Maybe, when the retrieval system appears, there will be a flurry of activity in the Guildhall Library. Meanwhile an initial prospectus has been provided by Schwarz and Jones in which they begin to analyse some of the data.[30]

The locating of other surviving insurance records has been facilitated by the sterling work of the Chartered Insurance Institute, which in 1972, through its Historic Records Committee, organised a national survey of the records of the insurance industry, with the assistance of its members throughout the country. The results of this survey were published in 1976 by H. A. L. Cockerell and Edwin Green under the title *The British Insurance Business, 1547–1970. An Introduction and Guide to Historical Records in the United Kingdom.*

However, it also seems likely that there has been some unwillingness to use fire insurance records as a result of the problem of interpreting and assessing the reliability of the information they contain. The purpose of the remainder of this chapter is to provide some insight to the business practices of insurance against fire between 1750 and 1840 and an assessment of the accuracy of the information contained in fire policy registers.[31]

III  *Competition and the practice of insurance*

With substantial collections of records surviving for just a few, mainly major, companies it is important to perceive the particular role of individual offices and how their practices and the extent and location of their activities altered.

Gradual development of knowledge, within the business, of risks and the pressures of, at times, intense competition brought changes to methods used by the fire offices and to the records they kept.

Between the early eighteenth century and 1840 four phases are discernible in the development of fire insurance. Up to about the 1750s the insurance of property against fire was almost entirely a London business. The pioneer company, the Hand in Hand Fire Office, and the Westminster Fire Office insured only London property. The Sun Fire Office, which had the most significant impact on the development of the initial principles and methods of fire insurance in the eighteenth century, and the Royal Exchange Assurance Company paid little attention to the provincial business and at first created only a few regional agencies. Small fire offices were founded at Bristol and Edinburgh but they had no real effect on London's dominance.

After half a century of gradual growth and slow experimentation the business of fire insurance began to enter a second phase from the 1760s. In that and the following decade new provincial offices generated business with apparent success in their respective areas, in some instances spreading the idea of insurance against fire risk to regions where it was hardly known. By 1780 there were fifteen fire offices operating, mainly quite well established concerns. But with a rapidly rising population, growing economic activity and the gradual spreading of the notion of fire insurance, provincial competition was as yet of little concern to the London offices.

In 1782 the government placed a duty on sums insured, in spite of substantial opposition from the fire offices.[32] The tax was severe; it equalled or exceeded premiums for much property, and there were fears that the whole idea of fire insurance would be irreparably damaged. The Leeds Fire Office declined further business, through fright of the consequences of the duty. The duty payments enable some indication to be obtained of the subsequent development of the business and the relative importance of the different offices. It has been estimated that in 1783, the first full year of the duty, property valued at over £170 million was insured, the sum rising to £211 million in 1800, £389 million in 1815 and over £478 million by 1830.[33]

With the fear that the imposition of duty and its effect on the cost of insurance would deter prospective insurance proposals 1782 was hardly a propitious year to launch a new office, but London sugar refiners had for long been unhappy about the treatment of their insurances. In that year they decided to establish the Phoenix Fire Office. They were quick to realise that, with the extent of competition within London, their success would lie in provincial and industrial business and even overseas. By January 1783 the Phoenix had appointed fifty-eight provincial agents, almost as many as operated for the Royal Exchange.[34] The Sun Fire Office had about 120 agents at that date. The impression emerges that the Phoenix agents were rather more active than those of the rival companies. Within just a few years the Phoenix was generating more business than the Royal Exchange.

Competition from the Phoenix started the third phase of development. Other major offices found themselves having to pay more attention to provincial business and to industrial risks. At last they began to try to develop an understanding of how to deal with industrial property. The main companies entered into joint discussions about industrial risks, sought independent advice and for a while, in the 1790s, operated an uneasy cartel in relation to some risks.[35]

Other local offices were founded in the closing years of the eighteenth century. In general they were very small and highly localised in their operation. The Salop Fire Office, formed in June 1780, with thirty co-partners and a capital of only £21,000, of which just £1,500 was called, was earning an annual premium income of only £590 in 1790 and £947 in 1800.[36] Although, through their local connections and generally lower rates, they gained business from the London offices, the latter do not appear to have been too worried about this competition before the turn of the century. They were clearly aware of their existence and at times deprecated some of their practices. Often the Sun disdained contact with the small, local offices, even to the extent of ignoring letters and refusing joint insurances.

But this lack of interest in new competition was not to last for long. From 1803 a proliferation of new London and provincial offices created a further stage in the emergence of the business, shaking the old established concerns and making great inroads in many areas of their business. The Imperial Insurance Office, set up by the directors of the West India Dock Company in

Table 3. *The relative importance of the business of the London and country fire offices, 1805*

| Office | Duty paid (£'000) | Property insured (£ million) |
|---|---|---|
| Sun | 93 | 74 |
| Phoenix | 59 | 47 |
| Royal Exchange | 44 | 35 |
| Imperial | 23 | 19 |
| British | 19 | 15 |
| Globe | 27 | 14 |
| Westminster | 12 | 10 |
| Hand in Hand | 12 | 10 |
| London | 6 | 5 |
| Union | 5 | 4 |
| Albion | 4 | 3 |
| *London total* | | 236 |
| Sixteen country offices | 31 | 25 |
| *Overall total* | | 260 |

Source. Cornelius Walford, *The Insurance Cyclopaedia*, III, 1876, p. 420.

1803 appointed twenty-one agents within three months. It was prepared to accept large risks at lower premiums, and within two years was the fourth largest office in terms of property insured. By September 1805 the value of its insurances in the West India Dock alone exceeded £1 million.[37] The Globe Fire Office, also established in 1803, and the British Fire Office, founded four years earlier, likewise set out to gain industrial and provincial risks. The Globe directors argued that 'the business of the office will, in a great measure, depend upon the due selection of proper persons as Country Agents'. They had duly appointed 140 agents by September 1804 and 158 by Christmas 1805.[38] Also in that first decade of the nineteenth century were founded another five London offices and at least twelve provincial ones, including some which rapidly became very successful in areas which had previously been strongholds for the Sun Fire Office.

The effect on the old companies was immediate. Royal Exchange income from fire premiums fell between 1802 and 1812.[39] The Sun was soon complaining that the Birmingham Fire Office was fighting for business at the expense of other offices, as if hinting that this was an ungentlemanly thing to do. It was recognising by November 1802 that it was not advisable to increase premiums, and two years later it was making great attempts to reduce costs, by cutting back advertising and by reducing its fire engine establishment.[40] In 1826 the Sun Fire Office premiums from its country business had fallen to half the peak level of 1798 and the value of the provincial property it insured had decreased from £42 million to £35 million over the same period.[41]

Manchester was one area where the Sun's business was badly affected. In 1803, the peak year, premium income from its Manchester agency was £9,060. By 1810 it had fallen to only £4,489. Its loss of business was particularly great for industrial property. In 1803 the Manchester agency had 125 cotton mills on its books, insured for a total of £258,461. By 1812 the number had fallen to just fourteen, insured for £17,850. In the country as a whole the value of cotton, lint and flax mill risks insured by the Sun Fire Office declined from £542,450 in 1803 to £240,900 in 1812. Thus Manchester business in particular had been adversely affected.[42]

The old established offices, of course, suffered in two ways. They lost insurances, some of which they had held for decades. On their remaining business they had to make do with much lower premiums. Sir Frederick Eden of the Globe claimed in 1806 that average premiums had fallen by over 25% following competition from newly established companies.[43] In response to the competition the Sun considered various measures. Rates were reduced for a wide variety of property. The secretary, Philip Bewicke, was sent on a tour of major agencies. Agents were exorted to make greater efforts and the directors resolved that the regulation of agents should no longer be looked on with 'prevailing apathy'.[44]

The wave of new formations came to an end in 1809. The fierce

Fire insurance and historical research 19

competition, higher duty rates and economic depression all discouraged further development in the next decade. However, in the early 1820s ferocious competition was again renewed. In that decade seven new London offices and at least thirteen provincial ones yet further challenged the supremacy of the main London businesses. The expansion resulted from the joint-stock mania in the capital market in 1824–25 and the minimal establishment costs for new offices. The impact of the local offices reached to all parts of the country. Whereas in 1806 the Sun, Phoenix and Royal Exchange offices carried out 68% of all English fire insurance, by the late 1820s their proportion had fallen to less than one-third.

Table 4. *The fire offices before 1840*

|  | Founded | Closed |  | Founded | Closed |
|---|---|---|---|---|---|
| *London offices* |  |  |  |  |  |
| Albion | 1805 | 1827 | West Middlesex | 1836 | 1840 |
| Alliance | 1824 | – | Licensed |  |  |
| Atlas | 1808 | – | Victuallers | 1835 | – |
| Beacon | 1822 | 1827 | London | 1720 | – |
| Benevolent | 1838 | – | London, |  |  |
| British | 1799 | – | Edinburgh |  |  |
| British |  |  | and Dublin | 1839 | – |
| Commercial | 1823 | 1824 | Minerva Universal | 1797 | 1799 |
| Church of England | 1840 | – | National | 1822 | 1822 |
| Clerical and |  |  | National Union | c. 1815 | c. 1817 |
| Medical | 1840 | – | Palladium (I) | 1797 | 1798 |
| County | 1807 | – | Palladium (II) | 1824 | 1830 |
| Eagle | 1807 | 1828[a] | Phoenix | 1782 | – |
| English and |  |  | Protector | 1825 | 1836 |
| Scottish | 1839 | – | Protestant |  |  |
| Globe | 1803 | – | Dissenters | 1837 | – |
| Guardian | 1821 | – | Royal Exchange | 1721 | – |
| Hand in Hand | 1696 | – | Royal Farmers | 1840 | – |
| Hope | 1807 | 1826 | Sun | 1710 | – |
| Imperial | 1803 | – | Union | 1714 | – |
| Independent and |  |  | Westminster | 1717 | – |
| *English country offices* |  |  |  |  |  |
| Anchor | c. 1808 | 1810[e] | East Kent | 1824 | 1828 |
| Bath | 1767 | 1827[b] | Coventry and |  |  |
| Bath Sun | 1776 | 1838[b] | Warwick | 1837 | 1839[b] |
| Berkshire, |  |  | Devizes | c. 1784 | 1824 |
| Gloucester and |  |  | Devon South | 1825 | 1827 |
| Provincial | 1824 | 1832 | District, |  |  |
| Birmingham | 1805 | – | Birmingham | 1834 | – |
| Bristol | 1769 | 1839[c] | Essex Economic | 1824 | – |
| Bristol Crown | 1719 | 1837 | Essex (and Suffolk) |  |  |
| Bristol Union | 1814 | – | Equitable | 1802 | – |
| Canterbury and |  |  | Finchingfield | 1804 | 1829[b] |

Table 4. *continued*

| | Founded | Closed | | Founded | Closed |
|---|---|---|---|---|---|
| Gloucestershire | 1825 | 1827 | Northern | c. 1840 | – |
| Hampshire, Sussex and Dorset | 1803 | – | Norwich General | 1792 | 1821[d] |
| | | | Norwich | 1785 | ? |
| Hertfordshire, Cambridge and Country | 1824 | 1831 | Norwich Equitable | ? | 1835[d] |
| | | | New Norwich Equitable | 1830 | – |
| Isle of Man | ? | ? | Norwich Union | 1797 | – |
| Kent | 1802 | – | Nottingham and Derby | 1836 | – |
| Leeds | 1777 | 1782[b] | Reading | 1823 | – |
| Leeds and Yorkshire | 1824 | – | Salamander (Wiltshire and Western) | 1790 | 1835[b] |
| Leicestershire (and Midland Counties) | 1834 | – | Salop | 1780 | – |
| Liverpool (I) | c. 1780 | 1795 | Sheffield | 1808 | – |
| Liverpool (II) | 1804 | – | Shropshire and North Wales | 1836 | – |
| Liverpool St George | 1802 | 1805 | Suffolk East and West | 1802 | – |
| Liverpool and London | 1836 | – | Surrey, Sussex and Southwark | 1825 | 1825 |
| Manchester (I) | 1771 | c. 1775 | West of England | 1807 | – |
| Manchester (II) | 1824 | – | Wooler | c. 1806 | ? |
| Newcastle | 1783 | – | Worcester | 1790 | 1818 |
| Newcastle and North of England | 1836 | 1838 | York and London | 1838 | – |
| | | | York and North of England | 1835 | 1837 |
| North and South Shields | 1826 | 1836[b] | Yorkshire | 1824 | – |

Notes.
a  Business transferred to Protector.
b  Business transferred to Sun.
c  Business transferred to Imperial.
d  Business transferred to Norwich Union.
e  Business transferred to Norwich General.
Where a closing date is not shown the office was still in business in 1840.

What happened in Yorkshire is indicative of the difficulties faced by the main offices throughout the country. In 1824 the Leeds and Yorkshire Assurance Company and the Yorkshire Fire and Life Insurance Company were both founded. The former gained great success in winning industrial and associated business in West Yorkshire in spite of treading very carefully initially. It issued 1,100 policies in the first six months of its life.[45] The latter company won a large proportion of the more important country properties in the county as well as competing well in more general rural insurance.[46] By 1826 the Leeds and Yorkshire was insuring property worth about £3·7 million

*Fire insurance and historical research* 21

and the Yorkshire property worth £1·4 million. This business was almost entirely in Yorkshire. Their competition was an assault on several fronts. Personal contacts of the directors were of great initial importance for both companies. Their more immediate knowledge of risks and, as I shall suggest below, their ability to check them gave greater security to their business. Care in the appointment of agents and closer contact with them promoted business. Both companies undercut on premiums. In a letter to an agent in November 1824 W. L. Newman, the secretary of the Yorkshire, requested:

> You will bear in mind that it is the object of this company to obtain as much business as possible from other offices and therefore you may fairly calculate that in almost all cases the premiums which will be charged by it will be somewhat under those of other offices.[47]

In and around Leeds competition was particularly fierce. At least eighteen fire offices had agencies in the town by 1824. There were other agencies in neighbouring villages. The Norwich Union opened a local agency in Leeds as early as 1802 and by 1824 was well established, with a range of industrial risks, including some very large property. Soon after the establishment of the Leeds and Yorkshire Fire Office the Norwich Union local agent wrote to his company secretary complaining of the large inroads that were being made to his business. Its Huddersfield agent drew the attention of the board of directors to the 'great loss of business arising from the establishing of the Leeds office which took at 3s 0d what this office charged 7s 6d'. In 1827 the directors, faced with this competition, decided to discontinue all woollen mill risks.[48] The Suffolk Fire Office had taken a similar decision some time earlier.[49] The Secretary's Minute Book of the Leeds and Yorkshire office shows a very clear familiarity with the processes and dangers of wool textile manufacture.

At times of previous onslaught from the provincial offices the response of the Sun Fire Office had been half-hearted and largely ineffectual. Now, however, it reacted more firmly. In 1824 agents were asked to make much greater exertions. The following year there was a reduction of premium rates in country districts. In 1827 there followed a huge shake-up of inefficient country agents. Many were sacked, new ones were appointed and new agencies were established, even in industrial districts where the Sun had not previously been represented — in Bradford and Huddersfield, for example. Twenty additional agents were appointed in 1826 and another twenty-nine in the first half of 1827.[50] By 1846 the Sun had 677 agencies in Great Britain, compared with 123 in 1786. In some districts agents were also given leeway to discount premiums. The Phoenix also resolved to fight, depending in the short term on its foreign business if necessary.[51]

On this occasion the Sun's exertions were successful; its business picked up. Its premium income began to rise from the low level reached in 1826. The number of provincial offices continued to increase; almost another thirty were founded in the 1830s. But many were forced to discontinue business, in some cases being taken over by larger offices which made use of their agency networks.[52] Moreover by the 1830s minimum-rate agreements on some high-risk property lessened the ferocity of previous competition.

## IV  The interpretation of fire insurance records

The interpretation and assessment of the reliability of the information contained in fire policies has been the subject of some debate. An understanding of the business practices of the fire offices does provide a guide to the accuracy of the various details they contain. As Ryan outlined on p. 46 below, fire offices were formed in three ways: those where proprietors put up the capital, carried all the risk and enjoyed all the profits; mutual offices or societies in which the insured effectively guaranteed one another and divided the profits after a period of years — often seven; and offices with capital put up by proprietors which divided some profits with the insured.

There were a number of substantial differences in business practice between the major companies, between the larger London offices and the smaller provincial ones, and between the provincial offices themselves. Moreover the methods used for country business by London offices were different in a number of respects from the conduct of London insurance. In general, with London business forming a large proportion of their activities for the major offices (an average of around 50% for the Sun Fire Office between 1750 and 1850), they were able to retain skilled and experienced staffs of inspectors, surveyors and others in the capital, whereas in the provinces the relatively small number of policies relating to any one place meant that it was rarely financially justifiable to regularly employ specialised local staff. Thus the major offices were able to maintain a greater degree of control and care over their London business.

Whereas it was the case that some of the London offices kept in very close touch with each other about their methods and problems, differences of approach to the business did arise from time to time. However, it is only too clear that many of the smaller, particularly the provincial, offices were founded and operated by persons who had no previous experience of fire insurance. The major companies often disdained contact with these smaller, country competitors and thus the latter were left entirely to their own devices in arranging their methods for establishing and operating their businesses. In spite of their lack of knowledge and wider experience, however, they were often able to operate much more effectively in their own localities because of their local contacts and their understanding of local problems and circumstances.

The complexity of the administration of the fire offices varied very much according to their size. In the case of many of the very small provincial offices, the administrative and secretarial duties were often in the hands of one man, although he rarely had much freedom of individual action, since, generally, all proposals had to be sanctioned by a committee of the directors. At each meeting of the directors of the Salop Fire Office, for example, the first business was to discuss the issue of policies. The Newcastle upon Tyne Fire Office required three or more trustees to sign policies.[53] In cases like these care was paid to the individual particulars and circumstances of proposals. Often the property concerned, or the proposer, was known to one or more of the directors. On occasions directors might decide to visit or the secretary would be sent to inspect.

But the administrative structure of the larger, national companies prevented them from taking similar care. Only very large proposals were individually considered. The vast majority were dealt with, as a matter of routine, by the office clerks, who doubtless built up considerable experience but who were unlikely to have had the time, inclination or knowledge to examine the details of every proposal carefully. In London more care could be taken. Surveyors were employed to visit property proposed for insurance. For provincial insurance, however, much reliance had to be placed on agents.

Up to the first decade of the nineteenth century, before the main London offices were being confronted with active provincial competition, decisions to set up agencies were generated on a very haphazard basis. Agencies were established either by a direct application to the office, or by the recommendation of someone already connected with the office – another agent, an important client or a director, or else by a head-office decision and a search for a suitable person. Early in its life the Royal Exchange decided to approach country postmasters.[54] Occasionally the Sun Fire Office actively sought agents or replacements. It asked for recommendations from respectable local citizens or, if necessary, despatched someone from head office to seek a suitable person. Much more frequently, however, the Sun Fire Office and others relied on requests and recommendations and only rarely turned down an application, and then often for the reason that the suggested agency was too close to an already well established one. There was often much opposition from established agents to the setting up of sub-agencies or other full agencies in their area.

This haphazard method of creating agencies led to many anomalous situations. Relatively small villages could have an agency for a major fire office whereas large and expanding towns could be without one. An example, here, was the Sun Fire Office in West Yorkshire at the beginning of the nineteenth century. It had active agencies at Sheffield, Wakefield and Leeds and established a small one at Gargrave. It was not until the 1820s that it set up agencies elsewhere in the industrial area. Until then it had no representation in the rapidly expanding towns of Huddersfield, Halifax, Bradford, Dewsbury and the surrounding areas.[55] Hence another reason why it was unable to maintain its share of industrial business in that district.

In the face of competition from the new local offices the major companies gradually began to pay closer attention to their agency networks. Agents were actively sought in new areas; more careful checks were kept on the amount of business individual agencies were doing and, if deemed necessary, replacements were made. Moreover the offices began to take rather more care in enquiring into the trustworthiness of prospective agents. The new offices paid much closer attention to their agency networks. Some local offices, the Suffolk Fire Office, for example, pursued a policy of trying to establish agencies in every town and large village in their locality, using their local knowledge and connections.

Agents came from many walks of life. The preference was for people with good local connections through their standing and other business activities. Agents generally ran their agencies as a second line to this major occupation. In the eighteenth century small traders and retailers, local clerks and other small local business people typically fulfilled the function. In the nineteenth century a broader range of persons got involved. Retailers, merchants, commission agents, teachers, surveyors of taxes, clerks in various professions, including banks, estate agencies, railway and canal offices, and persons from a wide range of occupations were recruited.[56] Solicitors took on agencies. They formed 25% of Sun country agents in 1846. The Licensed Victuallers Insurance Company, not surprisingly, actively recruited innkeepers.[57] The Leeds and Yorkshire favoured bankers and solicitors. By the 1840s some agents were representing more than one office. Women were occasionally recruited. In 1807 the Sun Fire Office grudgingly admitted that Mrs Buchanan, their Glasgow agent, was 'very active and as attentive to the business as a female can possibly be expected to be'.[58]

Perhaps the only thing these agents had in common, besides their respectability and local contacts, was their lack of experience or training in fire insurance. They were issued with printed instructions which rapidly became more complex as the nineteenth century progressed. Specific orders were often sent to them in alarmingly frequent fashion. There is plenty of evidence to show that agents were at times hard pressed, or insufficiently interested, to keep up. There are several recorded instances of disputes between offices and agents as a result of the failure of the latter to comply with instructions. Occasionally offices incurred substantial losses through the errors of agents. But, on the other hand, many agents did gain valuable experience and came to be highly respected by their employers, who were frequently willing to depend on their judgement. This experience was, at times, a family asset, as some agencies were passed on from father to son, husband to wife and occasionally through several generations. Agents were required, by most if not all offices, to provide a financial guarantor — the guarantee ranging from £100 to several thousand pounds, depending mainly on the size of the agency — but sometimes also on an assessment of the trustworthiness of the agent. In some offices — the Globe, for example — the agents could own shares instead.[59] But offices seem to have paid scant attention to their agents' guarantees. Often no great effort was made to check the financial standing of the guarantors. Even less was done to check that the guarantee remained viable. After a number of frauds and bankruptcies in the 1790s and the discovery that some guarantees were worthless the Sun Fire Office began to be much more careful and to institute regular checks as well as requiring prompter returns from agents. In 1804, out of 168 agents employed by the Sun, fifty-four were in default with their payments to head office, owing £10,000 in premiums.[60]

The London-based businesses, with their agents widely spread, had less control, however, than some of the provincial offices where the agent, his background and standing, would normally be better known and where a much closer eye could be kept on the agencies' financial situation. In view of the importance of the agency system and the problems the major offices faced as a result of the failings of agents, it is surprising that large offices, like the Sun, paid so little attention to the appointment and supervision of agents. By the 1840s and 1850s safeguards were being established, but up to then the majority of agents of the London offices were unknown personally to their directors — the only contact being through instructions and letter communication. Little supervision and control was exercised and there was little check that instructions were being obeyed.

The agents' duties appear to have been fairly similar, no matter which the office. They changed somewhat over time as property to be insured by fire became more complex. The list of functions, as set out in the various instructions of a number of offices, would seem to have been:

1. To canvass actively for business.
2. To make known the terms of the office and their advantages.
3. To accept proposals and, in certain circumstances, to check that the conditions under which they were accepted were complied with.
4. To forward proposals to head office.
5. To issue policies from head office to clients.
6. To supervise (in some agencies) the office local fire brigade.
7. In certain circumstances to supervise the fighting of fires and salvage.
8. Where required, to arrange the inspection, survey and valuation of fire loss.
9. To inquire into arson, fraud and other suspicious circumstances.

In return for these services the agent received:

1. A small, flat-rate fee for new policies, with certain exceptions.
2. A commission which early in the eighteenth century had normally been 5% but in the later decades began to rise towards 10%. This was certainly paid by newer offices, and after 1800 this rate increasingly prevailed throughout the market.[61]
3. Reasonable fire-fighting and other exceptional expenses, but not normally office and administrative costs.

4. Occasional honorariums where an agent had been called upon to do services extra to his everyday duties — such as prosecuting on behalf of the office.

With these duties and payments an agent clearly faced a number of conflicts of interest, and these conflicts do raise questions about some aspects of fire insurance policies. For many agents one might suggest that their main interest was maximum commission for minimum effort. It was to their advantage to canvass for business, without going to great expense, as long as the commission that they might receive would outweigh the cost of neglecting, for the time required, their other work. Fluctuations in the insurance activities of some agents may be explicable through fluctuations in the pressure of their other activities. Agents, of course, received commission on renewals. There was little incentive to check proposals carefully or to see that conditions were being complied with. Instructions to agents often put a considerable onus on them — as, for example, some of the requirements of the Globe office in the 1850s:

It is in the highest degree expedient and unprofitable to insure the property of persons of whose honesty and bona fide intentions there is any reasonable doubt ...

It is not desirable to insure property exposed to great or peculiar hazard, either from the kind of business carried on, the character of the occupants, the dangerous nature of the surrounding premises, the exposure of incendiarism, or any other circumstances or cause ...

Consider the character of the proposer ...

Be doubtful about insurances proposed by other offices.[62]

By the 1830s, with the greater competition, and the flexibility to discount premiums which many agents had, their responsibilities were increasing. Moreover agricultural incendiarism led to fire offices requiring their agents to pay much more careful attention to farming policies, which previously had been quite straightforward.

All the various instructions were no doubt in the interests of the fire offices, but there was no great incentive for the agent to be conscientious in carrying them out. If he accepted a doubtful proposal, so gaining his commission, and the property then sustained a loss, the agent lost nothing, except perhaps his reputation with the office in blatant cases. This conflict of interest between the agent and head office was possibly substantial for certain types of industrial property. By the early nineteenth century, when many conditions were being imposed on some industrial insurance, it was the duty of agents to check that proposals abided by the rules of the office. But rarely was anyone to know if they failed to do so. If the proposal did not meet the requirements and a loss was sustained, except in very serious fires it was the agent who dealt with negotiations over the loss, and thus discrepancies could be kept hidden. In mid-century one Sun agent, Mr Puddicombe of Moretonhampstead, got away for a while with fictitious claims on fictitious insurances.[63]

Perhaps the smaller offices with their greater local control were able to overcome the problem but not the big offices, nor others that operated over a wide geographical area. It was also in the agents' interests to settle losses quickly and without fuss. They were rarely paid any extra to make enquiries, and any reluctance to settle loss could detrimentally affect their other insurance business and, possibly, their non-insurance interests. Perhaps this pessimistic view does some agents an injustice. There are apparent instances of agents being very concerned and apologetic about mistakes or losses.[64]

This also suggests another area of conflict of interest between the agent and his fire office. Clearly the fire offices needed very large fire losses to be carefully checked and assessed. For large fires outside London the national companies occasionally sent their own surveyor and staff. When the Sun appointed two surveyors in 1773 they were explicitly told that they would be expected to travel into the country.[65] The Sun also retained local surveyors as fire assessors. John Barstard of Blandford did much fire loss assessment for it in Dorset in the eighteenth century.[66] John Jubb and John Sutcliffe, Yorkshire millwrights, assessed local fire losses for it on occasions. The engineer John Rennie surveyed fires for the Sun Fire Office in the 1790s.[67] The local offices, for which a very large fire might have been financially embarrassing, also had their retained experts. But the Sun, Royal Exchange, Phoenix and other offices relied, for most fires, on the local agent to arrange the assessment and settlement. The agent might obtain the services of a local surveyor — perhaps a local builder or millwright. But again there does not appear to have been much incentive for the agent to be very active in the matter, and the local surveyor might also have had divided interests — local loyalties and business versus the interests of the distant fire office.

Although the agency system had become essential to the fire insurance business by the middle of the eighteenth century, the organisation and control of agencies continued to be a weakness throughout the following century.[68] Inactive and inattentive agents continued to trouble the Sun. In 1872 thirty-eight agencies were abandoned, as no business had been received from them. The smaller offices increased the practice of requiring country agents to take shares. As the directors of the Licensed Victuallers recorded in 1836, 'it was thought that by giving them an individual interest in the concern it might make them more circumspect in the risks they took'.[69]

The implications of these problems for the interpretation and reliability of fire insurance policy records should not be overstressed. One might suspect that the information, excluding values which are discussed below, was not in itself inaccurate — that might have been too blatant. It was perhaps in details of risk left out of policies that the main scope for deception existed, and it was in this aspect that the inefficiency of some agents was of consequence.

It should be understood that there was no requirement for agents to check the details of proposals submitted through them, except on specific orders from head office. They were expected to look out for unusual circumstances, but the check on the accuracy of the information submitted only occurred if a loss was suffered. If when the loss was being investigated the property was found not to conform with the details of the proposal or the conditions of the office, then normally the offices resisted payment. For example, a claim for £11,000 resulting from the Customs House fire in 1814 was resisted by the Sun, Royal Exchange, London and Phoenix offices because the premises had contained gunpowder.[70] In 1838 the Licensed Victuallers refused a claim because of false information regarding occupancy of a building and dangerous risks.[71]

Occasionally the offices did make exceptions to this policy in order to retain 'that Character of Liberality which they have so long held with the public' or because the matter was 'of too trifling a character to become the object of a newspaper paragraph'.[72] Exceptions were made by the Sun Fire Office to avoid bad publicity, or where the client was well known to the office and where the belief was that the misinformation was unintentional. Losses were occasionally paid even though premiums were long overdue. Some offices were more liberal than others. The Globe, for example, appears to have been quite strict about adjusting losses if policy details had any inaccuracies.[73]

Thus it was not in the interest of the proposer to misstate details. Nor, for the vast majority of the information submitted in proposals, was there any purpose in falsification. It should, however, be remembered that details of the property, its ownership, terms and other information could change during the currency of the policy. All offices required changes to be notified to them at once. Some issued a new policy but most simply provided an endorsement note and recorded the changes in their endorsement register. Where they survive these registers need to be consulted in conjunction with the policy registers.

## V    The meaning and reliability of insured values

It is rather more debatable whether values recorded in fire insurance policies were always accurate. Moreover it is necessary to understand the basis of those values. As far as the fire offices were concerned, values were assumed to reflect replacement cost. It was on that understanding that risk was accepted, as the manager of the Phoenix Fire Office made clear in 1798:

> ... it has been decided again and again that the insurer is to pay so much (and no more) than the sum which will *reinvest* the Sufferer. Goods of various kinds, fancy goods in particular, are often manufactured in expectation of a demand which may or may not arise ... We therefore repeat that the true allowance is '*so much as* will replace the goods', and in this the Managers of the Royal Exchange and Sun Fire Office authorize us to say they coincide.[74]

Neither agents nor the head office normally checked or considered whether the values being proposed clearly reflected the true replacement value of the property. No instances have come to light of proposals being declined through suspicion of overvaluation.[75] There would have been little purpose in overinsuring. If a fire occurred the loss would be calculated by the property owner and submitted to the office. Until the beginning of the nineteenth century offices required claims to be accompanied by affidavits from a local clergyman, churchwardens, a justice of the peace and other local respectable citizens, stating that they were aware of no suspicious circumstances.[76] Some offices required the certificates to confirm that the loss 'is rated or valued to put them in the same conditions they were in before the fire happened'.[77] This practice was dispensed with by some of the new offices and was gradually abandoned by the older ones. The larger offices left most claims in the provinces to their local agent. If the sum involved was tiny the money would be automatically paid with little or no check. For larger losses the agent was expected to look into the circumstances and arrange for a valuation of the loss. For very large fires or fires damaging a lot of property of different ownership an inspector or director was occasionally sent. Surviving records of valuations of damage suggest that a very detailed approach was taken. Losses were carefully valued item by item in terms of their replacement cost. More than one independent assessment was sometimes obtained. The value of salvagable materials was deducted, or at times the fire office auctioned salvaged goods.[78]

Payment for losses was normally made quickly, often within a few days, but any suspicion of fraud could considerably hold up payments. As already suggested, the investigation of fraud depended on the conscientiousness of the local agent, and there is evidence to suggest that many suspicious cases were all but ignored through lack of investigators. Often all that the fire offices seem to have been able to do was to offer a reward in the hope that information would be forthcoming. There are, however, instances of agents going to considerable efforts to investigate suspected fraud, and some showed much detective ingenuity. One such case was at Beith, south of Glasgow, where the Phoenix agent spent several years investigating and finally prosecuting the owner of a printworks.[79]

Offices had the right either to make payment in cash or to reinstate the property themselves. In order to avoid fraud they had, from 1763, the statutory right to require property to be reinstated.[80] For example, the Globe agreed to settle a loss in 1811 subject to the company being given sufficient security that the sum would be expended in reinstating the premises according to the provisions of the Act of Parliament.[81] In general the main offices were better able to organise and supervise the making good of property in London, where they had professional staff available. In the country this was a task the local agent was often unwilling to perform, and thus cash payments were more usual.

The offices acknowledged that genuine disagreements could arise and had procedures for independent arbitration, which appear to have worked satisfactorily. But if disputes were not settled, the major offices were prepared to be taken to court and, from the instances recorded in their records, seem to have more frequently won than lost.[82] There are surprisingly few examples of legal action involving the smaller offices in the early nineteenth century. Perhaps they were more concerned about the publicity and were worried about the massive legal expenses. When the Suffolk resisted a 'fraudulent' claim in 1824 and lost, it incurred costs, expenses and legal charges of over £1,000.[83]

Whereas overvaluation of property was unlikely, except perhaps through the accident of the owner miscalculating replacement cost or through downward price changes, there are various reasons why undervaluation might have occurred. Until the end of the eighteenth century or later some offices considered it better for the proposer to underinsure and to accept some of the risk himself. Some small companies even insisted on this. The secretary of the Essex and Suffolk Equitable Insurance Society, for example, wrote to an agent as late as 1806, 'It is not novel nor fair for any person to insure buildings to the full value — two thirds or three fourths is a fair value.' Up to the 1780s most fire offices deducted a small amount, normally 3%, from loss payments so that clients were taking a small part of the risk themselves. The Phoenix never instituted the practice, the Sun abandoned it in October 1782.[84]

Another factor which may have created undervaluation at times was the risk limits on items insured, which varied according to risk classification and from office to office. They were quite regularly varied by the main offices, which did not necessarily strictly adhere to them. In the eighteenth century a maximum of £500 was accepted on some more dangerous risks by many offices. Risk limits were gradually increased to £5,000 or even more on less hazardous risks by the end of the century. These had two main effects on insurance. They encouraged the greater division and detailing of risks. In certain cases, however, they may have prevented property from being insured to its full replacement cost. Joint insurance was normally the way to overcome the limits but there are instances, for example in the Leeds and Yorkshire Fire Office in the 1820s, of offices asking for values to be reduced to conform with limits.[85] Joint insurance was very common, however, particularly between the three biggest offices. The major companies were sometimes less happy about insuring jointly with small national and provincial offices. All offices insisted that details of insurance with other offices should be specified in proposals, as a measure to prevent fraud. The Sun Fire Office, and no doubt the others, reacted very unfavourably if this rule was not obeyed. There are a number of instances of its refusing to pay losses when it had not been informed of policies elsewhere. The record of joint insurances is an important aspect of the information in the policy registers. It seems likely that the information was rarely omitted.[86]

Insurance could be spread between many offices. Joint insurance between two offices was most frequent, but the famous Albion Flour Mill at Blackfriars, London, was jointly insured by five offices when it burnt down in March 1791.[87] By the third and fourth decades of the nineteenth century the distribution of insurance between six or eight offices was not uncommon. There are instances in the 1830s of eleven offices sharing a risk.[88]

There are many other reasons why fire insurance might understate the value of property. Insurance was taken out only on combustible items. As George Coode pointed out in 1863:

It would be a mere absurdity for any owner of property to insure from loss by fire the value of the part of the property which is indestructible by fire, and in England it is never done or pretended to be done, except in some of the comparatively rare cases where the 'condition of average' is compulsory.

He argued that the ordinary experiences of actual losses by fire showed that the practice of insuring from one-third to two-thirds of the appraised value generally covered the losses incurred, although he acknowledged that for some types of property, and for contents or stock, fuller coverage was essential.[89]

Unintentional undervaluation may have occurred through the property owner underestimating replacement cost, through insufficient adjustment to price rises or through his not taking out extra cover for additions to property. During the rapid inflation of the early years of the nineteenth century the Sun Fire Office printed a handbill pointing out the great advance in prices and encouraging its clients to review long-standing policies to ensure their property was adequately covered.[90]

Intentional undervaluation could arise from a number of factors. Coode acknowledged that some property owners insured only what they would want to replace after a fire. At times premiums on some property were prohibitive. The introduction of, and subsequent increases in, government-imposed duty meant that for many types of property duty payments could be more than premiums. In 1782 the Sun Fire Office argued that underinsurance would be the result of the imposition of duty.[91] But the impact of the tax may well have been through property ceasing to be insured altogether rather than by its being reduced in insured value. There is, however, a suggestion that some offices connived with clients in the avoidance of full duty payments by allowing them to understate the value of property, although paying a premium appropriate to its full value. This could be done where there were a lot of unconnected risks and little chance of fire spreading. An attempt was made to stop this by an Act of Parliament in 1828 which required the separate specification of risks or, alternatively, the use of the 'average clause'.[92] There is little to suggest that this practice was common.

Another possibility was that insurance would be taken out for that amount of money owed to creditors — perhaps to recompense those who had lent money to build or purchase the property. Agreements for loans sometimes required the insurance of the security, just as some landlords required their tenants to take out insurance.

There was, however, a more significant reason for potential underinsurance. For most types of property it was not until the 1840s or even later that the 'average clause' was included in policies.[93] Under the 'average clause' the sum to be paid for fire damage depended on the relationship of the sum insured to the full value of the property. Thus for example, if property valued at £1,000 was insured for only £500, and £500 of the property was destroyed by fire, for a policy without the 'average clause' the fire office would have paid £500. In a policy with the 'average clause' only £250 would have been paid. The inclusion or exclusion of the 'average clause' clearly had implications on the recorded values of property for insurance purposes. Without the clause the proposer might calculate that if he suffered a fire it would be likely to destroy only a part of the property. Therefore he might save premiums and duty by only valuing the property to the amount likely to be destroyed. The offices tried to overcome the problem by insisting on a detailed specification of property into 'divisions' so that the risk was broken down in a way that allowed losses to be individually associated with these components. There is some evidence that offices did try to keep alert to being taken advantage of in this way. The Leeds and Yorkshire Fire Office refused to insure a textile mill at Oldham in 1828 because:

This amount, if one may judge by the size of the mill will not be one tenth of the real value and, therefore, if a fire were to happen ... we might suffer a loss equal to the whole amount insured and be receiving only one tenth of the proper premium.[94]

It is by no means easy, in the records of the various offices, to discern when and why the 'average clause' was being applied. The fact that it existed in a policy did not necessarily mean that it was applied after a loss. The notion of average in British fire insurance first appears in 1723, when the Royal Exchange decided to add the following clause to all policies for £500 and upwards:

if in case of Loss or Damage it appears that there was a greater Value than the Sum hereby insured and part thereof saved, then sd. Loss or Damage shall be taken & borne in an Average.

For ten years the Royal Exchange Assurance Company debated the clause and regularly changed its views. In 1733 it decided to omit it from all policies. In the 1750s its use was ordered again for foreign risks.[95]

By the beginning of the nineteenth century the 'average clause' had become a matter of much debate and a competitive issue between offices. In the 1790s the Sun had been requiring its inclusion in some warehouse stock policies. West Indian merchant goods at the Port of London were insured under 'average'. The Imperial Fire Office was using the clause in 1803 for warehouse contents policies.[96] The extent to which these companies insisted on its use is unknown. There was likewise great uncertainty for farming stock. The Sun appears to have been offering a reduced premium for its use in 1801 and, the following year, believed all fire offices were using it for farm stock.[97] In 1804, however, the Sun advertised the acceptance of farming stock risks without the clause.[98] The Globe accepted a farming stock proposal in 1809, subject to it.[99] Whether it continued to be used regularly for farming policies in later decades is again uncertain. The Phoenix was using it in 1831 but in 1850 a Sun farming stock policy included the clause:

The Office reserves to itself the right of applying the Average Clause to this insurance at the expiration of any period, when renewable, either by endorsement on this policy, or upon the renewal receipt.[100]

The clause was also applied in some other trades. In 1793 the Sun directors resolved to allow a lower premium for brewers accepting the clause. In 1805 they refused to insure a brewhouse without it. In 1819 they offered a reduced premium for printers if the clause was included.[101] In spite of these occasional recorded instances of the use of the 'average clause' there does not appear to be strong evidence to suggest that it was used in more than a small minority of policies before the 1830s. At that stage reference to it becomes much more frequent, although its use was still much debated. For example, the Licensed Victuallers and General Fire and Life Assurance Company decided to include the clause in all its policies in 1835 but the following year resolved to try to remove it.[102]

For warehouse policies, particularly where contents could not be easily divided into identifiable components, there were other problems, and new types of policies were developed to meet them. Where the value of property insured fluctuated as stocks increased or decreased the major offices were willing to issue what were known as 'general policies'. These did not require detailed identification of property and were really a type of blanket cover. General policies appear to have been used both with and without the 'average clause'. Occasional mention is also made in company records of 'floating policies'. These were apparently used only for mercantile risks and were an extension of the general policies, in that property could be insured without specification or information on location. Floating risks were also accepted with or without the 'average clause'.[103]

There was considerable demand from agriculture throughout the period for insurance for less than one year, to cover, for example, seasonal variations in stocks of produce held. Many offices were not keen to accept short-term agricultural risks. Some, at times, refused to do so but ultimately found they had to if they wanted to avoid losing their annual agricultural business. The dislike of short-term policies arose through the high administrative costs involved and the small premiums chargeable. Agricultural premiums were among the lowest of the rates, and the charge that could be made for a three-month or six-month policy was therefore tiny, even though premiums were not normally reduced proportionately. Offices found, however, that refusal to grant short-term policies could mean that they lost out on agricultural insurance. Duty was reduced proportionately for short-term risks. They are clearly identified in the policy registers.

Thus, whereas one may be reasonably confident that the general details recorded in policies are likely to be accurate, it is not clear that the values given are a true reflection of the replacement cost of the property. It seems reasonable to assume that the values are understatements and that their representativeness varies according to type of property concerned and the extent to which it could be totally destroyed. I have argued elsewhere that values given for textile mills may be reasonably reliable.[104] It is by no means easy to check insurance valuations against other sources. Occasionally newspaper comment after a fire mentions full insurance or underinsurance. But these reports were presumably often based on rumour and their reliability cannot be assumed. There are instances where newspaper statements are contradicted by fire office records. Comparisons which involve initial cost do not allow for price changes and depreciated conditions of property. Sale prices and liquidation values need bear little resemblance to replacement values. Comparisons with balance sheets and company accounts are likewise often dubious. The basis of accounting, historic cost or historic cost written down, for example, may not accord with 'replacement cost' values. Accounts may include non-combustible items, land values and land and water works and perhaps an assessment of goodwill.[105]

However, in spite of these reservations about the recorded values there is no doubt whatsoever that insurance policies and associated insurance records provide a mine of exceptional information on eighteenth and nineteenth-century property. Their use so far has been very limited. The worth of the information they contain, for research into many aspects of eighteenth and nineteenth-century Britain, has yet to be fully realised. But as access to the policies is facilitated by indexing so many areas of research will benefit from them. And it would seem that, with a few exceptions, there are no strong reasons to doubt the reliability of the information the policies contain.

## Notes

1 P. G. M. Dickson, *The Sun Insurance Office, 1710–1960. The History of two and a half centuries of British Insurance*, London, 1960.

2 Barry Supple, *The Royal Exchange Assurance. A History of British Insurance, 1720–1970*, Cambridge, 1970. Interest was also stimulated by the publication of the second edition of Harold E. Raynes, *A History of British Insurance*, London, 1964.

3 See P. M. Deane, 'Capital formation in Britain before the railway age', *Economic Development and Cultural Change*, LX, 1961; P. M. Deane, 'The role of capital in the industrial revolution', *Explorations in Entrepreneurial History*, 10, 1972–73; P. M. Deane and W. A. Cole, *British Economic Growth, 1688–1959*, Cambridge, 1962, 2nd ed. 1967; S. Pollard, 'The growth and distribution of capital in Great Britain, c. 1770–1870', *Third International Conference of Economic History, Munich 1965*, 1968; W. W. Rostow, ed., *The Economics of Take-off into Sustained Growth*, 1963.

4   Conference on 'The Sources and Methods for the Study of Capital Formation, 1750–1850', sponsored by the Social Science Research Council and organised by the Department of Economic History at the University of Sheffield in January 1969. The paper was subsequently published in J. P. P. Higgins and S. Pollard, eds., *Aspects of Capital Investment in Great Britain, 1750–1850. A Preliminary Survey*, London, 1971. It appeared in revised form under the title 'Fixed capital formation in the British cotton industry, 1770–1875', *Economic History Review*, 2nd series, XXXIII, 2, 1970.

5   S. D. Chapman, 'The Peels in the early English cotton industry', *Business History*, XI, 1969; 'The cost of power in the industrial revolution in Britain. The case of the textile industry', *Midland History*, I, 2, 1971; 'Industrial capital before the industrial revolution', in N. B. Harte and K. G. Ponting, eds., *Textile History and Economic History*, Manchester, 1973; 'The genesis of the British hosiery industry, 1600–1750', *Textile History*, 3, 1972; 'The textile factory before Arkwright. A typology of factory development', *Business History Review*, 48, 1974; 'Workers' housing in the cotton factory colonies, 1770–1850', *Textile History*, 7, 1976.

6   D. T. Jenkins, *The West Riding Wool Textile Industry, 1770–1835. A Study of Fixed Capital Formation*, Edington, 1975.

7   D. T. Jenkins, 'Early factory development in the West Riding of Yorkshire, 1770–1800', in Harte and Ponting, eds., *Textile History and Economic History*; 'The cotton industry in Yorkshire, 1780–1900', *Textile History*, 10, 1979.

8   D. T. Jenkins and K. G. Ponting, *The British Wool Textile Industry, 1770–1914*, London, 1982.

9   J. Butt, 'The Scottish cotton industry during the industrial revolution, 1780–1840', in L. M. Cullen and T. C. Smout, eds., *Comparative Aspects of Scottish and Irish Economic and Social History, 1600–1900*, Edinburgh, 1975. He also makes rather broader use of policies in S. G. S. Lythe and J. Butt, *An Economic History of Scotland, 1100–1939*, 1975.

10   M. J. Dickenson, 'The West Riding Woollen and Worsted Industries, 1689–1770. An Analysis of Probate Inventories and Insurance Policies', Ph.D. thesis, University of Nottingham, 1974; Patricia Hudson, 'The Genesis of Industrial Capital in the West Riding Wool Textile Industry, c. 1770–1850', D.Phil. thesis, University of York, 1981; G. Ingle, 'The Yorkshire Cotton Industry, 1770–1835', Ph.D. thesis, University of Bradford, 1981.

11   Kenneth Rogers, *Wiltshire and Somerset Woollen Mills*, Edington, 1976.

12   M. W. Beresford, 'Building history from fire insurance records. An autobiographical fragment', *Urban History Yearbook*, 1976.

13   E. J. Connell, 'Industrial Development in South Leeds, 1790–1914', Ph.D. thesis, University of Leeds, 1975; M. F. Ward, 'Industrial Development and Location in Leeds, North of the River Aire, 1775–1914', Ph.D. thesis, University of Leeds, 1972; K. Grady, 'The Provision of Public Buildings', Ph.D. thesis, University of Leeds, 1980; M. W. Beresford, 'Prometheus insured. The Sun Fire Agency in Leeds during urbanisation, 1716–1826', *Economic History Review*, 2nd series, XXXV, 3, 1982.

14   J. Orbell, 'The Corn Milling Industry of the Industrial Revolution', Ph.D. thesis, University of Nottingham, 1977. The brewing industry, which is well represented in the policy registers, has received some attention. See I. Donnachie, 'Sources of capital and capitalisation in the Scottish brewing industry', *Economic History Review*, 2nd Series XXX, 2, 1977.

15   Elizabeth Adams, 'The Bow insurances and related matters', *Transactions of the English Ceramic Circle*, 1973; 'Ceramic insurances in the Sun company archives, 1766–74', *Transactions of the English Ceramic Circle*, 1976.

16   I am grateful to Mr T. Ingram, chairman of the society, for the information.

17   See, for example, L. M. Wulcko, 'Fire insurance policies as a source of local history', *Local Historian*, 9, 1970; S. D. Chapman, 'Business history from insurance

36  *The business of insurance*

policy registers', *Business Archives*, 32, 1970; J. H. Thomas, 'Fire insurance policy registers, *History*, 53, 1968; M. J. Dickenson, 'Insurance policy registers, 1720–1750', *Bulletin of Local History* (East Midland Region), 1971, VI.
18   Guildhall Library (G.L.), MS. 11,936.
19   G.L., MS. 11,937.
20   G.L., MSS. 7,252–3; 7,255.
21   G.L., MS. 7,253, Vol. 32a.
22   G.L., MS. 14,116.
23   Dickson, *Sun*, p. 77. As policies forwarded by agents are recorded in often large batches Dickson's small samples may not be totally reliable.
24   Dickson, *Sun*, p. 77.
25   P.R.O., Chatham Papers, 30/8/187, Hugh Watts to William Pitt, 22 June 1797.
26   Dickson, *Sun*, p. 140.
27   In the Sun registers the name of the agent is recorded in the margin of each policy. In the Royal Exchange registers the location of the agency is given.
28   G.L., MS. 17,817.
29   S. D. Chapman, *The Devon Cloth Industry in the Eighteenth Century. Sun Fire Office Inventories of Merchants' and Manufacturers' Property, 1726–1770*, Devon and Cornwall Record Society, New Series, 23, Torquay, 1978; K. G. Ponting, 'Insurance valuations of textile mills, Dorset and Somerset', *Notes and Queries for Somerset and Dorset*, XXX, 303, March 1976.
30   L. D. Schwarz and L. L. Jones, 'Wealth, occupations and insurance in the late eighteenth century: the policy registers of the Sun Fire Office', *Economic History Review*, 2nd series, xxxvi, 3, 1983.
31   Much of the research on which this study is based was financed by a Social Science Research Council Grant. I am grateful to Oliver Westall and to Dr R. B. Weir for very helpful comments on an earlier draft.
32   Fire insurance duty per £100 insured: 1782–1797, 1s 6d; 1797–1805, 2s 0d; 1805–1815, 2s 6d; 1815–1864, 3s 0d; 1864–1869, 1s 6d. There were various exceptions. Foreign property insured in British offices was exempted from tax in 1786. Relief from duty was granted for agricultural stock in 1833. There were other minor exemptions, hospitals for example. Duty rates were lower for Ireland after 1816. The government allowed a small rebate for duty collection. Duty was abolished in 1869.
33   Revised Report on Fire Insurance Duties, B.P.P., 1863 (3118) XXXVI. The estimates relate to England and Wales. They are, of course, at current prices and are therefore of little value as a measurement of trends in the volume of fire insurance. See Supple, *R.E.A.*, p. 108.
34   Supple, *R.E.A.*, p. 99.
35   See G.L., MS. 11,931, Vols. 6, 7 and 8.
36   Shropshire County Record Office, Shrewsbury, Salop Fire Office, Minutes of Directors' Meetings, April 1780 – December 1794, and Income and Capital Accounts, 1780–1873.
37   G.L., MS. 12,160A, Vol. 1.
38   G.L., MS. 11,657, Vols. 1 and 2; MS. 11,685.
39   Supple, *R.E.A.*, p. 62.
40   G.L., MS. 11,935A, Vol. 1.
41   G.L., MS. 11,933A.
42   G.L., MS. 11,935A, Vol. 1.
43   Cockerell and Green, *The British Insurance Business*, p. 21.
44   G.L., MS. 11,935A, Vol. 1.
45   Leeds and Yorkshire Assurance Company, Secretary's Book No. 1, in the care of the Royal Insurance Group, Leeds.
46   Yorkshire Fire and Life Insurance Company, Board Minutes. I am grateful to Miss A. W. Knight for information relating to the business of the company.

47 Board Minutes, as above.
48 Norwich Union Fire Insurance Society, Minute Book No. 2, 11/10/1824; 25/4/1825; 24/12/1827. The records are in the keeping of the Norwich Union Insurance Group, Norwich.
49 Leeds and Yorkshire, Secretary's Book, November 1824.
50 G.L., MSS. 11,935S, 11,935A, Vol. 1, 14,116.
51 G.L., MS. 14,116.
52 The Sun incorporated fifty-five Salamander agents in 1835 and 149 British Fire Office agents in 1843.
53 Salop Fire Office; Directors' Minutes; Newcastle Fire Office, advertising leaflet, c. 1800, in my possession.
54 Supple, *R.E.A.*, p. 98.
55 It had previously tried to recruit agents at Bradford, Halifax and Huddersfield.
56 See Registers of Agents, e.g. G.L., MSS. 14,386, 11,932, Vol. 19; see also advertisements in contemporary trade directories.
57 G.L., MS. 11,661, Vols. 1 and 2.
58 G.L., MS. 11,935A, Vol. 1.
59 G.L., MSS. 11,657, Vols. 1 and 2, 11,685.
60 G.L., MS. 11,935A, Vol. 1.
61 E.g. Licensed Victuallers, 1836, which paid 10% to agents on fire policies. The Anchor Fire Office offered 10% on premiums and 5% on duty in 1808.
62 G.L., MS. 11,657.
63 Dickson, *Sun*, p. 134.
64 See, for example, Beiths Agency Notebook, Phoenix Assurance Company, March 1846, in the care of the company at 78 St Vincent Street, Glasgow.
65 G.L., MS. 11,931, Vol. 6.
66 Dorset C.R.O., MS. D.6. John Barstard and Thos. Gardner; surveys of buildings lost and destroyed, made for the Sun Fire Office.
67 G.L., MS. 11,932, Vol. 14.
68 See P. Chapman, 'The Agency System of Insurance Companies', a paper read before the Insurance and Actuarial Society of Glasgow, 3 December 1906.
69 G.L., MS. 11,661, Vol. 1.
70 G.L., MS. 11,931, Vol. 9.
71 G.L., MS. 1,661, Vol. 1.
72 Dickson, *Sun*, p. 81; Leeds and Yorkshire, Director's Minutes, Vol. 1.
73 G.L., MS. 11,657, Vols. 1 and 2.
74 Phoenix Assurance Co., Agents' Extra Letter Books, I, p. 16. I am grateful to Dr S. D. Chapman for the reference.
75 There were occasional suspicions of overvaluations of stock.
76 G.L., MSS. 11,657, Vol. 1; 11,931, Vol. 1.
77 Cockerell and Green, *The British Insurance Business*, p. 31.
78 G.L., MS. 11,932, Vol. 19.
79 Beith Phoenix Agency Notebook.
80 4 Geo. III, c. 14.
81 G.L., MS. 11,657, Vol. 2.
82 See, for example, G.L., MS. 11,932, Vol. 16, p. 411.
83 Suffolk Fire Office, Minute Book, Vol. 2, 15/6/1826. I am grateful to A. G. Ryley, Esq., Sun Alliance and London Insurance Group, Ipswich, for allowing access to the Suffolk's records.
84 Bernard Drew, *'The Fire Office', being the History of the Essex and Suffolk Equitable Insurance Society Limited, 1802–1952*, London, 1952, p. 23.
85 Leeds and Yorkshire, Secretary's Book, Vol. 1.
86 See, for example, G.L., MS. 11,932, Vol. 16, p. 411. There are instances in the Sun and Royal Exchange registers of joint insurances not being recorded. These may have been omissions on the part of the copying clerks.

87 Raynes, *History of British Insurance*, p. 197.
88 National Library of Scotland, MS. 5252, *Insurance Company of Scotland*, Ledger, January 1837.
89 *Revised Report on Fire Insurance Duties*, pp. 9–10.
90 G.L., MS. 11,932, Vol. 17, p. 62.
91 G.L., MS. 11,931, Vol. 6.
92 Raynes, *History of British Insurance*, p. 192; 9 Geo. IV, *c.* 13.
93 See R. Atkins, *The Average Clause*, London, 1866.
94 Leeds and Yorkshire, Secretary's Book, Vol. 1.
95 Supple, *R.E.A.*, p. 83.
96 G.L., MSS. 11,932, Vol. 16, 12,160A, Vol. 1.
97 G.L., MS. 11,932, Vol. 16.
98 G.L., MS. 11,931, Vols. 8 and 10.
99 G.L., MS. 11,657.
100 Cumbria County Record Office, Carlisle. Private circulars from Phoenix Fire Office to its Cockermouth agent in Benson papers.
101 G.L., MSS. 11,935H, 11,932, Vol. 16.
102 G.L., MS. 11,661, Vol. 1.
103 Dickson, *Sun*, p. 80, n. 1.
104 Jenkins, *West Riding Wool Textile Industry*, pp. 276–301.
105 This may account for some of the discrepancies identified by Butt, 'The Scottish cotton industry ...', p. 121.

ROGER RYAN

# The Norwich Union and the British fire insurance market in the early nineteenth century

## I Introduction

The Norwich Union Fire Insurance Society was founded in 1797 by Thomas Bignold, who then retained the key post of secretary in the firm until 1818. During that period the society emerged as the only country (i.e. provincial) fire office seriously to rival the large London-based insurance companies. An unmistakable sign of Bignold's ambitious aims appeared in 1808, when he also established the Norwich Union Life Insurance Society. By then virtually every fire office with an eye on expansion had come to appreciate the need to branch into the rapidly growing life insurance market. More prestigious agents could be recruited if they were offered the chance to sell life as well as fire insurance. Indeed, the wider circle of contacts opened up tended to be mutually reinforcing, with each of these branches of insurance[1] producing new business for the other. Certainly the Norwich Union Life Society used this opportunity just as readily as its 'sister' fire office. Taking the existing network of some 200 Norwich Union fire insurance agencies as a valuable starting point, the newly opened Life Society grew rapidly. By the early 1820s it ranked as one of the leading firms in British life insurance.

Meanwhile the decline of the Norwich worsted industry was well under way.[2] The city's leading manufacturers were diversifying into activities more closely associated with East Anglia's growing agricultural wealth. Brewing, food processing and distribution, as well as transport improvements, figured in this change of emphasis.[3] But the growth of country banks was particularly significant. During the late eighteenth and early nineteenth centuries, banking firms such as Messrs Harvey and Hudson's, Gurney's and Barclay, Tompson and Ives, became renowned far beyond Norwich for their stability.[4] Having established this reputation as one of the soundest financial centres in the provinces, Norwich became ideally suited to house a leading insurance office.

As historians of the city's economic and political development have explained, immense political and religious differences existed at Norwich between the local Tory Anglicans and the predominantly Nonconformist Whigs.[5] Normally this conflict was carried over to business life. In particular ill feeling between the rival parties intensified whenever unemployment rose to a peak in the declining worsted industry.[6] Moreover, each Norwich bank identified clearly with one side or the other of this partly religious but predominantly political divide.[7]

Yet any new local fire office could hardly afford to risk getting involved with these sectarian disputes. A powerful motive existed for compromise which outweighed local religious and political differences. Accordingly, when the Norwich General Assurance opened as the city's earliest fire office in 1792 it was backed by the leading local merchant manufacturers and bankers regardless of their political affiliation. In part, at least, this spirit of compromise might explain how Thomas Bignold came to be chosen as the new company's first secretary. He was a relative newcomer to the city and had not become actively involved in its turbulent political life. His appointment could hardly be seen as partisanship by either of the leading factions.

Thomas Bignold was born in 1761 at Westerham, in Kent, the eldest son of a prosperous farmer. Little is known about his early life except that he was well enough educated to gain a post as an exciseman. But that in itself is a useful pointer. Such work, with its long hours and close attention to detail, gave him an ideal grounding for his later role in the insurance business. Probably it was also this experience which governed his choice of occupation when he moved to Norwich in the early 1780s, married, and started business as a small wine and hop merchant with financial backing from his father.

By 1792 he had proved modestly successful, being worth perhaps £3,000, compared to less than £1,000 when he started. This obviously satisfied the city's leading businessmen on the Norwich General board sufficiently to appoint him as their secretary. Indeed, Bignold's experience and social standing would have been well suited to the role of chief officer in any country fire office. As D. T. Jenkins explains in his chapter, in these formative years provincial insurance officials seldom possessed the same degree of fire underwriting experience as their counterparts in the large London companies.[8]

Yet Bignold was chiefly responsible for the detailed work needed to launch the Norwich General. Within five years its premium income had reached £3,500 per annum and the company was producing good dividends (see Fig. 1). With some fifty agents, nearly all in East Anglia, it was the only local fire office serving this predominantly agricultural region. Moreover the company was solidly based on local wealth. Its capital of £160,000 — on the large side for a country fire office — had been fully subscribed within weeks.[9] In all, £32,000 was actually called up, to give an ample working reserve.

By contemporary standards Bignold had done well. Under his management the Norwich General was fully established as a profitable and very stable country fire office. But it soon became obvious that he was no ordinary insurance official. Indeed, he proved an extremely difficult man to get on

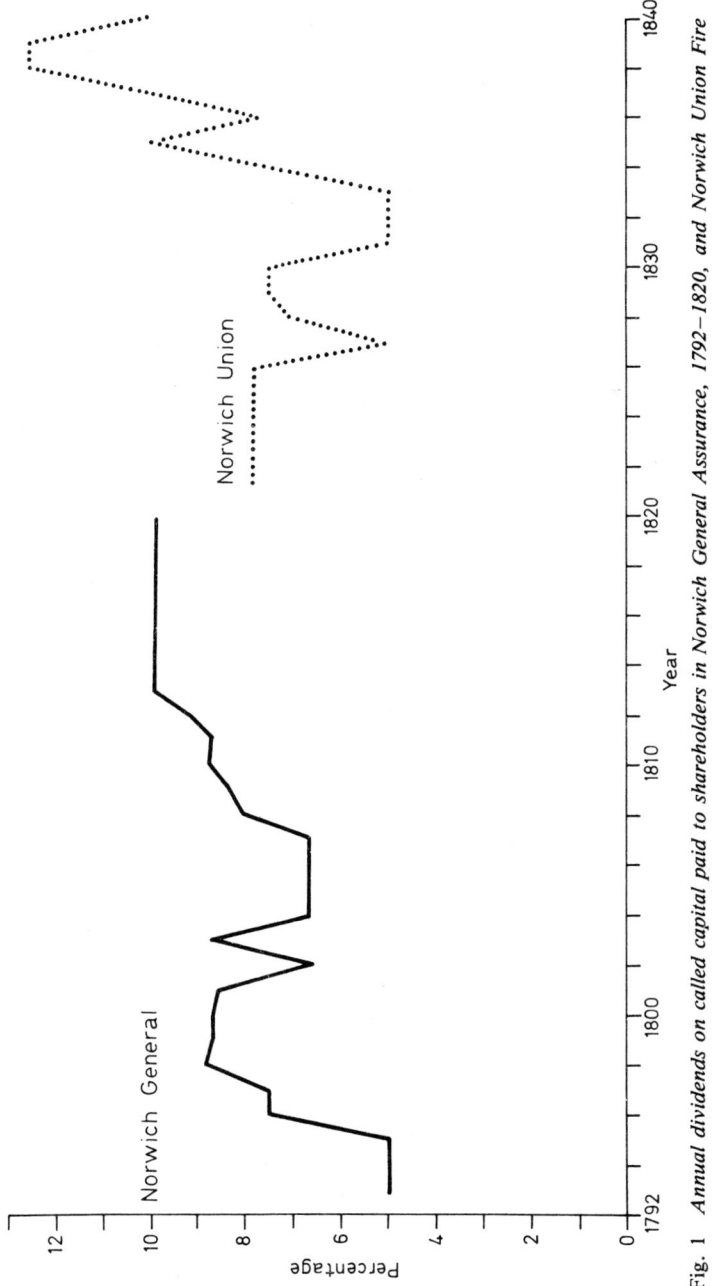

Fig. 1 *Annual dividends on called capital paid to shareholders in Norwich General Assurance, 1792–1820, and Norwich Union Fire Insurance Society, 1821–40.* Sources. Norwich Union Museum; Norwich General Assurance Company, Annual General Meetings of Proprietors, 1796 to 1821, dividend covering first three years, declared 1796, thus figures in Fig. 1 are an average of the total for 1792 to 1795; Norwich Union Fire Insurance Society, Finance Committee Minute Books, 1821 to 1840.

with. He preferred an unconventional style of management which was out of place in a business dominated by conservatism. Paradoxically, his independent approach got results but at the cost of producing head-on conflicts with his directors.

Yet the remarkable thing about Bignold is that for many years he surpassed the hostility and opposition aroused by his methods. His experience with the Norwich General board is a case in point. Few records survive to show how the Norwich General was managed. But there are clear signs of Bignold refusing to bow meekly to the authority of its directors. On at least one occasion he initiated an inquiry into their management of the funds. Also, he was undoubtedly at odds with them about underwriting policy. They preferred extreme caution, based on the local market, while he was looking towards the growing opportunities for expansion beyond East Anglia.

It was in this atmosphere of distrust and disagreement that he left the Norwich General without warning in February 1797. Within weeks he had organised the financial backing needed to launch the Norwich Union Fire Insurance Society. Moreover, once it had gained a foothold in the local market, the new Fire Society's premium income expanded at a tremendous rate, to reach almost £80,000 a year by 1817. Throughout this period it received no support from the wealthy Norwich merchant manufacturers and bankers. They came to play a significant part in the Norwich Union's business only after a three-year dispute in the society (between 1818 and 1821) which resulted in Bignold's being replaced as secretary by his third son, Samuel.

By then Bignold's efforts had pushed the Norwich Union into fourth position in the British market, in terms of sums insured (Table 1). Furthermore, the momentum of this outstanding early growth carried it to second place during the 1820s. Indeed, the Norwich Union remained among the leading four British fire offices until the 1860s, when it was overtaken by powerful new firms such as the Liverpool-based Royal.[10]

Meanwhile, Bignold was replaced in the Norwich General by Adam Taylor. Taylor proved better suited to the company's modest aims. He was a local attorney, and this remained his chief interest. As secretary to the Norwich General he acted efficiently but was neither innovative nor responsive to the competitive pressures arising in provincial insurance during the early nineteenth century. Premiums rose steadily to £5,000 per annum by the early 1800s. Yet under his management they were then allowed to remain at or near that level over the next twenty years. Indeed, there can have seemed little reason to do more. Dividends grew increasingly attractive (Fig. 1) and the company remained a local bastion of financial strength. Nevertheless its shareholders then found themselves in the totally unexpected position of playing a vital part in rescuing the Norwich Union from disaster in 1821. It was their capital, in fact, which guaranteed the Norwich Union's long-term survival as a leading fire office.

Accordingly, after outlining the organisation of the home market, the

Table 1. The British fire insurance market, 1805–51

| Share % of total market held by five largest firms | Individual years | | | | | | | Quinquennial averages | | | |
|---|---|---|---|---|---|---|---|---|---|---|---|
| | 1805 | 1810 | 1816 | 1820 | 1825 | 1829–33 | 1832–36 | 1837–41 | 1842–46 |
| Sun | 28·48 | 21·40 | 20·60 | 20·40 | 16·19 | 16·61 | 16·89 | 16·80 | 16·95 |
| Phoenix | 18·15 | 13·15 | 13·74 | 11·71 | 9·15 | 9·56 | 10·56 | 13·74 | 12·12 |
| Royal Exchange | 13·53 | 10·27 | 9·08 | 8·88 | 6·95 | 7·24 | 7·61 | 7·48 | 7·24 |
| Imperial | 7·10 | 8·06 | 6·62 | 6·18 | 4·60 | – | – | – | – |
| British | 5·75 | – | – | – | – | – | – | – | – |
| Globe | – | 6·24 | – | – | – | – | – | – | – |
| Norwich Union | – | – | 6·32 | 7·08 | 9·53 | 8·68 | 8·89 | 8·14 | 7·64 |
| Protector | – | – | – | – | – | 7·79 | – | – | – |
| County | – | – | – | – | – | – | 6·18 | 5·62 | 5·54 |
| Share % of total market held in total by: | | | | | | | | | |
| Five largest firms | 73·01 | 59·12 | 56·36 | 54·25 | 46·42 | 49·88 | 50·13 | 51·78 | 49·99 |
| Ten largest firms | 89·16 | 75·99 | 75·51 | 73·70 | 64·37 | 71·26 | 70·96 | 67·24 | 66·08 |
| Total No. of firms | 27 | n.d. | 36 | n.d. | 50 | 41 | 39 | 47 | 49 |
| Total amount of insurance each year, (averages from 1829–33, £ million) | 262 | 351 | 382 | 391 | 448 | 492 | 528 | 659 | 737 |

*Sources.* 1805: C. Walford, *Cyclopaedia*, III, pp. 420–1. 1810: S. Brown, 'On the progress of fire insurance in Great Britain', *Assurance Magazine*, VII, 1858, pp. 267–9; C. Walford, *Cyclopaedia*, III, p. 421; Norwich Union Museum, advertising pamphlet for Norwich Union figure. 1816, 1823, 1825: Norwich Union Museum, broadsheets showing duty payments. 1829–33: Colman and Rye Library, Norwich, broadsheet showing duty payments. 1832–36 to 1847–51: BPP's, Scottish offices included from 1837 to 1841; sums insured on farm stock but exempt duty are included in annual totals from 1834.

purpose of this chapter is to examine Thomas Bignold's influence on the early nineteenth-century fire insurance business in Britain. The discussion relates mainly to the Norwich Union Fire Society's growth between 1797 and 1818. The equally outstanding performance of the Life Society will be mentioned only where it clearly influenced the Norwich Union's fire insurance business. Finally, reference will be made to the contribution of Samuel Bignold, who reorganised the business in 1821 and brought its methods into line with those of the leading London insurance companies.

## II  The organisation of the early nineteenth-century fire insurance market

The British fire insurance market held obvious attractions for new firms like the Norwich Union during the 1790s and 1800s. Above all, the existing offices were by no means covering potential demand. Also, entry conditions were facilitated by the way the market was organised. New fire offices which might have found the going difficult, if not impossible, from the 1820s met fewer obstacles during these early years. Market size and organisation, therefore, determined the competitive framework for the Norwich Union's expansion between 1797 and 1821. This section discusses both aspects of the early nineteenth-century fire insurance market in turn.

Fire underwriting income is determined by the total value of sums insured as well as the average level of premium rates. Of course, sums insured were likely to grow as the industrialising economy accumulated capital. But it must also be remembered that insured values are always established at current price levels. Consequently, inflation and deflation could have a powerful effect on actual market size. Even this adjusted sum ignores the potential demand not actually being covered during the early nineteenth century. Many property owners had no fire insurance policy at all. Others often relied on cover well below their property's full value. According to an estimate by Sir Frederick Eden in 1802, some £557 million of insurable property existed in Britain.[11] Yet at that time only £223 millions, or about 40%, was actually insured.[12]

Assessing the impact of changes in non-insurance and underinsurance on market size poses immense difficulties for the historian. Both factors seemed to offer scope for expansion in the early nineteenth century. More fire offices were opening. In fighting for business they must have persuaded many property owners to insure for the first time. But their efforts in this direction probably did little more than keep the habit of insurance up to its existing level among Britain's rapidly growing population.[13] Certainly much of the property remaining uninsured consisted of the kind of small, badly built houses which fire underwriters instinctively avoided.[14]

Underinsurance is a more complicated problem which has received considerable attention from historians. D. T. Jenkins's chapter in this volume explains how companies tried to reduce it by applying strict divisions (detailed specifications) on the average clause.[15] However, the extent to which these techniques were applied in practice depended on the degree of competition for new business and the nature of the risk. Allowing underinsurance was an indirect way of reducing premiums and might easily take place in the face of competition.[16] All fire offices tended to be lenient on residential houses, farm stock and other low-risk properties. These brought a large volume of fairly safe business at low premium rates which could hardly cover the expense of a detailed valuation.[17]

Underinsurance was probably less extensive on large and complex industrial and commercial risks. London's dockside warehouses seem to have been fully covered as early as the 1800s.[18] It was only sensible to insist on full insurance when there was a substantial conflagration risk. There is less agreement about industrial risks. S. D. Chapman and D. T. Jenkins believe that a high degree of insurance was undertaken among textile mill owners in northern England during this period.[19] As Jenkins argues, few textile manufacturers would have deliberately underinsured to make a modest saving on their premiums when the risk of total loss was so high. Yet he has also pointed out that any factory's value could soon exceed the sum insured if prices rose rapidly, quite apart from the practical difficulties involved in making accurate valuations.[20] Making this point, J. Butt suggests that Scottish cotton mills were underinsured during the period by at least half their insurable value.[21] Donnachie's work on the smaller and less fire-prone breweries in Scotland assumes that for this type of risk the degree of underinsurance was even higher.[22] Indeed, Donnachie's views are probably generally true for British industry as a whole in the early nineteenth century. Most industrial output still came from small units with considerably less fire risk than large textile factories.[23] Competition for such business was often fierce, because it could easily be accepted by small country fire offices. This probably encouraged persistent underinsurance.[24]

On balance, then, it is unlikely that there was a dramatic change in either non-insurance or underinsurance during this period. In fact as late as the 1850s most insurance officials believed that the bulk of property was still covered only for up to half its insurable value.[25] Accordingly, the key factors determining market growth are likely to have been variations in price level and the rate of capital formation.

The price-adjusted value of property insured grew on average at only 1·1% each year from 1790 to 1814,[26] largely owing to the low rates of capital formation.[27] Between 1816 and 1840 this annual growth rate doubled to 2·2%,[28] with the return to higher rates of investment.[29] However, the actual values insured were strongly affected by price trends. Prolonged wartime inflation raised the annual average growth rate between 1790 and 1815 to 2·8%. Even with the buoyancy created by higher rates of capital formation after the French wars, the value of sums insured could grow only at a yearly average of 1·7% between 1815 and the early 1840s.[30] Clearly, from the point of view of sums insured, the earlier period offered the greater scope for expansion and entry.

Most of this potential lay in the provinces. Fire insurance was firmly established in London by the late eighteenth century.[31] In fact several leading London insurance companies were also expanding into the potentially far larger provincial market alongside the growing number of country fire offices.[32] Furthermore, new fire offices could open quite easily. There was a potentially huge mass market — known collectively as ordinary business — on housing, shops, farm stock and other non-hazardous risks. It enabled new offices to avoid the technical problems and large capital requirements of complex risks like textile mills — termed special business — which were in any case relatively few in number.[33]

Even so, all fire offices needed a large financial reserve to fall back on if their losses rose unexpectedly. Consequently, small partnerships were ruled out.[34] The larger organisations formed to give this cover also needed a secure legal status. Predictably they faced problems on this account before the 1844 Companies Act. The London Assurance and the Royal Exchange Assurance became incorporated, at great cost to their shareholders, by a clause in the 1720 Bubble Act.[35] Yet the chief aim of this legislation was to clamp down on new joint-stock ventures. It forced other insurance company promoters to seek refuge with the Chancery lawyers, who had already created a workable alternative to full incorporation in the form of the deed of settlement. This described the firm's purpose, listed its rules and vested its assets in named trustees.[36] Inadvertently, then, the Bubble Act made it easier for new insurance firms to start business once the deed of settlement had gained acceptance. If the only alternative had been for them to gain incorporation by private Act of Parliament, they would have faced high initial legal costs and close scrutiny by a parliamentary committee. Of course, powerful groups like those behind the flotation of the Globe would have easily gained incorporation.[37] But it is most unlikely that small provincial businessmen such as Thomas Bignold would have considered entering insurance. Admittedly, the deed of settlement could prove a cumbersome legal device if a dispute arose in a going concern, as happened to the Norwich Union in 1805 and 1818.[38] But it could be drafted quickly and at relatively little cost so as to allow any new insurance firm to open with remarkable speed.

Early nineteenth-century fire offices could be established in one of three ways: as a straightforward joint-stock company; on the mutual system; or as a joint-stock office dividing some profits among its policy-holders.[39] All but four of the sixteen fire offices open by 1800 were joint-stock companies of the first kind.[40] The Sun, Royal Exchange Assurance and Phoenix dominated the home market on this basis, taking nearly 80% of all business in 1802.[41] It is also known to have been used by about half the forty-five new offices opening in the first quarter of the nineteenth century, including powerful companies like the Imperial and the Globe.[42]

On the other hand, three early London mutual offices — the Hand in Hand, Union and Westminster — had survived.[43] They had virtually ignored the provincial market throughout the eighteenth century.[44] This reflected the difficulty of organising a large number of policy-holders in a mutual fire insurance society over an extensive area, particularly while communications and financial services remained poor. Yet in local provincial markets the mutual system offered an attractive alternative to joint-stock fire insurance. This possibility was realised only at the end of the eighteenth century, for Thomas Bignold was the first person known to have used the mutual system outside London and the home counties. Even he did so only when left with no workable alternative.[45] Yet once the Norwich Union had demonstrated the viability of mutual insurance in provincial districts Bignold's example was followed by at least another six offices, four within East Anglia alone, during the first quarter of the nineteenth century. By concentrating on their local markets, where there were few large commercial or industrial risks, the provincial mutuals could hold down losses in the early nineteenth century to yield regular surpluses of up to 50% which, when returned to policy-holders as a bonus, made them highly competitive.[46] Moreover Thomas Bignold used this initial advantage to extend the Norwich Union's business well beyond East Anglia from about 1805.

This method was so competitive that at least six joint-stock fire offices opening between 1800 and the late 1820s responded to the mutual system, and to the Norwich Union in particular, by returning part of their profits to policy-holders.[47] Understandably, these returns were lower than the mutual societies' bonuses, because their proprietors expected dividends comparable to those of other joint-stock fire offices. Yet they offered a most attractive compromise. Rates were effectively lower than those of the pure joint-stock companies on the one hand, while, on the other, policyholders accepted none of the liabilities taken on by every member in a mutual society. Certainly the County used this form of organisation very effectively from the company's foundation in 1807[48] (Table 1). It was also adopted from the start by the West of England in 1807, while the Atlas switched over to the system from a non-profit-sharing basis in 1816.[49] In fact the Norwich Union Fire Society took a similar decision in 1821, following growing difficulties with its extensive mutual organisation during the post-war depression.[50]

Entry was therefore possible in these three ways. Moreover, while so many other joint-stock ventures were ending in disaster during the late 1800s, the new fire offices — including the mutuals — proved remarkably stable.[51] Admittedly about a dozen small country fire offices closed in the first quarter of the nineteenth century. Generally, though, they had arranged in advance for a larger company to take on their risks.[52] Outright collapse was unheard-of in British fire insurance during the early nineteenth century.

Furthermore, though still in its infancy, life assurance was offering many agents attractive opportunities in association with fire insurance.[53] Consequently insurance company shares emerged as a very attractive investment. They were particularly favoured in periods of rising trade when capital was readily available. For example, no fewer than forty-three of the forty-five fire offices opening in the first quarter of the nineteenth century were launched during the two major cyclical upswings from 1802 to 1810 and 1820 to 1825.[54] Even though there were some closures and amalgamations, these bursts of new promotion were chiefly responsible for bringing the total number of British fire offices from twenty in 1800 up to fifty by 1825.[55]

It was far easier to raise capital for such ventures in London than in the provinces because of the city's vast financial resources, while many of its leading businessmen and M.P.s joined their boards or acted as trustees. London offices typically boasted subscribed capitals of between £1 million and £2 million. Even though this stock often covered life insurance commitments as well, it far exceeded the capital of provincial firms, where the range stretched from about £50,000 to £200,000, apart from the exceptional £600,000 of the Exeter-based West of England Fire and Life Insurance Company.[56]

In the provinces new fire offices were often closely linked with country banks.[57] In areas with surplus capital this proved an excellent complementary relationship. However, in capital deficit regions, such as the textile districts of Lancashire and Yorkshire, banking was less stable[58] and when such links existed local fire offices were prone to failure. The closure of the Manchester Fire Office in 1788 and probably the one at Liverpool in 1795 was linked with financial crises which hit local banks severely.[59] These problems, together with the fact that industrial risks in Yorkshire and Lancashire were larger and more hazardous than elsewhere in the provinces, meant that there was some reluctance to float local fire offices before the mid-1820s.[60] Yet both counties were among the fastest-growing fire insurance markets in Britain. The large London companies possessed the financial strength and technical expertise to take advantage of this growth and established a number of agencies in the north. The Norwich Union was the only country fire office to commit itself fully to these districts. The decision played a key part in its remarkable expansion. Generally, however, provincial fire offices concentrated on local markets and, as Table 2 shows, the result was that while many of them were formed, their total share of the British market was overshadowed by a smaller number of London firms.[61]

Finally, we turn to the competitive structure created by this pattern of market growth, organisation and entry. As explained earlier, the most rapid growth of insured values took place during the French wars. This undoubtedly stimulated entry, which in turn led to a significant fall in premium rates. Yet business appears to have remained profitable even though collusion was prevented by the continued entry of large, well financed London offices between 1810 and 1811. This meant that there were few barriers to expansion. However, when insured values began to grow more slowly after 1815 competition intensified. This problem was made even more severe by the additional entry which took place in the early 1820s. Premium rates were driven down,

Table 2. *British fire insurance market, 1805–45: total market shares held by London compared with other British fire offices (%)*

|  | 1805 | 1810 | 1816 | 1823 | 1825 | 1830 | 1835 | 1840 | 1845 |
|---|---|---|---|---|---|---|---|---|---|
| | London fire offices | | | | | | | | |
| No. of fire offices | 11 | 15 | 15 | 17 | 20 | 16 | 15 | 21 | 20 |
| Share % of market | 91·7 | 86·9 | 80·9 | 80·2 | 73·5 | 73·3 | 72·6 | 72·2 | 73·1 |
| | Country fire offices (plus those in Scotland from 1835 onwards) | | | | | | | | |
| No. of fire offices | 16 | n.a. | 21 | 20 | 29 | 25 | 36 | 35 | 36 |
| Share % of market | 8·3 | 13·1 | 19·1 | 19·8 | 26·5 | 26·7 | 27·4 | 27·8 | 26·9 |

*Source.* S. Brown, 'On the progress of fire insurance in Great Britain', *Assurance Magazine*, VII, 1858, pp. 267–9.

reinforcing the effect on business of declining property values. Insurers found themselves having to cover larger and more complex risks without a proportionate rise in premium income. In these circumstances it is not surprising that the 1820s saw the first really effective attempts to organise premium rate collusion across the market.[62] This posed problems for smaller companies wishing to expand, quite apart from the squeeze on profitability.

It is therefore evident that the Norwich Union, by entering the market in 1797, just before a period of rapid market expansion, could become well established before difficult market conditions and barriers to entry developed. Yet, on the other hand, the important advantages possessed by London offices which enabled them to retain market leadership have also been described. In this respect the Norwich Union ran against the pattern of concentration of business in the hands of the London companies. Certainly its emergence as the fourth largest British fire office before 1820 must have been primarily reponsible for reducing the London companies' market share from just over 90% in 1805 to some 80% fifteen years later. Figure 2 leaves no doubt as to the success of this effort, with annual premiums rising from £3,900 in 1804 to £78,000 in 1818, while there was a growth in membership (policy-holders) from about 5,000 to 70,000 over the same period. Furthermore, this was the only occasion when the mutual system received an extensive trial in British fire insurance on a fully co-operative profit and liability-sharing basis. The society's methods and development are therefore of particular interest.

### III. *The Norwich Union's early background, to 1805*

When Thomas Bignold left the Norwich General to found the Norwich Union in February 1797 conditions for raising capital could hardly have been worse, with the Bank of England suspending cash payments the very week the Fire Society opened. This probably influenced his decision to adopt the mutual system. But the main reason for his choice was that, having fallen out with the city's wealthy Tory and Whig leaders, he had turned to its extreme radical groups for help. They were small merchants and local tradesmen who, like himself, were prosperous enough, but not capable of financing a joint-stock venture. Moreover the co-operative nature of mutual insurance must have appealed to their radical outlook, especially at a time when the London companies were widely believed to be making excess profits from country business. The radicals not only supported the Norwich Union, they also provided members for its first board of twelve directors. Indeed, Thomas Bignold, in turn, never hesitated to emphasise the mutual system's profit-sharing principles in his new role as the Norwich Union's secretary. The Fire Society's well advertised practice of returning all profits as a bonus to its 'members' played a crucial role in its expansion during the early nineteenth century.

Like most fire offices, the Norwich Union's deed of settlement defined its purpose while naming the first board of twelve directors, half of whom

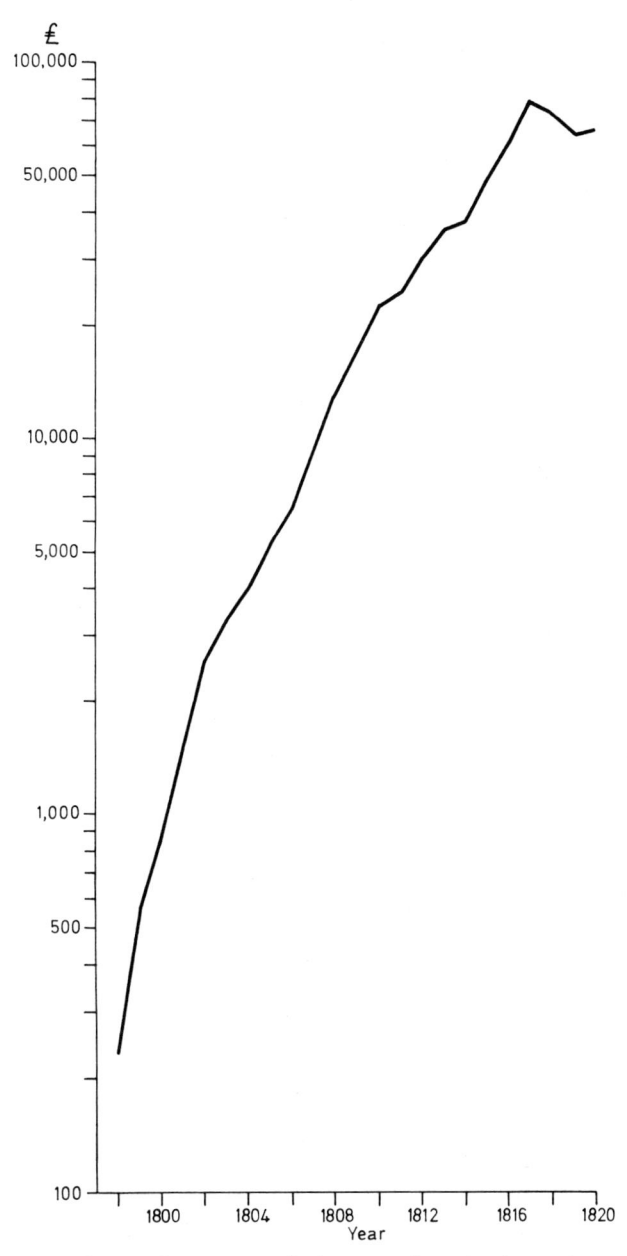

Fig. 2 *Norwich Union Fire Insurance Society: annual premium income between 1797 and 1821. Source.* Norwich Union Museum, Norwich Union Society; Statement of Receipts and Disbursements, 1797 to 1820.

also acted as trustees. But unlike the joint-stock offices ultimate control rested with the members, who could alter the deed as they wished. Some protection was given against arbitrary use of this power by requiring any proposed change to have the backing of at least twenty policy-holders with total insurances of over £10,000, who then had to secure the approval of a properly advertised general meeting of members. These principles of mutual control were also embodied in a requirement that four directors should retire each year. All elections had to be confirmed by the annual general meeting.

Of course, as secretary Thomas Bignold implemented decisions taken at the weekly board meetings. Like any full-time official he had the advantage of being in day-to-day contact with the business. This enabled him to influence the directors, who lacked a detailed knowledge of the society's routines. Also, in recognition of his role as founder he could be dismissed only by a majority vote of a general meeting. Compared to most other provincial fire office secretaries, who could be removed by their directors, this gave him an unusual degree of freedom to interpret his managerial role. In this respect he was in a similar position to the top officials in some of the large London companies. But he even had an edge over them, because he received 10% of all premium income in lieu of a fixed salary. By 1815 he was receiving some £5,000 per annum, gross, from the society plus a similar amount from the Norwich Union's 'sister' life office, which he founded in 1808. Certainly he was responsible for meeting routine head-office expenses from his own pocket. But these accounted for well under 10% of his total income from the societies. Together with the relative security of his appointment, this reflects the unusually powerful incentive that the arrangements had given him to expand the Norwich Union business.

Initially, though, it is unlikely that either Bignold or the other founding members appreciated the long-term implications of his conditions of appointment. His exceptional income was derived from the unprecedented way he expanded the Norwich Union after 1805. Initially his aim was to establish the society with a modest premium income from local sources. At best Bignold might have expected to receive some £200 to £300 a year.

Every mutual fire office goes through an initial period when survival depends on avoiding heavy losses until a reserve fund is accumulated from its premiums. Like the original London mutuals, the Norwich Union partly covered this danger with an initial commitment from its founding members, twenty-eight of whom apparently accepted a personal liability of £1,000 each.[63] It also followed the early mutuals' practice of issuing septennial policies. This gave every member a secure contract for seven years if he paid his annual premiums, while also allowing the society a reasonable time to determine its average loss ratio before having to declare the first bonus from profits.[64]

But the threat to solvency was more apparent than real. Bignold appreciated that the only way to establish the Norwich Union's credibility was to produce an impressive bonus after seven years. Initially, then, the society kept to ordinary business and followed the conventional practice of increasing premium rates according to both the class and size of each risk, as shown in Table 3. In fact the Norwich Union's underwriting remained distinctly conservative. It refused to insure any single risk beyond £3,000, excluded all London property and confined its remaining area of business to England and Wales.

Table 3 *Norwich Union Fire Insurance Society: premium rates, 1797–1805*

| Sums insured | Premium rate per £100 insured per annum | | |
|---|---|---|---|
| | Common risks | Hazardous risks | Doubly hazardous risks |
| Up to £1,000 | 2s 0d | 3s 0d | 5s 0d |
| £1,000 to £2,000 | 2s 6d | 4s 0d | 5s 0d |
| £2,000 to £3,000 | 2s 6d | 5s 0d | 7s 6d |

*Source.* Norwich Union Museum, Norwich Union Fire Insurance Society, copy Deed of Settlement, Amendments to Original Deed, enrolled in Chancery 1 March 1806.

But these restrictions had little impact at first, because initial growth relied chiefly on attracting the relatively safe business on housing, commercial and agricultural property in East Anglia. Of around seventy agents appointed by 1804, forty-five were in either Norfolk or Suffolk, and these counties had provided almost 75% of the society's new business since 1797 (see Table 5). Indeed, in 1804 the founding members were rewarded with a bonus of no less than 75%. As Bignold put it, the initial obstacles had been 'happily surmounted'.

Yet despite his success Bignold quarrelled with the directors a year later when it became obvious that he intended expanding the society well beyond East Anglia. Like his earlier argument with the Norwich General board, it began as a trivial matter. But it soon became clear that the real issue concerned the extent of Bignold's freedom to use his own judgement in running the society. The directors were well satisfied with the existing bonus results, which had been set at a more realistic 50% after the first declaration, and had no wish to take on riskier business. They all possessed other local business interests, as was common among eighteenth-century provincial entrepreneurs. An extraordinarily ambitious man like Bignold was bound to come into conflict with the modest aims of such a board at some stage. Differences of opinion are, of course, normal in any firm. But the secretary's strong position in the Norwich Union — not his stormy temperament — brought this dispute about the society's expansion before the public and prevented the directors from removing him quietly.

54  *The business of insurance*

In fact the decision on Bignold's future rested with those members who attended the general meeting called to settle the dispute. Among the city's tradesmen and small merchants support for the directors and for Bignold was evenly balanced. Indeed, Bignold proved himself totally indifferent to political ideals. He readily switched to the large group of local tradesmen and small merchants who were Tories in order to rally enough support to defeat his radical directors. As secretary he could also mobilise the 'country' members in Norfolk and Suffolk, who were impressed by his bonus results. Their support tipped the scales in his favour. The attempt to dismiss him was clearly rejected (by 279 votes to 64) at the crucial general meeting in April 1805. He actually strengthened his position by capitalising on their support a month later to secure three amendments in the deed of settlement. The first simply confirmed his appointment, with a specific reference to his role as founder. The second changed the society's premium rates for ordinary business and introduced special risks, thus bringing its practice into line with the most advanced London offices (Table 4). The final, and most important,

Table 4. *Norwich Union Fire Insurance Society: premium rates, 1806–25, 'For the Insurance of Property to any Amount, not exceeding £3,000'*

| Risks | Premium rate per £100 insured per annum |
|---|---|
| Common | 2s 0d |
| Hazardous | 3s 0d |
| Doubly hazardous | 5s 0d |
| Special | Rate 'adopted to the nature of the risk' |

*Source.* Norwich Union Museum, Norwich Union Fire Insurance Society, copy Deed of Settlement, Amendments to Original Deed, enrolled in Chancery 1 March 1806.

amendment replaced the existing board with eighteen new directors and created a separate group of nine trustees. Unlike the previous board, these new appointments were made for life. Closed recruitment was also secured by a rule allowing board vacancies to be filled by a vote among the trustees, while new trustees were appointed by the directors. In fact, whereas only eighteen directors could hold office at one time, there was no limit on the number of trustees. By 1818 there were around fifty.

Ironically, Bignold's earlier quarrel with the Norwich General strengthened his position at this stage. Although all the new directors were local men, mostly Tories, none of them belonged to the city's wealthy manufacturing or professional groups. His own family therefore managed to secure key positions within the Norwich Union. Already by 1804 he had opened the Union Bank with his eldest son, John Cocksedge Bignold. Gradually this firm secured most of the Fire Office's financial business together with that of its 'sister' Life Society after 1808. Then his second son, Thomas junior, qualified as a solicitor in 1809. With Bignold's son-in-law he took over the Norwich Union's legal business shortly afterwards. Finally, Samuel, the third son, joined the Fire Society in about 1811. Within three years the members had approved his appointment as joint secretary with the right to succeed his father.

Meanwhile, although no large landowners joined the new board, they provided about half the trustees appointed by 1818, and the help given by 'country' members in 1805 resulted in local farmers being well represented, with a third of the board consisting of owner-occupiers from Norfolk or Suffolk. Yet in practice they were seldom in close touch with events at head office, and the most active directors remained, as before, local small businessmen. The only difference was that they were all Tories instead of radicals. For all his personal influence within the Norwich Union, Bignold needed their support if he was to extend its business after 1805. In the event they gave him a virtually free hand to run the society over the next decade. Why they should have done so is not entirely clear, but it is likely that once drawn into the business they found the attractions of being associated with such an energetic character irresistible. Certainly despite lacking experience of insurance they immediately became a focus of public attention and enjoyed a rising social status as Norwich Union directors over a period when it evolved into a business of national rather than local significance. And in this respect they were perhaps better fitted to be directors than their predecessors, because, like Bignold, they avoided the burden of active involvement in local politics even though they were nominally Tory supporters.

IV. *Expansion; 1805 to 1818*

With the new table of rates, the Norwich Union could handle its business more easily up to the £3,000 limit (Table 4). London risks were still excluded. But with that market virtually saturated there was little point in a small country fire office opening agencies in the capital. Instead Bignold turned to the provincial market beyond East Anglia. He trebled the number of agencies by 1811 — a peak year for new appointments — to a total of 300, providing a network which covered most of England and Wales. Then in 1814 the members agreed to extend the business to Ireland and Scotland, to remove the ban on London risks, and to raise the ceiling on any single risk to £10,000. Meanwhile new agencies continued to open. More than 500 existed by 1818.

Initially the society had to compete with prestigious London companies in districts where it was virtually unknown. This must have tempted Bignold to resort to direct premium rate-cutting in an attempt to gain a foothold in new markets. In fact the Norwich Union's opponents regarded its bonuses as simply another form of rate-cutting and, as mentioned earlier, some companies responded by sharing profits with their own policy-holders. Nevertheless, compared with cuts on premium rates which had to be made *before* losses were known, the mutual system offered far less danger to solvency, because bonuses were paid only *after* the risk had been taken. As a purely mutual society, then, it would have been illogical for the Norwich Union to throw away this security by initiating a premium rate-cutting war if its bonuses, with the backing of non-price competition, could attract an adequate flow of new business.

Indeed, very little scope existed for direct cuts on ordinary business, which accounted for some 90% of the society's liabilities, because existing rates were already low enough to discourage further competition. The only time that Bignold reduced any of these rates, in fact, was in 1808, when he followed the Sun's lead and cut farm-stock premiums from 2*s* 6*d* to 2*s* 0*d* per cent, a predictable defensive move, bearing in mind that agricultural insurance was a major source of local business for the Norwich Union.

More room existed for rate-cutting on special risks. Yet these were already under severe pressure before the society looked beyond East Anglia for business after 1805. For example, the Phoenix had already accepted the need to reduce special rates below half those charged in the late eighteenth century. Although the few surviving Norwich Union policies on special business cannot show its response to these conditions in detail, they do allow the main trends in its special rating to be followed up to 1821.

Early Norwich Union policies on corn, paper, flax and woollen mills contain only basic details, with few divisions. Some of these risks were certainly taken at unduly low rates. But this was hardly surprising. With little experience of handling complex insurances remote from head office, Bignold, as secretary, must have found great difficulty in imposing an adequate method of classifying them across a rapidly growing agency network. The £3,000 limit remained Bignold's chief safeguard against serious error. After about 1812, however, Norwich Union policies were increasingly drafted with the greater detail needed to set rates accurately.

Some indications of this emerge on all special risks. But a substantial run of about sixty corn-mill policies give the best overall picture for the period 1805 to 1818. Variations according to type of building material and power source as well as the number of stones used began to appear in 1811. By then the Globe's corn-mill rates are known to have been in line with those charged by the Norwich Union. In 1812, for example, the Globe charged 7*s* 6*d* per cent for a five-storeyed water-powered corn mill with a kiln, a price which that company's agent, who wanted to confirm at 5*s* per cent, regarded as 'much higher than expected'.[65]

Indeed, the Norwich Union charged a steady base rate of 5*s* per cent on the safest corn mills, which would have been regarded as adequate by most offices. Moreover the increasingly detailed underwriting evident in the society's corn-mill policies from 1807 to 1818 brought an *upward* trend in rates on the more hazardous risks. By 1814, for example, water-powered mills were being rated at 10*s* 6*d* per cent if they housed a kiln; a steam-powered corn mill in turn was accepted at 13*s* per cent in the same year. As this coincided with a rapid expansion of the Norwich Union's business, it clearly suggests that deliberate rate-cutting played little or no part in Bignold's sales methods.

Admittedly, the society charged only 16s per cent for a sugar refinery in 1813. This lay well below the Sun's range of 21s to 32s on these risks at the time. Also, by charging 7s 6d per cent for woollen mills the Norwich Union had captured the business of eight leading Trowbridge factories from the Sun by 1815.[66] Yet rather than deliberate rate-cutting this probably reflects the Sun's reluctance to bring its prices down to current market levels until after the French wars. Certainly at 14s to 18s per cent from 1816 onwards the Norwich Union's cotton-mill rates lay well within the band then being charged by the Sun and Globe.[67] The overall impression, then, remains one of the Norwich Union avoiding direct rate-cutting on special business just as firmly as for ordinary risks.

Instead, by an intensive use of advertising throughout the provincial press, Bignold presented mutual insurance as a system which not only offered good bonuses but also had the support of influential trustees. He relied initially on local worthies like the wealthy Yarmouth brewer and banker Sir Edmund Lacon, but, as the society's connections widened, aristocratic policyholders and other prominent landowners or businessmen agreed to become trustees, including the radical Cumberland landowner John Christian Curwen, M.P., the Duke of Somerset and Earl of Craven.[68] No fewer than ten of the fifty appointed before 1818, in fact, belonged to the aristocracy, and their presence gave the Norwich Union a public image every bit as impressive as those of its chief rivals, the large London companies.

But, as Jenkins's chapter explains, good agents were vital to any sales effort. Bignold recruited them by inviting applications from likely candidates in new areas.[69] Those appointed were typical of most insurance offices, with attorneys figuring prominently, followed by local businessmen such as brewers, various kinds of merchants and shopkeepers. Many of those who became agents after 1808, particularly the attorneys, had doubtless been attracted by the opportunity to also represent the Life Society. Meanwhile they all received 10% commission on their fire premiums, with those in larger towns occasionally being paid expenses for supervising agents or surveying risks in surrounding districts. Very few had previous experience of fire underwriting. But, within the limits laid down by head office, they selected risks and settled most claims. Until 1811 few problems arose, as premiums grew rapidly and loss ratios remained low enough (Fig. 3) for a 50% bonus to be maintained with ease. This gave the Norwich Union a huge advantage over joint-stock rivals even if, like the County, they shared part of their profits with policy-holders.

The commercial crisis of 1810 brought two years of heavier loss ratios, and although there was a fall when trade recovered they rose to a new peak during the post-war depression (Fig. 3). Understandably, most insurers

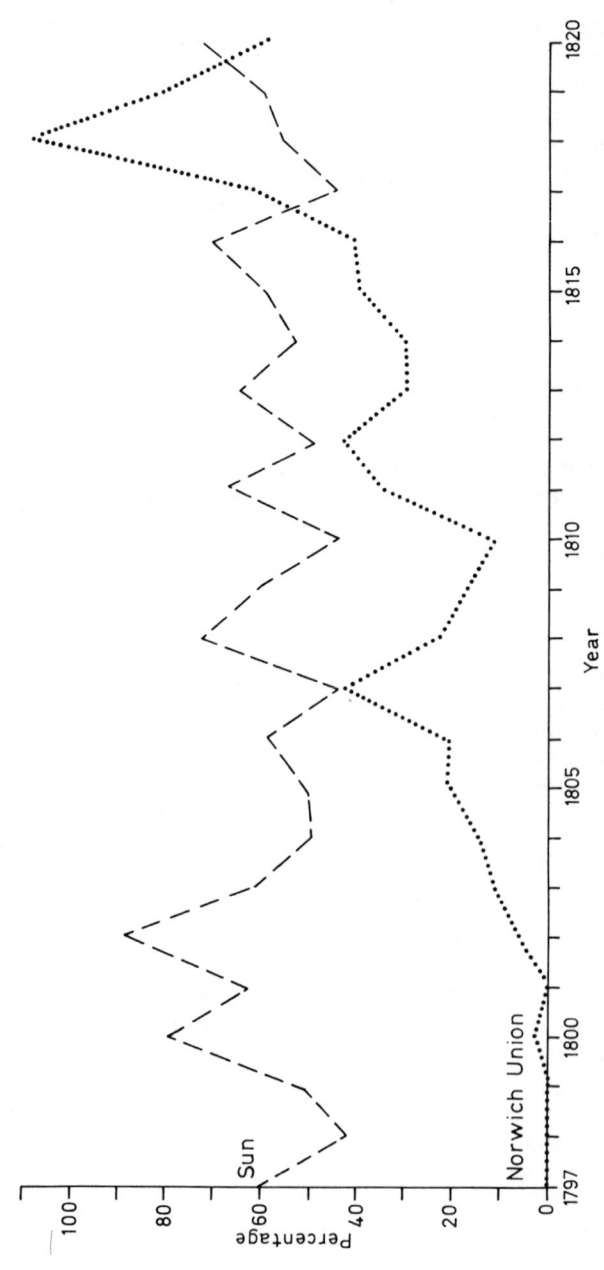

Fig. 3 *Norwich Union Fire Insurance Society: losses as a percentage of annual premiums, compared with the Sun Fire Office, 1797–1820.*
*Sources.* Norwich Union Museum, Norwich Union Society, Statement of Receipts and Disbursements, 1797 to 1820; P. G. M. Dickson, *Sun*, p. 302.

blamed this coincidence of high claims and trade recession on arson or what they termed the 'moral hazard' of policy-holders who took inadequate precautions against fire. Indeed, many industrial and commercial risks were growing more complex while forensic science remained in its infancy. Consequently, and policy-holder verging on bankruptcy could burn down his property and claim on his insurance with little chance of detection or, as probably happened more often, he merely needed to stop taking safety precautions so that a fire would occur of its own accord.[70] Meanwhile, in farming and industrial districts, the setbacks to local trade caused high unemployment which in turn brought outbreaks of incendiarism.

Obviously the Norwich Union was worried, because its bonuses were threatened unless the rising trend in loss ratios could be reversed quickly.

Bignold, therefore, responded to the first signs of trouble in 1812 with a plan to form local committees of members in districts remote from Norwich. He intended them to serve as a link between head office and the agencies by investigating local claims and new policy proposals in an attempt to reduce fraud. Moreover, by persuading prominent members to join the committees he also hoped to attract new business, an aim perhaps inspired by similar measures taken by the Atlas and County.

Originally, Bignold wanted to promote the scheme by visiting every large agency himself. He did so in Kent, which beyond East Anglia was the Society's largest market, but then showed less interest when trade recovered in 1813. Renewed enthusiasm came during the post-war depression, with nearly fifty committees being established by 1817. No records survive to indicate their effectiveness but, as most were formed after loss ratios had fallen during 1813 and 1814, they can hardly have contributed much to this improvement. Probably most had been appointed by the more resourceful agents after 1815 to strengthen the Norwich Union's image at a time of intensifying competition.

Nearly all the committee members appear to have been substantial insurers, often owning hazardous risks, and their chief motive for publicly backing the Norwich Union could well have been that its high bonuses were leading to a significant cut in their own running costs.

Whereas a variety of industries and trades were normally represented on the committees, those in northern England were dominated by textile manufacturers and merchants, including the prominent Leeds woollen merchant John Hebblethwaite,[71] the Todmorden cotton manufacturers Joshua and Samuel Fielden, and the Manchester cotton spinner Jonathan Pollard.[72] The most valuable members of the Darlington committee were the Quaker bankers and worsted manufacturers John and Edward Backhouse, whose firm, apart from its high repute throughout the north east,[73] brought previous experience of holding an agency with the Royal Exchange Assurance.[74]

This set the Norwich Union apart from other country fire offices. Some, like the West of England, the Newcastle, and even the Suffolk, accepted textile risks in these districts, but they lacked the wholehearted commitment[75] to

Table 5. *Norwich Union Fire Insurance Society: geographical distribution of new premium income, 1797–1814*

| County | % of total new premium income | | |
|---|---|---|---|
| | 1797–1804 | 1805–11 | 1812–14 |
| Bedfordshire | 0·29 | 1·54 | 1·27 |
| Berkshire | 1·77 | 1·64 | 2·28 |
| Buckinghamshire | 2·91 | 0·68 | 0·78 |
| Cambridgeshire | 2·91 | 5·83 | 4·57 |
| Devon | Nil | 2·96 | 2·69 |
| Durham | Nil | 1·93 | 2·28 |
| Essex | 3·74 | 2·25 | 1·96 |
| Gloucestershire | 0·88 | 5·33 | 6·70 |
| Hertfordshire | 0·11 | 4·42 | 2·90 |
| Huntingdonshire | 2·19 | 2·35 | 0·66 |
| Kent | Nil | 6·72 | 11·44 |
| Lancashire | Nil | 6·55 | 11·02 |
| Norfolk | 56·72 | 15·43 | 11·06 |
| Northamptonshire | 3·50 | 2·62 | 3·89 |
| Northumberland | 1·96 | 2·18 | 4·60 |
| Shropshire | Nil | 1·78 | 2·23 |
| Suffolk | 16·42 | 7·40 | 5·62 |
| Warwickshire | Nil | 2·12 | 2·41 |
| Yorkshire | 4·59 | 10·16 | 8·71 |
| Other counties | 3·08 | 16·11 | 12·93 |
| Total | 100·00 | 100·00 | 100·00 |

*Note.* All counties named provided over 1·5% of the Fire Society's total new premium income in at least one sub-period.
*Source.* These figures have been estimated from the individual agency returns in Norwich Union Museum, Norwich Union Society, Instituted 1797, statement of the Sums repaid to the Members whose Seven Years have expired, distinguishing the Agencies and Years (1804 to 1821).

them which is reflected in particular in the society's rapid growth in Lancashire and Yorkshire (Table 5). Insuring textile factory risks in both counties had its dangers, while as a newcomer the society could at best hope to charge the existing premium rates which in the Sun's opinion had been forced too low by competition to yield a profit.[76] Yet there was also much to gain. The towns of Yorkshire and Lancashire were expanding rapidly, and once a foothold had been established by taking high-risk policies a wide range of ordinary insurances followed, to bring a substantial volume to business.

This point is also indicated in Table 6, which shows the amounts insured through the Norwich Union's largest agencies in 1816 and 1821. Liverpool, Manchester and Leeds were clear leaders. The presence of cotton factory risks at Manchester led to a high average premium rate on its total business in 1821, which was approached only by Leeds, where many woollen mills were insured.

Table 6. *Norwich Union Fire Insurance Society: sums insured by the leading agencies, 1816 and 1822, showing the average premium rates for 1822*

| Agency | 1816[a] | | 1822[b] | | Average premium rate per £100 insured |
|---|---|---|---|---|---|
| | Sums insured (£ million) | % of total | Sums insured (£ million) | % of total | |
| Birmingham | 1·05 | 4·35 | 0·99 | 2·23 | 2s 2d |
| Bristol | 1·60 | 6·63 | 1·26 | 2·84 | 2s 11d |
| Canterbury | 0·66 | 2·73 | n.d. | n.d. | n.d. |
| Dublin | n.d. | n.d. | 1·00 | 2·25 | 4s 1d |
| Cambridge | n.d. | n.d. | 0·18 | 1·83 | 3s 5d |
| Edinburgh | 0·60 | 2·49 | n.d. | n.d. | n.d. |
| Leeds | 1·09 | 4·52 | 1·02 | 2·30 | 4s 6d |
| Liverpool | 1·86 | 7·71 | 2·30 | 5·18 | 3s 1d |
| London | n.d. | n.d. | 1·13 | 2·55 | 3s 1d |
| Manchester | n.d. | n.d. | 1·48 | 3·34 | 5s 0d |
| Newcastle | 0·57 | 2·36 | 0·51 | 1·15 | 3s 0d |
| Norwich | 0·96 | 3·98 | 2·30 | 5·18 | 2s 10½d |
| All other agencies | 16·71[d] | 69·22 | 31·57[f] | 71·15 | n.d. |
| Total insured | 24·14[c] | 100·00 | 44·37[e] | 100·00 | |

*Notes*
a The agencies named in 1816, although among the largest, are derived from a Norwich Union advertising pamphlet and there is no particular significance in the exclusion of Manchester and Cambridge. Also Dublin had just started and its business was still small in 1816.
b The unusually high figure for Norwich in 1822 probably reflects the fact that the society had just added the Norwich General Assurance's highly localised business to its own interest at head office.

*Sources*
a N.U.M., Books, General Association for the Prevention of Accidents by Fire and the Remuneration of Individual Sufferers, Norwich, April 1818, Bacon and Kinnebrook, p. 20.
b Norwich Union Fire Insurance Society, Finance Committee Minutes, 5 November 1822.
c Appendix, Fire Insurance Duty Return, 1816.
d Balance of (c) less individual agencies named.
d Norwich Union Fire Insurance Society, Finance Committee Minutes, 4 March 1823, Analysis of Amount Insured ...
f Balance of (e) less individual agencies named.

This resulted in Manchester's agency being the Norwich Union's largest single source of premiums. Indeed, local demand for life insurance was also expanding; so much so, in fact, that by 1820 one Norwich Union official described the north-west, centred on Manchester, as 'the Principal English District of the [Life] Society'.[77]

Meanwhile Bignold tried to hold down loss ratios by avoiding large single risks whenever possible, even for a year or so after the original £3,000 limit was raised to £10,000 in 1814. With many industrial and commercial risks growing in size — while their values were also rising, owing to wartime inflation — this might have checked the Norwich Union's expansion. It did not do so for several reasons. Above all, most factories and mills were still fairly small and a good market existed within the £3,000 limit. Beyond that, despite the intensity of the competition, fire offices were prepared to co-operate with one another to some extent. Co-operation took the form of co-insurance, with several firms splitting a large risk. Surprisingly, co-insurance could lead to closer ties between companies. This was certainly true of the Norwich Union by 1812, because when one of its agents asked whether he could accept a single risk of £20,000 Samuel Bignold replied:

We would go as far as £5,000 tho' the Directors normally restrict themselves to £3,000 ... But we can procure policies ... from the Phoenix and Atlas ... for the difference, say £15,000. And those offices have, by an arrangement which we have made with them agreed to allow our agents commission.[78]

Nevertheless, Bignold's overriding policy was to fight vigorously for new business, and, apart from raising the single-risk limit to £10,000 in 1814, expansion was maintained by extending the society's agency network into Scotland, Ireland and London. London was the most difficult of these new areas. An outsider stood far less chance of success here than in the provinces. But it was also the focal point of Britain's legal and financial services and the home of every large insurance office except the Norwich Union. Consequently, if the society's growth was to continue, it could not afford to remain out of touch with London. This alone might explain Bignold's decision to move there himself in 1815 to open an agency. By then he had once more quarrelled with his directors and could well have seen the move as an opportunity to evade attempts to control his activities. The background to his move is unclear, and it is not known how the society was organised during the next three years. Samuel Bignold certainly took over some of the provincial business, but his father was still regarded as *the* secretary, and retained control over the Life Society as well as the family's Union Bank. Nevertheless, this split in the management contributed to the build-up towards a second dispute in 1818.

## V  *The second dispute, 1818*

The Norwich Union's continued expansion after 1815 sharpened the resentment of rival offices, because for most of them the post-war depression brought at best a stagnation of premium income. The society's entry into new markets and acceptance of larger risks in these years also increased its loss ratio. They did not, however, exceed levels regarded as normal by well established large companies like the Sun (Fig. 3). Expansion itself, therefore, removed any chance of maintaining 50% bonuses. Yet high bonuses were central to Bignold's sales methods, and any reduction might easily have destroyed public confidence in the society at this crucial stage in its early growth. By 1817 the once remote danger that policy-holders might have to contribute towards losses was beginning to appear too close for comfort (Fig. 2). Despite the Norwich Union's reserves of £108,000, rival offices could now hit its mutual system at its weakest point; against the society's impressive bonuses, they argued, the public should contemplate the chaos that would arise if the Norwich Union needed to levy a call on 70,000 members. It was a prospect against which 'the price of security was of minor consideration'.[79]

Yet Bignold was not the man to give in without a fight. He boldly tried to resolve the problem in 1817 with a private Bill which aimed to limit the members' liability to the collective funds of the society. Greater credence was given to his proposal in June 1817, when the annual general meeting approved a plan for a yearly deduction of 7½% from premium income until the society had accumulated a reserve fund of £500,000.[80] Yet these belated efforts were in vain, because the House of Lords threw out the Bill and, if anything, the resulting publicity made matters worse.

With the members' growing unease about Thomas Bignold's business methods and judgement, the annual report in June 1818 dealt a final blow to their confidence in his management. Not only had the loss ratio risen sharply, but it was disclosed that two-thirds of these claims arose from either fraudulent or incendiary fires. This immediately caught their attention, especially in London where, out of the directors' reach but firmly in the public eye, they formed two rival committees of investigation.

One, chaired by John Thorpe, a City M.P. who was probably backed by rival insurance companies, originated with a complaint from some twenty members that Bignold's suspicions about frauds had led him to deliberately delay settling their claims. The other arose from a meeting of London members called to the York Hotel, Blackfriars, by head office to deny the allegations. From the start, this 'York Hotel Committee' showed more sympathy than Thorpe for the Norwich Union's difficulties. Understandably it received greater co-operation than he did from the directors and Samuel Bignold.

Yet Thomas Bignold further isolated himself by totally refusing to co-operate with either committee, and it was left to Samuel to foster the York Hotel Committee's goodwill. Indeed, Samuel offered to assist in every way possible at its first meeting. Over the next few months he also rallied support in the provinces, where he found most agents, local committee members and trustees willing to back head office rather than face the likely alternative of the Norwich Union losing its business to London companies if the York Hotel Committee's report was unfavourable.

Predictably the committees differed on many points when they reported two months later. But Thomas Bignold's obstructiveness, particularly when compared to the tactful co-operation of Samuel, brought strong criticism from both. Their most serious accusation was that he had taken two claimants to court on charges of arson without the directors' knowledge. Even when both cases went against the Norwich Union, he had still refused to settle the losses. As mentioned earlier, fire offices could normally do little against suspicious claims, owing to the technical difficulties of proving fraud. Neither committee, in fact, mentioned the prevalence of arson despite the emphasis on it in the society's last annual report. Although some of the contested claims were suspicious, they had since been quietly paid by the directors, who now understandably preferred the problem to be forgotten.

Serious mismanagement had also occurred in the handling of Norwich Union funds. Of £108,000 in the Fire Society and another £257,000 belonging to the Life Office, only a fifth was correctly vested in the names of the legal trustees, while the remaining securities were held by either Samuel or Thomas Bignold. Samuel immediately agreed to assign his to the proper trustees, but his father once more refused to co-operate.[81]

Such evidence led both committees to conclude that Thomas Bignold ought to retire, and this was supported virtually unanimously by a large special general meeting called to receive the York Hotel Committee's report. Their decision that he was, in effect, solely to blame was unjust. Hardly any decisions taken by him could have been effected without his sons' knowledge, even if they disagreed with them. Moreover those board members who claimed they did not know what was going on had no right to push the blame for their own inertia on to Bignold. But, unlike him, they realised that their society could not afford damaging public quarrels. Tact, diplomacy and compromise were now needed to play down the crisis and ensure the Norwich Union's survival.

Yet such attitudes were never part of Thomas Bignold's make-up. They ran counter to his style of management, and he showed no willingness to change. Indeed, he regarded Samuel's attitude as little more than misguided insolence, and claimed that in order to protect themselves the directors had turned his three sons against him. But this was totally untrue. Despite a veneer of regard for the board, Samuel quickly realised that it was incapable of decisive action. The burden of the Norwich Union's problems had fallen squarely on himself and his two brothers. Difficulties increased when Thomas Bignold rejected outright their suggestion that he should retire quietly on a good pension. Instead he opened a rival National Union Fire Association in London in 1819, while continuing to use his office as a Norwich Union agency, and keeping any premiums which strayed there by mistake.[82]

Faced also by rival firms keen to secure Norwich Union business, it became impossible for head office to operate effectively, and losses rose sharply (Fig. 3).

Meanwhile the dispute itself brought heavy legal costs, so that even a reduced bonus of 25% could be sustained only by drawing on reserves, which declined alarmingly from £108,000 in 1818 to £38,000 by 1821, bringing the society to the verge of collapse.

## VI  Amalgamation with the Norwich General Assurance, 1821

Realising the weakness of the society's position by 1820, Samuel Bignold had opened negotiations with the Norwich General directors for an amalgamation of the two offices to form a new joint-stock profit-sharing company. Obviously, given the chance, Thomas Bignold would have opposed this new threat to his persistent claims to be Fire secretary of the Norwich Union. Yet he was denied the opportunity. Just as his son's negotiations were nearing completion the directors of his own recently established National Union took out an injunction against him on an entirely separate issue.[83] Like their predecessors at Norwich, they had found him difficult to get on with, and following several quarrels with them he had refused to hand over the new office's funds. Ironically after so much trouble, this came at an ideal moment for the Norwich Union because, as Samuel Bignold dryly observed, 'It will leave a rod hanging over his head ... and our affairs will in the meantime be proceeding.'[84]

No records exist of Samuel Bignold's discussions with the Norwich General directors, but it is clear that the Fire Society's survival depended on his ability to attract a large injection of new capital. Furthermore, he must also have realised that this had to come from the wealthy elite families of Norwich if the society was to avoid being taken over by a large London company or, even worse, face total collapse.

Accordingly, his ability to reach a compromise with the Norwich Union's former opponents played a vital part in its survival. The Norwich General directors, in turn, persuaded their proprietors to close their company and take up most of the Norwich Union's capital of £550,000. With £30 of each £250 share called as a £66,000 reserve, any fears about its ability to meet liabilities quickly faded. Meanwhile the trusteeship of the new company's funds was held by the directors. Virtually all of them came from the Norwich General board. Many of the Norwich Union's former trustees agreed to act as patrons of the society. Although legally a completely separate organisation, the Norwich Union Life Society had inevitably been under pressure during the dispute, and it could now hope for a return to settled conditions.

Samuel Bignold became secretary of the company on terms similar to top officials in other large fire offices. Compared with his family's earlier position there was a loss both of control and of income. Thus the board could dismiss him, he was salaried (£400 p.a.) and major policy decisions were left to the directors. Yet none of these changes detracted from Samuel Bignold's growing reputation in the fire insurance business, where he proved an able official, noted for his tact and ability to negotiate with the secretaries of the large London companies.

Admittedly, as a profit-sharing office, complete harmony with non-profit-sharing companies like the Sun was impossible. In 1825, for instance, the non-profit-sharing fire offices reacted to growing competition by cutting their rates on ordinary risks by 6d per £100. Like all established profit-sharing companies, the Norwich Union reluctantly followed and so lost a small part of the home market as its bonuses to policy-holders became less attractive (Table 1).

On balance, though, as a well established company, the society's long-term interest now lay in co-operating with the London fire offices to minimise the impact of competition. Thus in 1826 it joined the earliest tariff, a base rate of 3s per £100 on Liverpool warehouses, and was party to virtually every subsequent tariff negotiation, leading ultimately to the formal creation of the Fire Offices Committee in 1868.[85] The outcome of these attempts to regulate the market is reflected in the Norwich Union's dividends (Fig. 1). Several reductions occurred before the mid-1830s, owing to greater competition and heavy losses from rural incendiarism. Thereafter they rose to over 10%, which in the long run fully vindicated the Norwich General shareholders' decision in 1821 to switch their capital into the far more extensive business of the Fire Society. Indeed, the remaining small fire offices in East Anglia ran into severe difficulties from the 1820s onwards, owing to incendiary losses, and it is most unlikely that the Norwich General Assurance would have survived in its original form.[86]

## VII  Conclusion

Thomas Bignold was an unconventional but outstanding entrepreneur. Against the odds, at a time of financial crisis in 1797, he founded the Norwich Union fire office as a mutual insurance society. Over the next twenty years he successfully challenged the powerful London insurance companies for a significant part of the British market well in advance of any other country fire office. His skill as an organiser and tireless advocate of the mutual system — when it was still a novelty beyond London — clearly impressed many influential people. They included those who gave their support as trustees or local committee members and so lent credibility to his ideas.

Inevitably he made enemies on the way. Sometimes their attacks bore the stamp of irrelevance and small-mindedness inherent in jealousy. One critic seeking Bignold's dismissal in 1805, for instance, complained about his flamboyant habit of wearing 'a green coat and a striped waistcoat'. As Bignold retorted, this could hardly be denied, 'for he had them on'.[87]

Yet his odd behaviour also invited more serious criticism. Too many people from widely differing backgrounds fell out with him for there to have been no substance in their complaints. Above all, he refused to accept that he was only the custodian of the society's funds and that however able he might be in his use of them he remained accountable to its members. Most legitimate criticism concentrated on this crucial weakness in his management. Unfortunately he also allowed the quarrelling to split his family. In fact the row with his sons in 1818 dragged on for at least ten years, in which he faced financial ruin, before a reconciliation allowed him to end his days in comfort in 1834. Moreover, only the caution and tact of Samuel Bignold prevented the society disappearing completely as a result of the 1818 dispute, and it was through his efforts that the Norwich Union remained a leading fire insurance company.

Nevertheless, for all Thomas Bignold's shortcomings, his imaginative approach towards the insurance business must be regarded as the key ingredient explaining the timing and speed of the Fire Society's growth beyond its local market. Furthermore, his drive to establish and expand the Norwich Union agency system for fire insurance also provided a framework for the later but equally rapid growth of its Life Society. Ironically, perhaps the kindest and most fitting tribute to this achievement came from a member who voted for his dismissal in 1818. Thomas Bignold was, he said:

the individual who by increasing activity had raised a society ... Yet it would also seem, that the same qualifications which enabled him to establish so useful and enlarged a concern, were of that peculiar kind which rendered him unfit to act as a subordinate instrument in carrying it on.[88]

## Notes

1 See, for example, H. A. L. Cockerell and E. Green, *The British Insurance Business, 1547–1970*, London, 1976, p. 38; P. G. M. Dickson, *The Sun Insurance Office, 1710–1960*, London, 1960, pp. 105–6; H. E. Raynes, *A History of British Insurance*, 2nd ed., London, 1964, pp. 223–9; B. Supple, *The Royal Exchange Assurance. A History of British Insurance, 1720–1970*, Cambridge, 1970, pp. 51, 98–100, 153–4, 178–84, which also emphasises that difficulty sometimes arose with agents who did not appreciate the complexity of the actuarial techniques for life insurance.

2 See, for example, J. H. Clapham, 'The transference of the worsted industry from Norfolk to the West Riding', *Economic Journal*, XX, 1910; D. C. Coleman, 'Growth and decay during the industrial revolution. The case of East Anglia', *Scandinavian Economic History Review*, X, 1962; P. J. Corfield, 'The Social and Economic History of Norwich, 1650–1850. A Study in Urban Growth', unpublished Ph.D. thesis, University of London, 1976; J. K. Edwards, 'The Economic Development of Norwich, 1750–1850, with Special Reference to the Worsted Industry', unpublished Ph.D. thesis, University of Leeds, 1963; M. F. Lloyd-Pritchard, 'The decline of Norwich', *Economic History Review*, 2nd Series, III, 1950–51.

3 Corfield, *Norwich 1650–1850*, pp. 410–15, 576–8; J. K. Edwards, *Norwich 1750–1850*, pp. 157–9.

4 W. H. Bidwell, *Annals of an East Anglian Bank*, Norwich, 1900, principally a study of Messrs Gurney's Norwich and Norfolk Bank, but an account of the other Norwich banks opening in the eighteenth and nineteenth centuries is also included.

5 See, for example, Corfield, *Norwich 1650–1850*, pp. 352–3, 620; R. W. Davis, *Dissent in Politics, 1780–1830. The Political Life of William Smith, M.P.*, London, 1971; D. Hayes, 'Politics in Norfolk, 1750–1832', unpublished Ph.D. thesis, University of Cambridge, 1957; C. B. Jewson, *The Jacobin City*, Norwich, 1975.

68  *The business of insurance*

6   Corfield, *Norwich 1650–1850*, pp. 335–6, 352–3, 585–6, 620; Hayes, *Norfolk Politics*, pp. 58–62.

7   Bidwell, *East Anglian Bank*, especially pp. 35–6, 127–8, 140–6, Messrs Harvey and Hudson's Crown Bank was the leading Tory bank by the 1800s; Messrs Gurney's and Messrs Barclay Tompson and Ives were Whig firms.

8   See p. 22–3 above.

9   Norwich Union Museum, 'Original Documents on the Establishment of the Norwich Fire Insurance Office'; Committee Meeting 7 October 1792.

10  Raynes, *British Insurance*, pp. 265–6; Supple, *R.E.A.*, p. 214; the growing strength of the *Royal* and other companies such as the Liverpool London and Globe, Commercial Union and North British and Mercantile was partly based on their readiness to exploit foreign markets, particularly the U.S.A., while the established companies were less keen to do so in the mid-nineteenth century.

11  C. Walford, 'Fires and fire insurance considered under their historical, financial, statistical and national aspects', *Journal of the Statistical Society*, XL, 1877, pp. 403–4, gives Eden's estimate of insurable property in Great Britain and Ireland in 1802 as £612,975,000. But the Irish portion was estimated simply by adding 10% to his detailed calculation for Great Britain, which came to the £557,250,000 total used here.

12  This figure is based on evidence from government fire insurance duty returns; see p. 16 above; also, Supple, *R.E.A.*, p. 109, on the need to treat fire insurance duty payments with caution, 'owing to the erratic way in which insurance companies paid in the fire insurance duties before the early 1850s'.

13  C. Walford, *The Insurance Cyclopaedia*, London, 1874, III, pp. 553–4, gives a series of annual stamp duty on fire insurance between 1809 and 1861. Duty was levied on each new policy; the number of new policies issued each year is recorded. When compared with population this gives a rough indication of trends in the habit of fire insurance. New policies per 1,000 population in England and Wales were according to these figures; 1811, 6·57 per 1,000; 1821, 6·51; 1831, 7·13; 1841, 6·73; 1851, 8·45; 1861, 11·64. This suggests that little was done between about 1811 and the 1860s to increase the proportion of the population taking out fire insurance policies.

14  Walford, 'Fires and fire insurance', p. 415.

15  See p. 32–3 above.

16  The Insurance Institute of London, Report HR.2, *Development of Mercantile Fire Insurance in the City of London*, London, 1962, pp. 45–6; if used this could enable a policy-holder to evade a large part of his fire insurance duty.

17  This type of insurance was known as 'ordinary' business. It provided fire offices with the bulk of their business throughout the eighteenth and nineteenth centuries. As shown in Tables 3 and 4, fire insurance was priced as a 'rate' per £100 insured (referred to as per cent in this chapter). Ordinary business was then accepted on a predetermined scale of rates, divided into three standard classes, common, hazardous, doubly hazardous. From the 1720s to 1800s rates on ordinary business then varied according to four criteria, (1) type of building material, (2) the building's contents, (3) the nature of any trade carried on there, (4) the amount insured on each risk up to a maximum limit, normally, of £3,000.

From the late eighteenth century onwards variable 4 was dropped by a growing number of fire offices. As shown in Table 4, the same rate was then charged within each of the three classes of ordinary business, while the larger companies also raised their 'limit' on individual ordinary risks up to as much as £10,000.

Meanwhile, throughout the eighteenth and nineteenth centuries, risks on particularly fire-prone buildings — such as cotton mills or sugar refineries — were treated separately as 'special' business. Premium rates were set on the basis of a detailed survey and often by subsequent negotiation between the fire office and property owner.

Further details on the development and use of these rating methods are given in Dickson, *Sun*, pp. 78–83, 140; B. Drew, *The Fire Office, being the History of the Essex and Suffolk Equitable Insurance Society Limited, 1802–1952*, London, 1952, pp. 21–2; Supple, *R.E.A.*, pp. 85–6, 128, 158–60; Walford, *Cyclopaedia*, III, pp. 400, 573–4.

18 Dickson, *Sun*, pp. 79–80; Insurance Institute of London, Report HR.2, 1962, pp. 16–21, 44–50; Supple, *R.E.A.*, p. 84.

19 S. D. Chapman, 'Fixed capital formation in the British cotton industry 1770 to 1815', in J. P. P. Higgins and S. Pollard, eds., *Aspects of Capital Investment in Great Britain, 1750–1850*, London, 1971, pp. 57–8, 60–1, 89–91; D. T. Jenkins, *The West Riding Wool Textile Industry, 1770 to 1835*, Edington, 1975, pp. 276–301.

20 Jenkins, *West Riding Wool Textile Industry*, pp. 287–8, 291–4.

21 Higgins and Pollard, eds., *Capital Investment*, pp. 115–16, discussion on S. D. Chapman's paper. See also remarks of M. M. Edwards, pp. 108–9, who points out that Chapman's examples were drawn heavily from steam-powered mills. Edwards believes that insurance cover on water-powered mills was probably a lower percentage of insurable value.

22 I. Donnachie, 'Sources of capital and capitalisation in the Scottish brewing industry, c. 1750–1830', *Economic History Review*, 2nd Series, XXX, 1977, pp. 279–80.

23 See, for example, S. Pollard, 'Fixed capital in the industrial revolution in Britain', in F. Crouzet, ed., *Capital Formation in the Industrial Revolution*, London, 1972, p. 147, on small size of most units where 'the fixed-capital equipment was relatively simple and cheap'.

24 Drew, *The Fire Office*, pp. 50–1, on Essex and Suffolk; see below on the Norwich Union, pp. 55–7.

25 Walford, 'Fires and fire insurance', p. 415.

26 Calculation of linear trend of sum insured is based on annual fire insurance duty returns in B.P.P. 1870, XX, p. 1303. The periods 1790–1814 and 1816–1840 are chosen. These are chosen to allow use of the Gayer, Rostow and Schwartz price 'index of domestic and imported commodities', published in B. R. Mitchell and P. Deane, *Abstract of British Historical Statistics*, Cambridge, 1962, p. 470. Supple, *R.E.A.*, p. 108, discusses the application of capital formation and price series estimates to the fire insurance data. Given the elements of uncertainty in all these figures, the statements on market growth presented here can be regarded only as broad indicators of trend. Certainly none of the price indexes of this period can fully represent the property insured by fire offices. But Gayer *et al.* include a wide range of raw materials which despite the heavy weighting given to grains makes it fairly representative of the stocks covered by fire offices as well, in the long run, as the value of insured fixed capital. See also A. D. Gayer, W. W. Rostow and A. J. Schwartz, *The Growth and Fluctuation of the British Economy*, Oxford, 1953, pp. 462–82, 509–14, on the composition of their price index.

27 R. A. Church, *The Dynamics of Victorian Business*, London, 1980, p. 4, discusses the various estimates of capital formation for the early nineteenth century — including Feinstein's 1968 figures — on which this statement is based.

28 See n. 26.
29 Church, *Victorian Business*, p. 4.
30 See n. 26.
31 Raynes, *British Insurance*, pp. 187–9.
32 Dickson, *Sun*, pp. 73-99; Raynes, *British Insurance*, pp. 191–3; Supple, *R.E.A.*, pp. 81–95.
33 See n. 17.
34 Dickson, *Sun*, p. 15; Raynes, *British Insurance*, p. 73.
35 B. Drew, *The London Assurance*, London, 1949, pp. 15–16; Supple, *R.E.A.*, pp. 32–3.

70    The business of insurance

36    C. A. Cooke, *Corporation, Trust and Company*, Manchester, 1950, pp. 84–7; A. B. DuBois, *The English Business Company after the Bubble Act, 1720–1800*, London, 1971 ed., pp. 59–60.
37    Raynes, *British Insurance*, pp. 211–13, on the Globe's very well financed efforts to secure a charter between 1799 and 1806.
38    See pp. 52–5, 62–5.
39    See p. 22 above.
40    The four non-joint-stock companies were mutual societies; the Hand in Hand, Union, Westminster and Norwich Union. This statement is based on the following references to the organisation and number of fire offices. Raynes, *British Insurance*, pp. 223–38; F. B. Relton, *An Account of the Fire Insurance Companies*, London, 1893, *passim*; Walford, *Cyclopaedia*, six vol., 1871–78, see I, pp. 54, 214, 303, 376; II, p. 285; III, pp. 299, 422, 426–8, 491–5; IV, p. 153; V, p. 568.
41    Dickson, *Sun*, p. 73.
42    Raynes, *British Insurance*, pp. 223–38.
43    E. A. Davies, *An Account of the Formation and Early Years of the Westminster Fire Office*, London, 1952; Relton, *Insurance Companies*, pp. 71–80 on Hand in Hand, pp. 95–111 on Union, pp. 112–14 on Westminster.
44    Davies, *Westminster*, pp. 19, 56, 59, on radius of Westminster business from London, which did not exceed twenty-five miles before 1800; Relton, *Insurance Companies*, p. 79, on Hand in Hand, p. 110, on the limited scope of the Union's business before 1805.
45    See p. 50 below.
46    The six other known mutuals were the Essex Equitable, Finchingfield (of Essex), Wooler (Northumberland), Norwich Equitable, Anchor (Norwich), Devizes (Wiltshire); B. Drew, *The Fire Office*, appendix IX, Essex and Suffolk paid 50% as its first septennial bonus in 1809 (date estimated by comparing advertisement, appendix IX, with list of directors on p. 135); Norwich Equitable paid quinquennial bonuses of 40% in 1813 and 50% in 1818; see *Norwich Mercury*, 14 May 1814, 15 August 1818; Norwich Union bonuses, after an initial return of 75% in 1804, remained at 50% from 1805 to 1818.
47    Raynes, *British Insurance*, pp. 223–38.
48    A. Noakes, *The County Fire Office, 1807–1957*, London, 1957, pp. 1–25, the company's first septennial return was paid at 25% in 1814.
49    Raynes, *British Insurance*, pp. 226–8; Supple, *R.E.A.*, pp. 122–3.
50    See p. 65 below.
51    B. C. Hunt, *The Development of the Business Corporation in England, 1800–1867*, Harvard, 1969 ed., pp. 14–16.
52    See, for example, Relton, *Insurance Companies*, pp. 232–3.
53    Supple, *R.E.A.*, pp. 110–11, 130–1, an influx of unsound schemes in the speculative mania 1824–26 ended this earlier record of stability.
54    See Walford, *Cyclopaedia*, III, pp. 438–515, on opening of new fire offices. Privately published fire insurance duty returns, 1813–17, 1823, 1825, enabled some corrections to be made to Walford's statements. See D. H. Aldcroft and P. Fearon, eds., *British Economic Fluctuations, 1790–1939*, London, 1972, pp. 11–13; the major cycles were taken from table 2, p. 12. There are good reasons for taking the period 1802 to 1810 as one of sustained investment, for example, Hunt, *Business Corporation*, pp. 14–17, 21–2, emphasises the growth of speculative promotions, including fire and life insurance offices throughout the period 1801 to 1808. Growth in new insurance promotions did not slacken until about 1810, as G. Clayton points out in his study *British Insurance*, p. 97. See also R. C. O. Matthews, 'The trade cycle in Britain, 1790–1850', in D. H. Aldcroft and P. Fearon, eds., pp. 97–130; p. 112 emphasises the vastly differing experience of various sectors of the economy during the French wars but, p. 113, he identifies the 1800s as a decade of strong confidence and high

private investment. This decade lay between two bouts of high-deficit spending by the government, in the mid-1790s and 1811–14, needed to finance heavy wartime costs. Clayton, p. 97, points out that new promotions of insurance offices from 1815 to 1820 were discouraged by high levels of fire losses and an increase in the fire insurance duty.

55  Relton, *Insurance Companies, passim*; Walford, *Cyclopaedia*, III, pp. 438–515.
56  Raynes, *British Insurance*, pp. 223–38.
57  L. S. Pressnell, *Country Banking in the Industrial Revolution*, Oxford, 1956, pp. 55–6; comparisons of local banking histories with those of country fire offices indicate that the involvement was extensive. This is true for Norwich. See also M. Christy, 'The history of banks and banking in Essex', *Journal of the Institute of Bankers*, 1906, pp. 319–25, and Drew, *The Fire Office*, pp. 11–12, 133–40, on links between Colchester bankers and the Essex Equitable. They were behind its initial launch and were prominent directors; L. H. Grindon, *Manchester Banks and Bankers*, Manchester, 2nd ed., 1878, p. 4; Relton, *Insurance Companies*, pp. 209–12, Manchester's first bank and fire office were opened simultaneously in 1771 at the initiative of Messrs Byrom, Sedgewick, Allen and Place, the bankers; J. Hughes, *Liverpool Banks and Bankers, 1760–1837*, Liverpool, 1906, pp. 92–110; Relton, *Insurance Companies*, p. 213, link between the bankers Messrs Arthur Heywood Sons and Co. and the Liverpool Fire Office, founded in 1777; West Suffolk Record Office, Alliance Insurance Company Ltd, Suffolk Fire Office, Board Minutes, 24 November, 2 December, 31 December 1802, 8 August 1803; Pressnell, *Country Banking*, pp. 54, 79, 156, the leading Suffolk banking families, Alexanders, Browns and Oakes were all closely involved with the launching of the Suffolk Fire Office and served as prominent directors.
58  See, for example, Grindon, *Manchester Banks, passim*; W. C. E. Hartley, *Banking in Yorkshire*, Clapham, 1976, *passim*; Hughes, *Liverpool Banks, passim*; D. F. E. Sykes, *The History of Huddersfield and its Vicinity*, Huddersfield, 1898, p. 291; Pressnell, *Country Banking*, p. 19.
59  Grindon, *Manchester Banks*, pp. 45–7; Hughes, *Liverpool Banks*, pp. 116–17, 143–56; Relton, *Insurance Companies*, pp. 213–14.
60  See, for example, Jenkins, *The West Riding Wool Textile Industry*, pp. 136, 291–4.
61  On the London companies see, for example, anon., *Phoenix Family Story*, London, 1949, p. 4, by 1797 the Phoenix had nearly 300 agents covering the British Isles; Dickson, *Sun*, pp. 67–70, 78, 90–3, by 1786 the Sun had 123 agents including coverage of the northern textile districts; Supple, *R.E.A.*, pp. 89–100, the Royal Exchange Assurance had 195 agents in 1788, rising to 316 in Britain by 1805: these also included agencies in the northern textile areas. On the country fire offices, some did open agencies in these districts but normally withdrew before they had taken on a heavy commitment; Relton, *Insurance Companies*, p. 207, refers to the Bristol Fire Office opening agencies in all towns in north and west England in 1787; and, p. 226, the Newcastle Fire Office insured complex industrial risks from 1783 to 1819, when it refused to cover flax and cotton mills; West Suffolk R.O., Suffolk Fire Office, Board Minutes, show an active extension of agencies in the 'Manufacturing Counties and Towns', 21 January 1803. But after 1815 it withdrew from cotton-mill insurances, see 16 January 1818. Even the West of England, the second largest country fire office in this period, had only a modest connection with the north. Overall, its total home market business was no more than a sixth the size of the Norwich Union's by the 1820s.
62  Dickson, *Sun*, p. 146; Supple, *R.E.A.*, pp. 126–8.
63  See, for example, Relton, *Insurance Companies*, p. 112, on the Westminster fire office.
64  See, for example, Relton, *Insurance Companies*, pp. 72, 95, 107, 112; Walford, *Cyclopaedia*, III, p. 469.

72  The business of insurance

65   Liverpool City Library, Royal Insurance, Box No. 5, Globe Letters, correspondence between J. G. Denham, Globe Secretary, and D. F. G. Mahoney, Limerick agent, ref: the insurance of Manister Mills, 2 December 1809, 10 December 1809, 23 December 1809.

66   The basic rate for corn mills of 5s per cent in the early nineteenth century is referred to in Walford, *Cyclopaedia*, III, 1874, p. 199; for the Sun's rate on sugar mills in 1813 see Dickson, *Sun*, p. 145; on Trowbridge mills, S. D. Chapman, 'Fixed capital formation in the British cotton industry, 1770–1815', *Economic History Review*, 2nd Series, XXIII, 1970, p. 238.

67   Dickson, *Sun*, p. 145, Sun cotton mill rates c. 1816 were 12s 6d to 18s per cent; Brotherton Library, Leeds University, Box 21, Marriner Family, Globe insurance policy 51,350, £3,000 on cotton mill at 17s per cent ran from 1812 onwards, with annual receipts to 1816.

68   See H. Perkin, *The Origins of Modern English Society, 1780–1880*, London, 1969, p. 237, on Curwen.

69   Northumberland Record Office, ZLK Insurance Papers (Norwich Union), 28 September 1808, a printed circular letter to J. Bell, Junr. Esq., solicitor, Hexham, Northumberland, from Thomas Bignold, offering Bell an agency in the Fire Society. But ZLK Insurance Papers (Albion), 20 October 1805, Table of Rates, sent to J. Bell, Junr, by the Albion Fire and Life Office, suggest that he was already an agent for that company. A Norwich Union agency list for 1811 does not include him. He seems therefore to have ignored Bignold's offer despite the chance of holding a Norwich Union Life Society agency, founded April 1808; no other examples of these circulars have been traced.

70   Dickson, *Sun*, p. 142, S. J. Fletcher, *Sun* secretary, evidence to 1867 Select Committee on Fire Protection, held the view that higher claims were linked to recession. See also B.P.P., 1867, X, 1, *Report from the Select Committee on Fire Protection*, most other insurance officials agreed, e.g. Swinton Boult (Liverpool London and Globe), qq. 3408–13, although some did not, see Shaw's evidence, qq. 6339–41. On the 'moral hazard' see D. Deuchar, 'The necessity for a tariff organisation in connection with fire insurance business', *Journal of the Federation of Insurance Institutes*, 6, 1903, p. lxi; J. Ostler, 'The cost price of fire insurance', *Journal of the Federation of Insurance Institutes*, 3, 1900, p. 267, refers to the policy-holders' use of 'a little judicious laxity' in increasing fire risk; Supple, *R.E.A.*, p. 159.

71   See R. G. Wilson, *Gentlemen Merchants*, Manchester, 1971, p. 244, on Hebblethwaite.

72   R. Lloyd Jones and A. A. Le Roux, 'The size of firms in the cotton industry. Manchester, 1815–1841', *Economic History Review*, 2nd Series, XXXIII, 1980, p. 81, lists the firm of J. Pollard as the second largest of ninety cotton mills in Manchester c. 1809–12.

73   C. R. Fay, *Great Britain from Adam Smith to the Present Day*, London 1957, 4th ed., p. 109, 193; Maberly Phillips, *A History of Banks, Bankers and Banking in Northumberland ... 1755 to 1894*, London, 1894, p. 134.

74   Pressnell, *Country Banking*, p. 55.

75   See n. 61.

76   Dickson, *Sun*, p. 93.

77   Norwich Union Life Insurance Society, Board Minute, 10 April 1820.

78   Norwich Union Correspondence, Samuel Bignold to Bishop Wearmouth Agent, 25 July 1811.

79   Anon., Norwich Union Fire and Life Insurance, *Proceedings of the Meetings of Members*, London, 1818, p. 7.

80   *Norwich Mercury*, 21 June 1817, gives detailed annual report of Norwich Union. The draft copy of the private Bill, *An Act to Amend an Act passed in 1813 ...*, J. S. Goodife, House of Commons, is held in the Norwich Union museum.

81 The York Hotel's Committee's findings and recommendations, and the general meeting on 25 September 1818, were fully reported in *The Times* as well as many other national and provincial newspapers.
82 Walford, *Cyclopaedia*, I, 1872, pp. 278–9, gives extracts of the National Union deed of settlement.
83 E. Green and Sons, *English Law Reports*, London, 1904, Chancery, 37, pp. 720–4, Ellison *v.* Bignold, 7, 9 March 1821.
84 Norwich Union Correspondence, Samuel Bignold to John Cocksedge Bignold, undated letter, but there is a reference to Guardian Fire Office, opened 1821, and it was written prior to the amalgamation with the Norwich General Assurance in September 1821.
85 Dickson, *Sun*, pp. 147–56.
86 See, for example, West Suffolk Record Office, Suffolk Fire Office, Board Minute, 28 July 1849, explaining why the company had been absorbed by the Alliance; 'The want of success of the Suffolk Fire Office of late years has arisen from the spirit of incendiarism in the agricultural districts and from the circumstance of the risk on Farming Stock being one fifth of the whole business of the office and the risks on Farming Buildings in proportion ...'.
87 Reported in *Norwich Mercury*, 25 April 1805.
88 Reported in *Norfolk Chronicle*, 14 November 1818.

*Acknowledgements*

This chapter is based on chapters 1–6 of my forthcoming thesis, 'A History of the Norwich Union Fire and Life Insurance Societies, 1797 to 1914', which has been supervised by Dr R. G. Wilson of the University of East Anglia. It has been financed by generous grants from the Social Science Research Council and the British Insurance Association. All references to the Norwich Union in the essay are based on my thesis research. Notes to these sources have been omitted to save space. A fully annotated version of the chapter is held at the University of East Anglia Library. I shall also be pleased to answer any specific enquiries about these references. I am very grateful to Mr H. Scurfield, general manager and secretary of the Norwich Union, for allowing me to have access to the society's archives, and to Mr D. Dorling (assistant secretary), Mr J. Lamb (museum curator) and Mrs C. Thurston (archivist) for their help in locating many of the Norwich Union records which I have used in my research. I should also like to thank Richard Wilson and Oliver Westall for their detailed comments and advice on an earlier draft of this chapter.

SARAH PALMER

# The Indemnity in the London marine insurance market, 1824–50

## I  Introduction

Already by the nineteenth century marine insurance was a well established business. With the expansion of Britain's trade and shipping in the seventeenth and eighteenth centuries the practice of insuring goods carried by sea and, later, of insuring ships had become common and methods of insurance, including forms of policy, standardised. The contribution of marine insurance to the development of the shipping industry has long been recognised by maritime historians; without the security it offered there would have been fewer willing to risk their capital.[1] But as a subject in its own right it remains very incompletely explored. Two studies of the chartered companies, Supple's *The Royal Exchange Assurance* and John's article on the London Assurance are exceptional in describing this form of marine insurance. The early history of Lloyd's was well covered by Wright and Fayle in a study published in 1928, but little is known of the conduct of insurance by private underwriters. House histories of non-chartered companies are not lacking, but the economic setting is often obscure. Hull clubs have been almost entirely neglected by historians.[2]

However, with the deposit in recent years of many more insurance records, the opportunity for new research has been provided, particularly in respect of the nineteenth century.[3] In the meantime the most valuable subjects for study are those which permit some background as well as foreground to be filled in. The Indemnity Marine Insurance Company was one of the few joint-stock companies formed before 1860 which succeeded in capturing a remunerative share of the marine insurance market early on. This makes it worthy of attention in its own right, but an analysis of its success casts valuable light on the marine insurance business generally.

II  *The institutions of marine insurance*

London dominated the British marine insurance market in the early nineteenth century, handling perhaps three-quarters of all transactions.[4] In part this was the result of the capital's central commercial role. As a contemporary commentator noted,

> London ... particularly from the operation of public commercial regulation and revenue laws, which draw to it exclusively the whole of the East India, and a great proportion of the many other branches of foreign trade, possesses such a pre-eminence over all other maritime cities of Great Britain that her market for marine insurance regulates that of the whole country.[5]

But it was also the result of the development of successful insurance institutions over the previous century, notably the emergence of Lloyd's, which attracted business both from the outports and overseas. Significantly, foreign centres, particularly Hamburg, were regarded by underwriting interests as a far greater threat to London marine insurance than other British ports.[6]

Until 1824 there were three distinct types of institution supplying insurance for sea carriage: the private underwriter; the chartered companies (Royal Exchange and London Assurance); and the mutual insurance association or 'hull club'. After this date alterations in the law permitted a fourth type of enterprise, the joint-stock company. Throughout our period the private underwriters dominated the insurance market, although the development of joint-stock companies reduced their share. The majority of private underwriters did their insurance business at Lloyd's, though some writing was still done at the Jerusalem and Jamaica coffee houses, at the Coal Exchange and at other places where merchants gathered.[7] Membership of Lloyd's had been on a subscription basis since 1771, and after 1800 depended also on recommendation by existing subscribers. The Committee of Lloyd's, formed first in 1772, was for early decades mainly concerned with accommodation, but during the French wars became increasingly involved in general questions of members' interests, particularly in relation to the government. A trust deed of 1811, together with bye-laws introduced at the same time, gave the committee more formal powers for the management of subscribers' interests, for example power to appoint Lloyd's agents.[8] The powers did not touch on the freedom of underwriters and brokers to do business on whatever terms they wished, for insurance at Lloyd's was always a private transaction.

Lloyd's strength as a market for marine insurance was in part a result of the Bubble Act of 1720, which gave two chartered companies, London Assurance and Royal Exchange, a monopoly of company insurance.[9] At the time there was no recognised centre for effecting insurance, but by restricting all underwriting other than that undertaken by these two companies to private individuals, impetus was given to development of a common meeting place for underwriters and their clients. Critics of the Bubble Act, including the 1810 Select Committee on Marine Insurance, believed that it put Lloyd's in a privileged position. But business advantage, not compulsion, brought Lloyd's its subscribers.[10] The two chartered companies offered private underwriters no effective competition; in 1810 their joint share of marine insurance business amounted to at most 4% of the total market. A cautious commercial policy led them to confine themselves to regular, straightforward risks and to charge higher premiums than those generally prevailing at Lloyd's. The select committee of 1810 emphasised lack of capital as a factor in the chartered companies' poor performance, but in view of the fact that the capital requirements for underwriting were not large, this seems unlikely to have been a significant factor. Rather it is probable that these institutions, with marine insurance only a part of their interests, were content with their market share and lacked incentive to pursue the business more vigorously.

The privileged position of the London Assurance and Royal Exchange remained unchanged but not unchallenged until 1824. Attempts were made in 1806 and 1809 to open marine insurance to other company enterprises. In 1806 the Globe Insurance Company tried unsuccessfully to obtain a charter. Three years later a proposal, backed by leading shipowners and merchants, to set up a company with nominal capital of £5 million, presented a more serious threat to existing interests. Both this proposal and a renewed application from the Globe were referred to the Select Committee on Marine Insurance, but although this recommended abolition of the chartered companies' monopoly, the Bill to do this was narrowly defeated after a vigorous campaign of opposition led by the Committee of Lloyd's.[11]

Surprisingly no attempt was made to reverse this decision until 1824, when the newly formed Alliance petitioned in favour of the removal of restrictions on marine insurance to allow it to add this to its other interests. Supported by merchants and bankers, the Alliance promoters included Nathan Rothschild, Samuel Gurney, Alexander Baring and Moses Montefiore. As before, Lloyd's formed a special committee to fight the proposal but the political atmosphere was now different; the government was in favour of the removal of restrictions on business and prominent members like Huskisson gave their support in debate. Despite attempts by Lloyd's defenders to refer the matter to a select committee and to introduce restrictive amendments, the Bill was passed.[12]

Yet the impact of the change in law was not as great as had been anticipated by those who had opposed it. Twenty years later there were only five London-based marine insurance companies in existence besides the London Assurance and Royal Exchange: the Alliance and the Indemnity, both of which began business shortly after the ending of the monopoly; the General Maritime, established in 1830 and surviving only to 1848; the Marine Insurance, set up in 1836 in hope of acquiring risks formerly underwritten by the East India Company; and the Neptune of 1839, which handled Liverpool risks.[13] Even McCulloch, an advocate of company underwriting, could claim in 1844 no more than that these companies drew to themselves 'more than half the marine insurance business effected in London'; a marked increase in market share over the situation in 1810 but testimony to the continuing power of the private underwriters doing business at Lloyd's.[14]

What were the problems faced by these new companies in their early years? What were the sources of their capital? On what terms did they conduct their business? How did their operations differ from those of the private underwriters? What determined their profitability and hence survival? This study attempts to answer these questions for the Indemnity, a company exceptional in its success but by no means exceptional in the market conditions it confronted.

### III  The formation of the Indemnity

The Indemnity began business in August 1824. According to the first chairman, Robert Rickards, it owed its existence to the initiative of the shipowner John Staniforth. 'Mr Staniforth is in fact the founder of the institution, he planned it at its outset, the soundness of its principles, its chief excellence we owe chiefly to him.'[15] The laudatory judgement was to be reversed within two years, but initially Staniforth's proposal was sufficiently attractive to gain the support of several prominent members of London's shipping community. The committee which set up the company consisted of Robert Rickards, George Lyall, J. H. Palmer, Thomas Murdoch, W. D. Dawson, John Innes and V. H. R. Davis; the first board of directors included among its members Ralph Fenwick and George Hibbert.[16]

In an early history of marine insurance Frederick Martin suggested that the Indemnity originated in 'a society of shipowners'.[17] This is probably a reference to the London-based association later known as the General Shipowners' Society, for George Lyall was chairman of that body between 1823 and 1825 and several of the Indemnity's directors were active members in the early 1830s.[18] The connection is significant, but not quite in the way it might appear. At the time of the Indemnity's foundation the Shipowners' Society was not the influential pressure group which it was later to become; it enjoyed only a fragile, intermittent existence after its formal creation in 1811 and lacked support. After some show of activity in the early 1820s, when representatives gave evidence to several select committees, it was defunct by 1828.

However, a few years later some of those shipowners involved before set up a new association on a firmer financial basis, in order to ensure 'a constant and efficient attention to all questions in which British Maritime interests are involved'.[19] These active members of the Shipowners' Society, always few in number, were not typical of the shipowning interest in general, being drawn from the still small group of investors in shipping who held a large amount of tonnage and regarded themselves as specialist shipowners. In the late eighteenth century the same group had been instrumental in developing a classification register for use in assessing shipping at Lloyd's, in opposition to that published by underwriters, and in the 1830s played an equally central role in organising the new, allegedly fairer, Lloyd's Register of Shipping.[20] Dislike of the growing influence of Lloyd's underwriting interests as spokesmen for the shipping industry as a whole during the war years may well have been a factor promoting the formation of the Shipowners' Society in 1811. It is therefore not surprising that the prominent owners involved in this should also have been associated with the formation of a company which would compete with the private underwriters at Lloyd's, particularly when the Indemnity's mode of organisation was based not upon the chartered companies but on the older shipowners' insurance institution — the hull club.

Hull clubs were a distinct branch of marine insurance in which underwriting of risks was not a service performed for profit but a system operated by shipowners themselves to meet the need for protection. Club members paid an annual premium which then formed part of a common fund used to settle claims made in the year. Unfortunately there is little information available on such clubs based in London beyond the description of the Friendly Assurance and the London Union given to members of the 1810 Select Committee on Marine Insurance, and occasional odd references, such as that in an advertisement of 1859 to the formation of seven mutual insurance clubs in London in 1854.[21] However, whether or not clubs were *based* in London, it is probable that in certain London shipping trades this was the normal mode of insurance. The shipowner J. L. Thompson told the Select Committee on the Coal Trade of 1837 that colliers were generally insured in clubs, but at the 'other end', that is, in the north-east.[22] Edward Solly, a timber merchant, claimed in 1820 that insurance in clubs gave English vessels in the timber trade an advantage over Prussian ships, which could not be insured so cheaply.[23]

Hull clubs developed, as the secretary of the London Union explained, from 'the confidence which shipowners entertained in one another'.[24] In consequence, mutual insurance was confined to regular trades, such as coal and timber, where risks were well understood and participants known. With membership typically small — under a hundred shipowners — and policies arranged on a specific day each year, clubs presented few organisational problems. Resultant low administrative costs, reinforced by the ability of club committees to identify bad risks and false claims more readily because of their personal involvement in shipping, allowed clubs to offer lower premiums than their competitors. In 1810, for example, the London Union rate for colliers was £5 10s per cent as against £18 – £20 at Lloyd's.[25] Club policies also tended to be more comprehensive; the conventional Lloyd's policy did not cover collision unless a 'running down' clause was specifically inserted, whereas this was a normal feature of club policies, which tended to be, as a member noted in 1839, 'copies of each other', most clubs using a similar form.[26] Payment for damages was one of the prime benefits of club insurance — a point of particular significance for colliers where this risk was especially high.[27] Insurance with a club, being on an annual basis, was convenient in trades where vessels made a large number of repeated voyages over the year.

As originally planned the Indemnity was an association for mutual insurance. Its revised prospectus paid tribute to the club principle — '... premiums paid for effecting Insurance by the ordinary means have always formed a heavy charge upon Ship Owners, who have found that they could insure their property at less expense by a plan of MUTUAL INSURANCE' — but noted that lack of capital led to inconvenience and delay 'before the amount of the losses could be obtained from the other members', arguing that a company would overcome this problem. It was therefore intended to set up a company for 'mutual insurance of merchandize as well as ships', with projected capital of £5 million, raised through the issue of 50,000 £100 shares. Every investor was 'bound annually to insure a specific sum', with holders of one share insuring capital to the value of a minimum £500 and holders of a hundred insuring at least £10,000 annually. Initial payment per share was set at £5, with provision for further calls to be established every July on the basis of the year's business. It was anticipated that settlements would be made within eight days. Profits were to be distributed on the basis of a complex scheme which took account of number of shares and premiums paid after payment of 5% interest on shares. A sixth of profits so allocated was to be retained as a reserve fund.[28] In taking legal advice prior to setting up the Indemnity, the promoters were particularly concerned to establish that no investor would be liable beyond the proportion of his share, and the final clause provided for dissolution should future legislation affect this limited liability.[29]

Although at the commencement of business in August 1824 the Indemnity's capital resources were by no means fully developed — by the following March only a quarter of the allocated shares had been taken up — the nature of the company allowed it to start 'as speedily as possible upon such a scope as should be proportional to the subscribed capital'.[30] Issue of shares was much complicated by the need to judge the character of investors as insurers. Thus, when a prospectus was dispatched to William Moxon of Hull, the clerk sent an accompanying letter:

... in the event of your influencing any of your friends become shareholders, and should you do so, Mr Staniforth feels assured that you will only recommend those who can be depended upon for their general respectability, as it is a fixed rule with the directors to admit no-one to become the member of the society who is not qualified in this respect, and who does not particularise the precise line of business he is engaged on, and the nature of the insurance he may wish to effect.[31]

By March 1827 13,453 shares had been issued, over half to the twenty-six directors, and the names and addresses of shareholders, together with the nature of their business, names of referees where appropriate, largest credit and security were noted in a Private Index to Proprietors. This index shows that a good many shareholders taking up shares in 1825 invested in a small number, typically five, which suggests that share purchases were for some an 'entrance fee' permitting them to insure with this company.[32] Checks on proprietors did not prevent the accumulation by 1827 of debts to the Indemnity totalling £9,290, most arising from insolvency and bankruptcy.[33] But bad debts were not the only problems facing the company. On 11 July 1826 the directors reported to a meeting of proprietors that losses on the first sixteen months of insurance were such that only interest on shares could be paid; a further call of 13s 6d per share was necessary which would bring paid-up capital to £5 13s 6d per share.[34]

In public the directors were at pains to place responsibility for the Indemnity's difficulties on circumstances beyond their control; 'the autumn of that year [1824] was one of the most disastrous in respect of sea losses in the European seas'.[35] In private blame was attached to the managing director, underwriter and founder of the company, John Staniforth. Investigation into his conduct, minuted in a secret book, revealed not only that the business of the office had been loosely conducted, hence the long list of bankrupt proprietors, and that unsuitable risks had been accepted, but also that he had deceived the directors as to the state of profits. Staniforth himself was in debt to the Indemnity to the tune of £1,174, with little prospect of paying it off, having pledged both ships and earnings to support speculative enterprises.[36]

Termination of Staniforth's appointment in 1827 marked the beginning of a new, more successful phase of the company's development.[37] Fortunately for its future, the chairman, Robert Rickards, took the lead in calling for a re-examination of the basic principles governing its business. 'The necessity of preparing annual statements to be laid before proprietors, the difficulties which have occurred in each year in the arrangement of these accounts, the inconvenience of an annual division of profit or loss, with the consequent impossibility of replacing profits of one year from the accruing profits of following years' — all, in Rickards's view, argued for a simpler system.[38] Recognising that much of the complexity associated with the Indemnity's operations arose out of the mutual insurance element, and no doubt having regard to the success of the Alliance in getting business, it was decided to dispense with this. The office was opened to the public, the obligation for shareholders to insure with the company was ended and share issues ceased after 25 October 1827.[39] The Indemnity's subsequent progress suggests that it was a wise decision. The number of policies written annually rose from 6,417 in 1827 to 11,068 in 1830, when profits were deemed sufficient to allow a bonus to be paid. By 1832 the Indemnity was handling insurance on ships and cargoes valued at £10,477,347, a figure which compares well with the £7,142,500 underwritten in the same year by the much longer established London Assurance.[40] Payment of bonuses after 1831 brought shares up from £5 13s 6d to £20 by 1840. In the following decade payments to shareholders (dividend plus bonus) averaged about 10%, only falling below this in 1845, when 7½ % was allotted. Table 1 indicates the long-term growth in the earnings of Indemnity shares from a dividend of 5s in the first year to £3 in 1850.

## IV  The basis of competition

By 1827, then, the club principle was no longer considered necessary to success. Rather, it may have seemed positively disadvantageous — limiting, not promoting business. With capital resources adequate (£72,214 after the 13s 6d call), to compel insurers to be shareholders amounted to an unnecessary handicap.[41] The cost benefits of mutual insurance enjoyed by more conventional hull clubs were necessarily denied to the Indemnity, with its interest in wide-scale operation. As the company enlarged its market so the degree of personal contact, the essence of club insurance, diminished and with it the economic attraction of the scheme. Indeed, it may be doubted whether mutuality was ever an appropriate basis for a company of such a size.

Yet the first two years of the company's operation should not be regarded as a false start. The original mutual scheme laid the foundation for the Indemnity's later development by giving it an initial competitive edge. This was crucial because the company faced all the long-standing advantages possessed by Lloyd's in a market which remained depressed until mid-century.

Lloyd's benefited from its accepted role as a meeting place and source of commercial intelligence for all those connected with the shipping industry. For merchants and shipowners it served as a kind of club, providing a vital personal as well as business focus for those who met there. Companies, conducting business on their own premises, offered no comparable attraction.

Even more significant was the absence at this time of any great economic advantage in insuring with a company rather than with private underwriters. Supporters of joint-stock insurance had placed much emphasis on the greater security offered by the capital resources of companies.[42] Such a guarantee was not unimportant to merchants and shipowners; writing in 1834, Henry Vaucher strongly disputed that 'merchants have become indifferent to every one consideration in insurance and look alone to comparative rates of premium' and argued that men were willing to incur extra costs for the knowledge that a risk was safely underwritten.[43] But trust in an insurer did not depend solely on capital resources; the limit on risks accepted was as important. Capital of £10,000 pledged against risks limited to £400 offered the same security as £100,000 where the risk limit was £4,000.[44] Moreover the 'line' system at Lloyd's, with its spread of risks between underwriters, offered considerable protection to the insured, as did the short-term nature of their liability. 'Within twelve months from any risk commenced it has generally run off and therefore any underwriter who is considered responsible enough to stand for twelve months or more is freely accepted as an insurer,' explained a witness before the 1844 Select Committee on Joint Stock

Companies.[45] Finally, the complicated structure of insurance finance involving merchant, broker and underwriter meant that at any one time the private underwriter, no less than the company, had valuable reserves of credit.

While companies' larger reserves did not therefore necessarily confer any special benefit in respect of security, they did offer other potential advantages. Greater capital resources meant that companies could accept larger risks, even to the extent of underwriting the total value of a ship. Not all chose to exploit this, preferring to increase their safety margin. In 1837, for example, the Marine Insurance Company set fairly unambitious limits; £8,000 for cargo; £5,000 for coasting and near Continental trades; £3,000 for the transatlantic and £5,000 for steamers.[46] The Indemnity set its limit much higher, £30,000 in 1838, but until the rise in shipping values which accompanied the shift from sail to steam after 1850, few vessels can have required such cover.[47]

Nevertheless, the ability of companies to accept larger lines had implications for their costs, by reducing the proportionate share of administrative expenses, while larger reserves enabled them to take on risky but potentially profitable business without threat to survival if the venture proved unsuccessful. In both cases companies could force market rates down or earn higher profits. Evidence to test these suggestions is hard to come by, though the Indemnity's establishment costs remained at 2% when there were assertions that underwriting and brokerage at Lloyd's was as high as 5%.[48]

In these difficult and ambiguous circumstances, with competition not only from private underwriters but also from the newly formed Alliance, the Indemnity's success depended on establishing a special attraction in the market. By espousing the mutual principle it defined a distinctive territory for customers: men already familiar with the club as a way of insuring ships who would welcome its extension to freight and cargo. As the Indemnity prospectus emphasised, what was proposed was not in essence a novelty but a beneficial enlargement of an existing practice. The fact that investors were also clients guaranteed custom, enabling it to begin business on a larger, more ambitious scale than might have been the case. Mutuality, then, provided a firm foundation for the Indemnity in terms of support, giving those associated a familiarity with its services which stood it in good stead in the long term. For a few years after dropping the requirement that insurers should also be investors the company noted the amount of capital insured by proprietors and non-proprietors. The latter overtook proprietors as the main customers in 1831, when they accounted for £6,612,429 out of a total of £12,360,292 underwritten, but until then those who had put money into the company continued to provide the bulk of its business.[49]

Table 1. Indemnity Marine Insurance Company accounts, 1826–50 (£'000)

| | Capital insured | Net premium income[a] | Settlements less salvage | Discounts[b] | Establishment | Profit or loss[c] | Cash dividend (£)[d] |
|---|---|---|---|---|---|---|---|
| 1824–26 | 7,801 | 194 | 150 | 12 | 7 | 25 | [e] |
| 1827 | 5,796 | 142 | 126 | 11 | 6 | (1) | 0·28 |
| 1828 | 8,217 | 201 | 162 | 17 | 6 | 16 | 0·28 |
| 1829 | 10,301 | 220 | 184 | 19 | 7 | 11 | 0·28 |
| 1830 | 11,280 | 237 | 206 | 20 | 7 | 4 | 0·28 |
| 1831 | 12,359 | 269 | 247 | 21 | 7 | 4 | 0·28 |
| 1832 | 10,477 | 205 | 137 | 15 | 6 | 48 | 0·33 |
| 1833 | 10,161 | 181 | 146 | 14 | 6 | 16 | 0·33 |
| 1834 | 10,836 | 206 | 151 | 15 | 6 | 34 | 0·38 |
| 1835 | 11,815 | 225 | 168 | 17 | 6 | 35 | 0·43 |
| 1836 | 13,321 | 248 | 210 | 19 | 7 | 12 | 0·53 |
| 1837 | 15,652 | 315 | 216 | 24 | 7 | 69 | 0·60 |
| 1838 | 19,447 | 384 | 362 | 31 | 7 | (15) | 0·70 |
| 1839 | 22,044 | 408 | 300 | 33 | 8 | 67 | 0·85 |
| 1840 | 18,590 | 359 | 296 | 33 | 9 | 22 | 1·90 |
| 1841 | 16,268 | 290 | 239 | 22 | 9 | 21 | 2·00 |
| 1842 | 13,678 | 255 | 281 | 20 | 9 | (55) | 3·00 |
| 1843 | 13,938 | 252 | 202 | 22 | 9 | 21 | 2·00 |
| 1844 | 13,903 | 237 | 183 | 24 | 8 | 22 | 2·00 |
| 1845 | 14,745 | 263 | 184 | 22 | 8 | 49 | 1·50 |
| 1846 | 15,210 | 284 | 214 | 23 | 9 | 39 | 2·00 |
| 1847 | 20,061 | 388 | 287 | 29 | 9 | 64 | 2·00 |
| 1848 | — | 412 | 295 | 29 | 9 | 80 | 2·00 |
| 1849 | — | 335 | 235 | 31 | 8 | 61 | 2·50 |
| 1850 | — | 283 | 214 | 27 | 9 | 34 | 3·00 |

Notes
a Premiums net of 5% brokerage.
b Discounts on premiums and duty stamps.
c Losses bracketed; this column refers to declared profits in any year, which will depend on the outcome of previous years' underwriting in part, so it will not always correspond with the sum of previous columns.
d Payments made on each original £5 share. This includes cash bonuses paid from 1840 but not capital bonuses. These increased the paid-up value of each share from £5·68 in 1831 to £20 in 1841.
e In each of the years 1824, 1825 and 1826 a cash dividend of £0·25 was paid.

## V  The development of the Indemnity

The achievement of the Indemnity in gaining acceptance as an insurer is reflected in the growth in the value of the capital it insured. But, as Table 1 shows, progress was not uninterrupted. Premium income growth and profitability were determined not simply by the company's business competence, but also by general influences on the marine insurance market, which led to fluctuations in the underlying upward trend.

Two interrelated factors were important in determining the market environment: the demand for insurance by merchants and shipowners and the level of premium rates. Both were influenced by the generally depressed state of the shipping industry from 1815 until the mid-century. The supply of shipping space ran ahead of demand as vessels continued to come on to the register and existing vessels were used more productively.[50] The consequent depreciation in shipping values and falling freight rates reduced the values on which premiums were based. The premium income earned by the market, which fell in the 1820s and 1830s, reflected this problem, although the need to relate sums insured to commodity values limited the fall. Furthermore, not all those with capital tied up in shipping customarily insured their property to its full value. In 1810 an estimate suggested that one-seventh of marine risks remained uninsured, but this was in wartime when the need for protection was great and the return to those in the shipping business exceptionally remunerative.[51] When profits fell after 1815 there was a real disincentive to spend money on insurance. As the merchant Henry Neilson explained to a select committee in 1833, 'two per cent would not have insured the freight, it would have swept it away altogether'.[52]

Average annual premium rates derived from the records of the Indemnity and London Assurance show a convincingly similar record. Between 1815 and 1820 they fell sharply, adjusting to peacetime conditions. They then fluctuated between 2% and 3% until the early 1830s, subsequently settling at a lower rate of 1¾% later in that decade, where they remained until mid-century. Yet this stabilisation did not check the fall in premium income, for the depression in shipping in the 1840s again seriously reduced the value of capital insured. Thus, over the period as a whole, these falling values were the principal source of contraction, apart from the immediate post-war years and the mid-1830s, when rate reductions were temporarily important. Not surprisingly, the income of the market as a whole mirrored the prosperity or otherwise of the shipping industry which it existed to serve.

Some contemporary commentators connected this depressed period with the introduction of joint-stock enterprise. As far as the market was concerned this could only have been through lower premium rates and we have seen that these were of only intermittent significance compared with the falling demand for protection. On the other hand, the expansion of the company sector from some 4% in 1810 to over one half in 1844 must have greatly exaggerated the effect of a contracting market on the private underwriting sector, and it would have been an obvious connection to make from the latter's point of view. Certainly, the historians of Lloyd's describe the decade after the repeal of the Bubble Act as characterised by 'dwindling membership, declining revenues and decreased individual profits' and regard 1846 as the year which heralded a new phase of business.[53] Of course, this is not to argue that the companies took all their business direct from Lloyd's; in many ways they probably opened up new markets, as the development of the Indemnity shows.

In the case of the Indemnity Table 1 makes it clear that the trend of business was upward, though subject to cyclical fluctuations. There were turning points in 1831, 1833, 1839 and 1844. These correspond with the experience of the two other companies for which there is information, the Royal Exchange Assurance and the London Assurance. In the case of the latter the cycles are less extreme, the Indemnity benefiting more from periods of buoyant demand but tending to suffer a more rapid decline in business when the market was depressed. Possibly this was associated with differences in the nature of the risks underwritten by the two companies, some trades being more affected cyclically than others, but without comparative information on the insurances accepted by each this cannot be proved.

Whatever competitive advantage the Indemnity may have had was not the result of lower premium rates. Comparison with the average premiums charged by London Assurance shows general consistency, and setting the rates charged by the Indemnity in March 1836 against average figures for this month which appeared in the *Shipping Gazette* shows no tendency to lower rates.[54] This fits with the instruction given to the original insurance committee of the company in 1824 that premium rates should be fixed 'with reference always to the rates prevailing for such risks at Lloyd's and other insurance offices'.[55] Initially the Indemnity's premium rates included the stamp duty, but this was not normal practice and gave rise to misunderstanding, and after 1826 stamp duty was levied separately.[56]

The Indemnity may have benefited, however, from another distinctive practice. It adopted the basic form of policy used at Lloyd's, drawn up in 1779 and prescribed by law since 1795, but, 'considering the practice of clubs upon which the Indemnity Marine Assurance Company was established', included a 'running down' clause which allowed the shipowner to insure against claims made against him in case of collision.[57] This was not a normal feature of policies issued by private underwriters at Lloyd's, but eventually came to be widely inserted after it appeared that failure to effect this cover was a handicap to business.[58] At the time of its introduction by the Indemnity the clause was still exceptional outside hull clubs, and the additional protection it offered shipowners may have worked to the company's advantage.

As far as it is possible to judge, the day-to-day business of the Indemnity was conducted efficiently, and there was evidently concern that this should be so. Monthly reports by the secretary to the directors regularly included information on the time it took to write policies up; four days in the 1830s when about forty policies were handled a day, rising to five days in the 1840s when some forty-five to fifty were dealt with.[59] Unlike the Alliance and London Assurance, the Indemnity made no attempt to extend business through the employment of agents in the outports, perhaps because of unwillingness to pay extra commission.[60] Indeed, there was great resistance to effecting insurance other than directly. Those who tried to obtain insurance through correspondence were firmly directed to employ someone to contact the Indemnity office in person.[61] This may reflect the influence of the company's underwriter, William Ellis, in arguing for the value of personal contact in accepting business.

What were the characteristics of the Indemnity's insurances? An adequate answer to this question could be provided only by analysis of the risk books, some of which survive for periods in the 1830s, but the number of policies issued and variety of details noted present a not inconsiderable problem of data handling. In the meantime a breakdown of risks according to trade, a procedure undertaken by underwriters themselves, is informative. Table 2 shows the proportion of premium arising from income from various voyages and types of risk for the year 1839, as recorded by the Indemnity's clerk.[62] The most striking feature of the table is the wide range of risks covered. Comparison with risks underwritten by private underwriters shows that this was by no means exceptional. The prudent underwriter desired to spread his interests so that losses due to adverse weather conditions or other localised factors did not affect the whole. However, the Indemnity's portfolio of risks reflects the disproportionate demand for insurance from different trades more than any conscious selection. Thus high-value cargoes, such as those in the East Indies trade, would be expected to be more often the subject of insurance than cargoes and vessels in the Baltic trades, and to yield higher premiums, despite the large share of Baltic traders in United Kingdom shipping entries, and this is reflected in the Indemnity's accounts. What is noteworthy is that the club trades, timber and coal, are not apparently as prominent as the early history of the Indemnity might lead us to expect, although it is probable that some of the separately noted time risks may belong to these trades.

The large share of time risks is the most obvious contrast between the Indemnity's business and that of two private underwriters whose risk books have survived.[63] In 1823 only twenty-six out of 1,893 policies on which Clagett and Pratt wrote a line were time policies and in 1846 De Rougement had an interest in ninety-seven out of a total of 2,373. Insurance of vessels could be for a specific voyage or for a period of time, most commonly a year. One of the main contrasts between marine insurance practice at the beginning of the nineteenth century and at its end is the replacement of voyage policies by time policies as the typical form. In the case of the Indemnity the share

Table 2. *Indemnity risks of 1839 (%)*

| | |
|---|---:|
| Coal | |
|     Cargo | 0·3 |
|     Ships | 0·5 |
| Coasters | 2·2 |
| Irish | 1·0 |
| Non-Mediterranean Spain and Portugal | 2·9 |
| France, Holland, Hamburgh | 2·2 |
| Baltic | 11·8 |
| White Sea | 0·5 |
| North Sea | 0·1 |
| Africa | 2·5 |
| Atlantic | 0·4 |
| Mediterranean | 3·0 |
| Turkey | 2·0 |
| Black Sea | 3·0 |
| Cape | 1·8 |
| Mauritius | 0·9 |
| Leeward Islands | 2·6 |
| Jamaica | 1·4 |
| Cuba | 3·9 |
| Spanish main | 1·9 |
| Newfoundland | 0·4 |
| British North America | 5·8 |
| United States | 6·0 |
| Brazil | 2·4 |
| West Coast of America | 3·3 |
| Greenland | 0·1 |
| Whalers, South Seas | 1·5 |
| Australia | 4·1 |
| East Indies | 7·3 |
| Hudson's Bay | 0·1 |
| Cross-risks | 5·8 |
| Time | 18·3 |

Total premium income: £408,132

of time risks may reflect simply preponderance of coastal insurance, but it may equally be a result of a disproportionate (relative to Lloyd's underwriters) share of steamship insurance. Time policies were always common in respect of coastal risks, where the repetitive nature of local voyages made separate policies impracticable. As steam propulsion was adopted, foreign-going vessels came increasingly to operate regular scheduled services, for which time policies were more suitable. In general it seems probable that steamship companies, when they were not their own insurers, would tend to opt for company insurance, not only because companies could carry a larger share of the risk but also because of the very familiarity of this form of business organisation.

However, the true test of underwriting is not the ability to attract business but the skill to make that business pay; the balance between income and expenditure, in which the major factor is the level of claims. Table 1 (column 8) shows annual profits and losses on the Indemnity's underwriting account, calculated after the lapse of three years when settlements and returns could be taken into account. A loss occurred in three of the years in the period under consideration but only in 1827 did this seriously affect reserves. The general, though by no means always spectacular, profitability of the underwriting account in the ten years after 1827 and the policy of carrying bonus payments to the capital account before 1840 (see Table 3) were sufficient to offset occasional reversals.

Although marine insurance could never possess the actuarial stability associated with life assurance, underwriting success, irrespective of institutional context, owed much to the exercise of skilled judgement in assessing the probability of loss involved in any particular proposal and relating this both to the premium charged and to the terms on which the policy was issued. As Joseph Marryat commented:

The underwriter must be well versed in geography; must be informed of the safety and danger of every port or road in every part of the world; of the nature of the navigation to and from every country and of the proper season for undertaking different voyages; he should be acquainted not only with the state but with the stations of the naval force of his own country and of the enemy; he should watch the appearance of any change in the relations of all foreign powers, by which his interests may be affected and, in short, constantly devote much time and attention to the pursuit in which he is engaged.[64]

In William Ellis, assistant underwriter to the company from 1824 and its chief manager from 1827 to 1876, the Indemnity found just such a paragon. Under the original arrangements for the conduct of business it was intended that terms of insurance should be determined by a committee of six directors in daily attendance. In practice responsibility devolved on the secretary, and when Ellis took charge this became the recognised procedure. Resisting from the first any division of responsibility for writing risks — 'the business of underwriting is in its nature open enough to difficulties and inconsistencies without extraneous efforts to add to this' — Ellis acted in relation to the company's underwriting business with almost as much influence as a private underwriter commanded over his own business.[65] On occasion the committee of management issued general directives. In January 1832, for example, it ruled that no more ships-of-war carrying Bank of England specie should be insured until existing risks were run off.[66] But inspection of the minutes shows that such intervention was rare. The twelve-man committee's prime role was determining complex settlements, nicely illustrated by the following laconic note, presumably made by one of the clerks:

Mr Gilmore had a long interview with Mr Ellis respecting a case of most extreme hardship to him, as regards the condemnation of a ship of his in Africa, which the captain condemned without (in the opinion of Mr Ellis and Gilmore) sufficient cause for so doing. The ship was insured with us and being condemned there can be no *legal claim* upon us, but the case is under the merciful consideration of the Directors.[67]

William Ellis's special role in determining the company's success was recognised by the committee of management by payment of special annual bonuses additional to his salary. From 1837 to 1850 sums paid to Ellis, 'upon whose sound judgement and wise discretion the vital interests of the company vitally depend', normally amounted to £1,000 annually.[68] Since his salary after 1840 was £2,000, itself an immense sum by contemporary standards, Ellis's career as company underwriter made him a very wealthy man.[69] Presumably for the Indemnity such generous payment was proportionately a small, and necessary, price to pay for continued profits.

What principles governed the company's conduct of insurance? Apart from the limitation on risks, set at £6,000 in 1824 and raised in 1838 to £30,000, it may be assumed that these were no different from those adopted by underwriters generally.[70] The season of the year, the trade, the cargo and the character of the vessel were all taken into account. Some notes made on the first pages of a voyage book for 1836–37, apparently for the clerk's own guidance, are informative on the factors affecting premiums and policy terms;

About the month of March the trades of the Baltic and British America open.
The Best season for Calcutta is from March forward, September is not a favourable one. Ships are usually restricted from sailing from West Indies after 1 August, and from the Baltic, White Sea and British America (Newfoundland excepted) after 1st October. From the middle of May throughout the whole of June is a bad season in the Bay of Bengal.
Wood is less worth writing than Tallow on account of the low value of wood, the Salvage being so heavy in wood it is not worth saving. Freight in River St. Lawrence less than risk on ship, the charges are so enormous if she gets on shore there.[71]

In common with private underwriters, the Indemnity made use of a variety of sources of information on shipping matters. Subscriptions by the company in 1834 included payment for customs bills of entry, Lloyd's List, Westenhall's List and for the ship classification register published by Lloyd's Registry of Shipping. Although companies were barred from underwriting at Lloyd's, the Indemnity subscribed both to Lloyd's and to the Jerusalem Coffee House in order to benefit from the intelligence service both offered.[72]

In 1837 the Alliance directors explained that company's enlarged business in terms of three factors contributing to success: 'cautious and prudent selection of risks', 'fairness and liberality in settlement of losses' and 'introduction of new and respectable connections'.[73] The part played by the first and third in respect of the Indemnity having been discussed, what of the second — 'generous and just settlements'? Again the clerk's notes are instructive — 'the company never offers a compromise for they say you either are or are not entitled to your money' — but perhaps a reputation for equity at least can be inferred from the continued ability to attract business.[74]

It is evident that the Indemnity's skill in underwriting was matched by sound financial sense. Lending on ship mortgage ceased in 1826 and from then on until the early 1840s investment of company funds, above the balance of £5,000 kept at the bankers, was restricted to government stock.[75] The directors were concerned that interest earned on this was too low, but in 1836 when alternatives were considered they were rejected on grounds of security and liquidity.[76] A minute of 1841 summarises the considerations determining the Indemnity's investment: 'the principal object has been to combine with unquestionable security that mode of investment which appears the most readily available and at the same time the least liable to suffer depreciation from the breaking out of war or any other cause which might concur simultaneously with the existence of large demands upon the company's assets'.[77] However, by this date reserves were considered sufficient for cash bonuses to be paid to shareholders. In 1844, apparently for the first time, the Indemnity invested in another company, the London and North Western Railway.[78] By 1850, when reserves stood at £672,477, the Indemnity portfolio included a number of railway and public utility investments (see Table 3).

Table 3. *Indemnity Marine Insurance Company investment portfolio, 1850 (£)*

|  | Value at cost | Date of first purchase |
|---|---|---|
| Government stock | 426,375 |  |
| Bank of England stock | 40,098 | 1845 |
| Railway bonds | 163,705 | 1844 |
| Dock company bonds and debentures | 40,623 | 1847 |
| Waterworks debentures | 1,676 | 1849 |
| Total | 672,477 |  |

## VI Conclusion

At mid-century the Indemnity was an established and trusted insurer, but still something of a rarity; the great expansion of company insurance was not to come until the 1860s. Operating at a time when private and company underwriters alike found survival difficult, it succeeded in taking a share of the insurance market sufficient to give its shareholders a good return. The original mutual scheme contributed to long-term growth by enabling the company to commence on a larger scale than would otherwise have been the case, but was wisely dispensed with. Not only did the scheme necessarily limit further growth, but the spirit of experiment which it reflected was alien to success in marine insurance. Indeed, what is most striking about the Indemnity under William Ellis's direction is the extent to which the conduct of business proceeded upon traditional lines. Yet to say that scale of operation alone distinguished the Indemnity from the private underwriter does not sufficiently emphasise the significance of that likeness. Either poor or over-conservative judgement of risks would have reduced the Indemnity's profits. Faulty, uncertain business judgement had ensured the demise of some other joint-stock companies, while company insurance in the past, as exemplified by the London Assurance and Royal Exchange, had tended towards excessive caution. In its developed state the Indemnity manifested neither tendency. Company insurance for the Indemnity referred to the mode of raising the initial capital; it meant little that was distinctive in terms of conduct of business. Rather than representing a new direction in marine insurance, as its founders had intended, the Indemnity was in many respects little more than the private underwriter writ large. As such it found a place in the London marine market.

### Notes

1  See, for example, references to marine insurance in Ralph Davis, *The Rise of the British Shipping Industry*, Newton Abbot, 1962, and Patrick Crowhurst, *The Defence of British Trade*, Folkestone, 1977.

2  B. Supple, *The Royal Exchange Assurance. A History of British Insurance, 1720–1970*, Cambridge, 1970; A. H. John, 'The London Assurance Company and the marine insurance market of the eighteenth century', *Economica*, XXV, 1958, pp. 126–41; C. Wright and C. E. Fayle, *A History of Lloyd's from the Foundation of Lloyd's Coffee House to the Present Day*, London, 1928.

3  On these see H. A. L. Cockerell and Edwin Green, *The British Insurance Business, 1547–1970*, London, 1976.

4  *Report from the Select Committee on Marine Insurance*, B.P.P., 1810, IV.

5  Anon., *Considerations on the Dangers of Altering the Marine Insurance Laws of Great Britain ...*, London, 1811.

6  In 1828 the Committee of Lloyd's alleged that stamp duties were driving insurance to foreign centres. See Wright and Fayle, *History of Lloyd's*, p. 320.

7  *S.C. Marine Insurance*, p. 58.

8   Wright and Fayle, *History of Lloyd's*, pp. 112–274.
9   6 Geo. I, c. 18.
10  See anon., *Considerations*, p. 21, for discussion of this point.
11  *S.C. Marine Insurance*, p. 5.
12  Wright and Fayle, *History of Lloyd's*, pp. 240–60; 307–14; Supple, *R.E.A.*, pp. 189–99.
13  Henry M. Hozier and E. Puttock, *Lloyd's General Report for 1884*, London, 1884, p. 64; Marine Insurance Company, *Prospectus*, London, 1836, p. 17.
14  J. R. McCulloch, *A Dictionary of Commerce*, London, 1844, p. 713. Given McCulloch's bias in favour of the companies, this may be an overestimate.
15  Guildhall Library (G.L.), MS. 11,833/1, 2 March 1825.
16  G.L., M.S. 11,833/1, 22 April 1824. Directors appointed in 1824 were Robert Rickards, George Lyall (deputy chairman), William Astell, David Barclay, Cornelius Butler, John Buckle, Richard Hart Dawes, William Dawson, John T. Dauburg, Edward Ellice, Ellis Ellis, Ralph Fenwick, George Harthorn, George Hibbert, John Hodgson, John Innes, Niven Kerr, Thomas Murdoch, Stewart Marjoribanks, John Horsley Palmer, Robert Scott, John Staniforth, Andrew Thompson, Henry Usborne, William Wilson, Samuel Winter. Among investors who were not directors was Joseph Somes, possible the largest individual shipowner in the country.
17  F. W. Martin, *History of Lloyd's and Marine Insurance*, London, 1876.
18  On the nature and origins of the Shipowners Society see Leonard Harris, *London General Shipowners Society, 1811–1961*, London, 1961, and S. R. Palmer, *The Character and Organisation of the Shipping Industry of the Port of London, 1815–1849*, unpublished Ph.D. thesis, University of London, 1979, pp. 61–70.
19  General Shipowners Society, General Meeting Minutes, III, April 1828.
20  On history of ship classification see anon., *Annals of Lloyd's Register*, London, 1884.
21  *S.C. on Marine Insurance*, pp. 360–1; Insurance Institute of London, *The History and Development of Protection and Indemnity Clubs*, London, 1957, appendix I.
22  *Report from the Select Committee to whom the Coal Trade (Port of London) Bill was committed ...*, B.P.P., 1837–38, XV, qq. 500–5.
23  *Report from the Select Committee on improving the Foreign Trade of the Country*, B.P.P., 1820, III, p. 14.
24  *S.C. Marine Insurance*, p. 361. At this time the London Union had eighty to eighty-four members and insured about 100 vessels.
25  *S.C. Marine Insurance*, p. 312.
26  *Report from the Select Committee on Shipwrecks of Timber Ships*, B.P.P., 1839, IX, q. 1100.
27  Insurance Institute, *Protection and Indemnity*, p. 7.
28  Indemnity Marine, *Prospectus*, London, 1824. A facsimile copy is bound into the official company history, J. F. Mainland and E. F. Howard, *The Indemnity. A Centenary Retrospect*, London, 1924.
29  G.L., MS. 11,833/1, 24 July 1824.
30  G.L., MS. 11,833/1, 2 March 1825; MS. 11,833/1, 16 July 1824.
31  G.L., MS. 11,880/1, 31 August 1824.
32  G.L., MS. 11,842.
33  G.L., MS. 11,840.
34  G.L., MS. 11,836/1, 11 July 1826. The call was authorised by an extraordinary meeting after the defeat of a contrary amendment.
35  G.L., MS. 11,836/1, 11 July 1826.
36  G.L., MS. 11,840. The name of Staniforth was omitted from the official list of directors which appears in Mainland and Howard, *The Indemnity*, which makes

The Indemnity and marine insurance 93

no mention of the circumstances surrounding his conduct of company business.
37 G.L., MS. 11,833/1, 3 February 1827.
38 G.L., MS. 11,833/1, 20 June 1827.
39 G.L., MS. 11,836/1, 24 July 1827.
40 G.L., MS. 11,841/1, London Assurance, MS. 8,749/4.
41 G.L., MS. 11,841/1, 8 March 1827.
42 See, for example, anon., *Letter to Jasper Vaux*, London, 1810, p. 10.
43 H. Vaucher, *A Guide to Marine Insurance*, London, 1834, p. 202.
44 Vaucher, *Marine Insurance*, p. ii.
45 *Report from the Select Committee on Joint Stock Companies*, B.P.P., 1844, VII, q. 2065.
46 Cockerell and Green, *British Insurance Business*, p. 14.
47 G.L., MS. 11,833/2.
48 MS. 11,833/1, 17 July 1824.
49 MS. 11,841, 1828–32.
50 On the state of the shipping industry see *Report from the Select Committee on the Present State of Manufactures, Commerce and Shipping in the U.K.*, B.P.P., 1833, VI; *Report from the Select Committee on British Shipping*, B.P.P., VIII, 1844.
51 *Letter to Jasper Vaux*, p. 32.
52 *Report from the Select Committee on Manufactures, Commerce and Shipping*, B.P.P., 1833, VI, q. 6493.
53 G.L., Wright and Fayle, *History of Lloyd's*, p. 319.
54 *Shipping Gazette*, 9 March 1836.
55 G.L., MS. 11,833/1, 17 July 1824.
56 G.L., MS. 11,833/1, 17 July 1824; 11,835/1, 27 September 1826.
57 See R. Stevens, *Essay on Average*, London, 1822, and J. Arnould, *Treatise on the Law of Marine Insurance*, London, 1850; G.L., MS. 11,835/1, 14 November 1827.
58 Insurance Institute of London, *Institute Time Clauses — Hulls*, London, 1962, p. 2.
59 Calculated from figures appearing in G.L., MS. 11,841/1/2/3.
60 Bernard Drew, *The London Assurance. A Second Chronicle*, London, 1949, pp. 89–90. G.L., Alliance Company, MS. 14,842/1, 5 January 1831, 11 December 1833.
61 G.L., MS. 11,880/1, letter dated 14 March 1842 to William Barnard.
62 This appears on a loose sheet in G.L., MS. 11,843.
63 Lloyd's Library, Risk Book for Clagett and Pratt, 1823; Risk Book for De Rougement, 1846.
64 J. Marryat, *Marine Insurance*, pp. 27–8.
65 G.L., MS. 11,833/1, 8 March 1827.
66 G.L., MS. 11,833/1, 10 January 1832.
67 G.L., MS. 11,843.
68 G.L., MS. 11,833/1, 9 August 1831.
69 Details of salaries appear in G.L., MS. 11,833/1/2/3. From 1827 to 1840 Ellis's annual salary was £1,500. In the years 1844–46, when profits were poor, his bonus was set at £500. Bonus payments to him were taken from underwriting profits and do not appear under 'Establishment' in Table 1; Junior clerks with the Indemnity earned £60 annually in 1840; William Ellis was benefactor of the Birkbeck Schools. See *Dictionary of National Biography* for details of his philosophical and philanthropic interests.
70 G.L., MS. 11,833/1, 1 September 1824. The limit on regular Indiamen and government packets was £10,000 and on men-of-war £15,000.
71 G.L., MS. 11,843.
72 G.L., MS. 11,837/1, 10 December 1834.
73 G.L., MS. 14,089, January 1837.

74 G.L., MS. 11,843.
75 G.L., MS. 11,833/1, 12 October 1826; 13 September 1831.
76 G.L., MS. 11,835/2, 9 June 1836.
77 G.L., MS. 11,838, 25 February 1841.
78 G.L., MS. 11,866/1.

J. H. TREBLE

# The record of the Standard Life Assurance Company in the life insurance market of the United Kingdom, 1850–64

## I  *Introduction*

Founded in Edinburgh in 1825, the Standard Life Assurance Company had emerged by 1850 as one of the three principal offices — measured in terms of the volume of new annual business which it had secured — operating in the United Kingdom market. Yet its rise to a position of national stature from an initially circumscribed geographical base had not been without serious setbacks. During the years 1825–32 internal organisational problems and the lack of a dynamic management had led to a succession of profoundly disappointing results.[1] Within less than two decades, however, it had not merely absorbed the lessons of its major errors of judgement; it was also positively committed, under the leadership of William Thomas Thomson, its third and longest-serving manager (1837–74), and a reforming board of directors, 'not only to try to keep up, but if possible, to surpass the measure of success we have achieved'.[2] This objective was to be realised during the course of the ensuing quarter of a century. Between 1845 and 1860 it transacted 'a larger amount of Business ... than any other Office'.[3] Between 1864 and 1875 this achievement was in its turn to be decisively eclipsed when it never failed to obtain a total of less than £1 million of new life contracts in any of its financial years. This last trend owed much to those major discontinuities in policy which embodied the Standard's response to the challenges posed by the stresses of heightened competition within the boundaries of the United Kingdom and the lure of the white settler market in the far-flung territory of the Empire.

The aim of this article is not, however, to examine these changes of direction in any detail. Rather it is concerned with the more limited problem of analysing those factors which, between 1850 and 1864, helped to maintain the office's competitive position in the life insurance market within an organisational and technical framework which had been erected and tested during the 1830s and 1840s. This framework consisted of three interrelated strands. First, largely following the lead of other major companies, the opportunity had been taken to liberalise participating policies over time.

96    The business of insurance

Secondly, operating through its Edinburgh-based Agency Committee and its London Committee, set up in the mid-1840s when the York and London Insurance Company had been taken over, the directorate increasingly realised the importance of agency revision and expansion in the search for business. Finally, in order to attract new custom for its participating scheme the Standard ensured that at each quinquennial valuation the major share of the ensuing surplus went to its with-profits policy-holders.[4] It is against this backcloth and those modifications in this inheritance from the past which were to be made in the 1850s and early 1860s that the contours of the office's annual returns have to be set.

II    *Directions of development, 1850–64*

The company's overall performance during the period 1850–64 was primarily determined by an intricate interaction between numerous endogenous and exogenous variables. Yet since some of those forces influencing the office's annual returns had been equally important determinants of the contours of new premium income in its first twenty-five years of existence, it was inevitable that the aggregate picture should have some statistical continuity with that of the immediate past. In the first place the amount of new life business won during 1850–55 and 1855–60 conformed in certain respects to an already familiar pattern, with peak results being recorded in the final twelve months of each quinquennium — in this case 1854–55 and 1859–60 — when the declaration of the bonus was imminent.[5] Again, the decline in the volume of annual business which had hitherto usually occurred in the period immediately after the conclusion of an Investigation was faithfully reproduced in 1850–51, 1855–56 and 1860–61, while the trend towards expansion which had emerged strongly in the 1840s was sustained, although the quinquennial percentage rate of increase tended to slow down during the 1850s. Whereas £2,146,641 of new assurance had been won in 1845–50, that total was to rise to £2,492,988 in 1850–55 and yet again to £2,815,455 in 1855–60. But if these points of similarity with the Standard's earlier history should be stressed, it is equally necessary to highlight discontinuities in experience. For example, while during the 1840s the upward surge in the number of new transactions was for the most part unaffected by the adverse movement of the trade cycle, the impact of the 1857–58 crisis was faithfully recorded in the decline in business in that year and in the relatively static level of returns in 1858–59. Furthermore, much of the period was marked by a greater element of stability in the Standard's results than had been true of the 1840s. Thus during 1850–53 the volume of new business fluctuated remarkably little from an annual mark of £450,000, while 1853–54, 1855–56, 1857–59 and 1860–62 conformed to a similar pattern, with the volume of the office's transactions moving between a low point of £503,854 (1860–61) and a high point of £516,351 (1855–56). This stability reflected in part the impact of those new companies

## The Standard and life insurance 97

Table 1. *New annual business secured by the Standard Life Assurance Company*

| Year | No. of new policies | Amount of new business £ s d | New premium income £ s d |
|---|---|---|---|
| 1850-51 | 822 | 467,499 18 1 | 15,240 2 11 |
| 1851-52 | 777 | 445,799 6 6 | 15,145 15 6 |
| 1852-53 | 875 | 455,248 17 1 | 14,886 9 3 |
| 1853-54 | 1,046 | 515,117 7 0 | 16,650 0 2 |
| 1854-55 | 1,088 | 609,323 7 11 | – |
| 1855-56 | 938 | 516,351 6 7 | – |
| 1856-57 | 840 | 574,839 7 5 | 17,916 3 6 |
| 1857-58 | 791 | 507,522 9 0 | 16,695 11 10 |
| 1858-59 | 896 | 510,845 0 0 | 16,580 1 0 |
| 1859-60 | 1,207 | 705,897 0 0 | 22,565 4 0 |
| 1860-61 | – | 503,854 18 0 | 16,082 5 10 |
| 1861-62 | – | 506,120 0 0 | 15,158 1 6 |
| 1862-63 | 1,119 | 643,960 0 0 | 21,482 15 5 |
| 1863-64 | 1,428 | 805,980 6 6 | 25,396 16 11 |

*Source.* Policy registers, annual reports, investigation reports and extant manuscript material of the Standard.

whose numbers, in the wake of the 1844 Joint Stock Act, multiplied rapidly between 1844 and 1852. These newcomers brought a more dynamic approach to the industry, spending heavily on advertising campaigns, raising the level of commission payments to agents and introducing changes, designed to stimulate business, in participating contracts. Reaction to these developments by older companies was predictably mixed. Some, among them the Royal Exchange Assurance, lost ground by continuing to cling to largely traditional guidelines when they were less relevant to changing market conditions. Others were to make adjustments to their existing assurance package and to parts of their administrative structure in a bid to improve their position in a highly competitive market.[6] Into this last category came the Standard, although it had to wait until 1862-64 for a sharp upswing in its fortunes. Even then this upswing has to be kept in perspective, since in the first of those years there were at least eight offices, including its great rival, the Scottish Widows' Fund, which secured over £650,000 of new business. It was only in 1863-64, when it won in excess of £800,000 of new proposals for the first time in its history, that it could claim that 'no Scottish Office has ever before issued so large a number of Policies in any one year as the STANDARD has done'.[7]

Nevertheless, while these data indicate that the company was able to maintain its hold on the United Kingdom market, they shed no light upon any of the significant shifts which took place over time in the geographical areas where it was achieving its greatest degree of success. Fortunately this problem can be effectively solved in this period from the extant policy registers, which enable the historian to chart with reasonable accuracy the distribution of its business according to country. These returns, embodied in Table 2, differ from the aggregate statistics which have so far been discussed since they include not merely policies issued in return for a uniform annual premium but also contracts which lapsed in their first year and proposals which had been accepted on a single-payment basis. The effect of this change is to inflate the ensuing figures above those for the United Kingdom as a whole, but the difference does not alter the underlying trend.

Table 2. *New United Kingdom business of the Standard Life Assurance Company, by country (£)*

| Year | Scotland | England | Ireland |
| --- | --- | --- | --- |
| 1850–51 | 206,694 | – | 68,871 |
| 1851–52 | 222,198 | 182,042 | 60,008 |
| 1852–53 | 188,637 | 182,372 | 102,441 |
| 1853–54 | 221,997 | 237,430 | 70,291 |
| 1854–55 | 235,780 | 272,266 | 102,478 |
| 1855–56 | 219,447 | 210,449 | 107,229 |
| 1856–57 | 229,189 | 265,061 | 92,839 |
| 1857–58 | 189,347 | 216,954 | 112,121 |
| 1858–59 | 218,195 | 227,300 | 82,601 |
| 1859–60 | 193,900 | 387,162 | 132,525 |
| 1860–61 | 158,396 | 239,360 | 128,580 |
| 1861–62 | 199,802 | 228,357 | 87,301 |
| 1862–63 | 183,779 | 349,020 | 124,050 |
| 1863–64 | 221,598 | 468,382 | 142,488 |
| 1864–65 | 213,990 | 596,064 | 182,075 |

*Source.* Policy Registers of the Standard Life Assurance Company.

Perhaps the most striking feature to emerge from these results is the relatively static record of the company in Scotland. Throughout these years the amount of new business generated within Scottish society displayed no tendency to rise. Indeed, if an analysis of these statistics was extended to include 1864–65 so that a quinquennial comparison could be conducted, it is clear that the best Scottish performance took place in 1850–55, when an annual average of £215,000 of new business was secured, and that the worst result was achieved in 1860–65, when the relevant figure was slightly under £200,000. Although, therefore, the amount of business in Scotland remained on a *per capita* basis consistently above what the company managed to achieve in England in the same time span, it comes as no surprise to find that Scotland was to lose its former position of the principal territorial contributor to the growth of new premium income. In part these runs of disappointing results stemmed from the fact that, compared with the Standard's formative years, competition had markedly increased in Scotland both through a multiplication in the number of indigenous offices in the subsequent quarter of a century and a more systematic penetration of the Scottish market by their English rivals. But, as will be argued later, the company's hold on its home base was also weakened by the greater financial attractions of the Scottish Widows' Fund's with-profits scheme for the younger elements of Scottish middle-class society and by the failure of head office to act expeditiously against apathetic agents in several of the major Scottish towns.

On the other hand the trend of business in England and Ireland was much more buoyant. In each country the secular trend was unmistakably upward, with the poorest returns occurring in the opening quinquennium — in Ireland during 1850–55 the annual average was slightly in excess of £80,000, while in England the corresponding result for 1851–55 was approximately £218,000, — but with a sharp increase thereafter. By 1860–65 almost £133,000 of assurance was on average being annually obtained in Ireland and £376,000 in England. There was thus a strong element of synchronisation about the timing and intensity of the upswing in both localities. This, however, was by no means the sole source of comfort which was derived from this picture. For as important as the overall pattern was what lay behind these aggregates. In the first place, the basic resilience of Ireland's middle and upper classes was amply demonstrated by the fact that the volume of new proposals from that country had as early as 1850–51 attained a level — £69,000 — which had never been surpassed at an earlier point in time. By the late 1850s, when the Irish landowner was once more regarded with favour and when intensive efforts were made to broaden the geographical coverage of the office's agency network, it was only rarely that an annual total of £100,000 of business was not won in Ireland. In the case of England the nature of the Standard's achievements was in large measure a reflection of the willingness of the board to heed the promptings of its London-based officials. The relatively modest results of the early 1850s, for example, stemmed primarily from the uncompetitiveness of the company's pre-1854 commission rates and the absence of an inspector of agencies. With the appointment of Bentham as inspector and the adoption of new commission scales in 1854–55, improvement was immediately discernible, although it was not to be continuous, the level of business on occasion falling away either, as in 1857–58, in response to the downswing of the trade cycle or as the aftermath to the division of the quinquennial surplus. Furthermore the relatively poor results from several major English towns and cities were still regarded as late as 1862 as a significant decelerating influence upon the Standard's performance.[8] Indeed, it was only when the strength of its English inspectorate was raised to two in 1862 that its English business surged decisively ahead, although the dimensions of the advance were impressive, with a record total of almost £470,000 of new proposals being secured in 1863–64.

It is with a more detailed analysis of these influences which shaped the Standard's response to changing market conditions that the remainder of this chapter is concerned.

## III  Organisational and technical development

Throughout this decade and a half the board of directors continued to uphold the company's original tontine scheme as the main basis of its appeal to the insuring public.[9] But, as Thomson himself was well aware, it did not follow that the Standard could look forward on these grounds alone to an automatic secular rise in its volume of annual business. For while potential customers were influenced by the size of the bonuses accruing to with-profits policies, they were also to some extent affected by the progressive liberalisation of the insurance contract which was taking place elsewhere. It was for this reason that the office took steps, in the more competitive atmosphere of the 1850s, to broaden the terms under which it issued its contracts.

A start was made in 1851, when the proprietors accepted Thomson's advice to establish two distinct categories of select assurance. Broadly defined, this decision meant that those whose contracts had been in force for five years could apply to the board for 'a certificate of admission' to either the First or 'Second Class of Select Assurances'. In the former case all applicants 'whose pursuits hold out no prospect of their going abroad, having at the same time no intention of leaving Europe, should have their policies relieved of the clause as to forfeiture or payment of Extra Premiums, in the event of their going abroad'. Furthermore, provided only that the annual premiums were maintained, such policies were to be 'unchallengeable upon any grounds whatever'. Those deemed eligible for a Second Class certificate were also held to possess an unchallengeable contract, subject to the vital qualification that if they wished to venture beyond the confines of Europe they became immediately liable to pay the appropriate scale of extra premiums levied by the office.[10] In 1856 this process of liberalisation was extended when it was resolved that 'Policies of five years' duration ... shall not be forfeited in consequence of non-payment of any ordinary premium, notwithstanding the expiry of the thirty days of grace, provided payment shall be tendered before the expiry of thirteen months from the date of such premium falling into arrear.'[11] Settlement of this obligation within that time span was not to involve any fresh medical examination, although a fine of 5% per month was added to the outstanding debt. Finally, in 1861, and borrowing from Thomson's earlier work for the Colonial Life Assurance Company, the so-called 'free assurance' category was introduced, which was effectively to supersede the First Class scheme of 1851. Under its terms an individual who at the time he was making his proposal could satisfy the directorate that he 'has no intention of proceeding beyond the limits of Europe, from his occupation and other circumstances ... he being ... not under 25 years of age' was in future to be free to travel to, 'and reside in, any part of the world without license [sic] or payment of extra Premium'.[12] In addition, it was accepted that all contracts upon which five or more annual premiums had been paid should automatically be granted 'unchallengeable' status.

None the less, despite these positive improvements to the insurance contract the board recognised that improved returns depended upon a broader-based appeal than simply emphasising the virtues of innovation *per se*. In particular, in the aftermath of the failure of the West Middlesex Company and of the distrust engendered by the proliferation of new life offices in the late 1840s and early 1850s, there was a need to reassure clients about the Standard's underlying financial strength. Translated into practical terms, the company's spokesmen had to demonstrate that the Standard's concern with a measure of innovation did not involve discarding those precepts of sound management characteristic of its immediate past, which were acknowledged to be the hallmark of all 'first class' offices. Among other things they sought to show that the company's investment decisions were invariably sound, producing yields which were on average 1% – 1½% 'above the rate on which the calculations of the Company are based'.[13] Again, attention was drawn to the conservative nature of the Standard's valuation procedure, to the future benefit of all with-profit policy-holders.[14] In the board's view, therefore, it was logical to conclude that the labour it bestowed upon husbanding the office's resources afforded the best guarantee that all contracts would be honoured; that those who possessed participating policies could anticipate receiving substantial tontine reversionary bonuses at the end of each quinquennium; and that the company was fulfilling its pledge 'to be nearly as possible a Mutual Association without all the drawbacks to which Mutual Assurance is liable'.[15]

It is a more difficult task to evaluate the contribution which these two approaches made to the overall pattern of the office's new life business during the period under review. On the positive side the select scheme was warmly welcomed in the first five years of its existence by a proportion of the Standard's existing clients, for between 1851 and April 1856 550 First and Second Class certificates were issued. This trend continued throughout the second half of the 1850s. By 1861 the number of certificate-holders had almost doubled from its 1856 base and must have included many who had taken out policies in the early 1850s.[16] Similarly between 1856 and 1863 some 700 policy-holders were beneficiaries of those resolutions governing the revival of policies which had previously been declared forfeit for non-payment of the appropriate premium.[17]

Yet, despite these data, the historian should not inflate the overall impact of such changes upon the company's performance. In this context there are at least three factors which justify such caution. In the first place, given the Standard's claim that no applicant was ever refused admission to the select category, it is obvious that only a small minority of those who had sealed their policies with the office between 1851 and 1856 had taken advantage of this privilege. Secondly, even among those middle-class elements who were preoccupied with such matters, the company was not to enjoy a long-lived monopoly of those improvements it had been responsible for pioneering.[18]

Thirdly, the general tenor of the comments of the Standard's salaried officials leaves little room for doubt that the prime generators of new business were the quality of its management and the financial probity of its operations. William Bentham, its Inspector of English Agencies, was one who was to argue that the office's results in the 1850s and early 1860s were largely attributable to 'the attractive bonus' and 'the distinguished ability and increasing energy of the Management'. Conversely only ephemeral gains had followed in the wake of policy innovations, since their rapid spread elsewhere 'takes away our special advantages from us'.[19] In the last analysis, therefore, the aura of respectability, achieved through adhering to well tried practices, not only resulted in the Standard's being accorded an honoured place in the *Post Magazine*'s list of 'pure vintage companies ... that stand upon their original base';[20] it was also a potent lever in directing clients into the offices of its agents. Nevertheless, while the company's integrity facilitated the work of its widely scattered representatives, it did not automatically follow that the agents themselves were sufficiently dynamic in forwarding its interests in their own towns and districts. In a word, in an imperfect market the volume of new business accruing to any office was probably more powerfully shaped by the quality and spread of its agency network than any other single factor.

In the Standard's case it can be legitimately argued that the contours of its post-1850 whole-life business can in large measure be interpreted in terms of the degree to which its directors were sensitive to the deficiencies, revealed over time, in its administrative infrastructure; for even if it was thought expedient to leave intact the main outlines of the pre-1850 agency system, there was a need to reform certain aspects of managerial practice in order to raise the efficiency of its agents. Among the more pressing of these requirements was a radical revision of its commission rates. In the early 1850s its commission scheme consisted of two distinct layers. A uniform rate of 5% was paid upon all new and renewal premium collected by the individual agent. In addition, an incentive system, introduced in 1851, offered an ascending scale of rewards to those representatives who had obtained in excess of £1,000 of new with-profits business in any year. By 1854–55, however, reasoned criticism was being voiced at the uncompetitiveness of those terms, while dire consequences were predicted if a substantial overhaul of these levels of remuneration were long delayed. These points were most forcibly expressed in an 1855 memorandum from H. Jones Williams, the Standard's new London secretary, in which he pointed out that while the company's commission plan 'works well in some instances', 'in others [it] is much objected to'. Such objections, whenever they were encountered in an English setting, were based upon rational grounds, since quite apart from the exorbitant rewards offered by some of the newer offices, 'almost all the old established English Companies allow a commission of 10 per cent on first premiums and 5 per cent thereafter'. What, therefore, was required if the office was to retain its present representatives and to attract a good class of agent in the future was the adoption of commission rates comparable to those offered by its principal English competitors.[21]

The reaction of the directors to these suggestions was an interesting commentary upon their determination to enlarge their share of the lucrative English market. For notwithstanding complaints about the disappointing level of English results in 1851–52,[22] the Edinburgh board quickly endorsed Jones Williams's blueprint in its entirety. Commission rates on first premiums were at once raised to 10%, while the existing incentive scheme was henceforth only to become operational when the particular representative had won at least £5,000 of participating business in any twelve months' period.[23] This process of change, once begun, was continued in 1856 when minor modifications in the system of remunerating 'occasional agents' were sanctioned and in the following year when solicitors in Scotland were allowed to claim the usual commission upon insurance proposals taken out in connection with loan transactions with the office.[24]

Taken together these alterations were designed to stimulate the Standard's agents to greater exertions on its behalf. Yet if much was expected from the implementation of this programme, the board was not content to allow its performance in the assurance field to be entirely determined by the responsiveness of its representatives to increased incentives. Drawing on its own previous experience, it realised that the recurrent problem of poor annual results from a significant proportion of its agents had still to be faced. In some localities the office's interests could suffer because it had appointed men who had too many alternative outlets to give them time to do justice to their connection with the Standard, while in yet other cases the high socioeconomic status of the agent could mean a relative reluctance on his part to seek out 'first class' lives. These reforms, therefore, in no way superseded the obligation of the directors to maintain, and in certain respects to expand, the controls which had hitherto been exercised over the developing agency network. The need to define market opportunity in a given area, to remove the inefficient, and to extend the spatial spread of the agency network was as pressing in promoting the economic health of the company in the post-1850 era as it had been in the first twenty-five years of its existence.

Throughout the 1850–64 period preoccupation with administrative efficiency was most marked in England, where the guidelines for future action had been finalised in 1849.[25] None the less it was not until the appointment of Bentham as Inspector of English Agencies in 1853 that the enforcement of the 1849 programme was effectively mounted. Bentham's period as inspector was to last little more than a decade. Yet by the summer of 1863, when he was moved to Ireland to assume the post of Resident Secretary in Dublin, it is possible to point to a substantial improvement in the company's English results and to highlight the part played in that process by a judicious use of the powers of inspection. Those powers consisted of three interdependent strands. In the first place the necessary task of revising the existing agency lists had to be carried out. Such work was in fact a fundamental precondition for growth, since it was clear that 'many' of the Standard's appointments 'have fallen miserably short of my expectation of them'.[26] During 1855–60, for example, only twenty-nine out of a total of more than 200 English agents had forwarded proposals in each year of that quinquennium. If the period of comparison was extended to embrace 1850–60, the figure was reduced to a mere sixteen. It is against this sombre statistical backcloth that the drastic nature of Bentham's work has to be set. Between 1850 and 1855 no fewer than fifty-three out of 177 new representatives had their contracts cancelled, while a further fifty-two out of 152 pre-1850 appointments were dealt with in a similar fashion. Over time, however, such pruning, accompanied by the installation of new agents, produced beneficial results. Whereas 199 representatives had sent in business in at least one year during 1850–55, that total rose to 256 in the following quinquennium. Moreover, in the latter period, 38½% of the business secured in England had been won by agents appointed in the second half of the 1850s. Nevertheless it would be a mistake to suggest that the apathetic were always removed. As had occurred in the pre-1850 era, inefficient officials in certain districts tended to be left undisturbed unless a more suitable replacement could be found, while in some of the major cities it was sometimes hoped to circumvent the problem altogether by appointing additional correspondents.[27]

The two remaining aspects of the inspection process were of much less general application. In order of significance they were the establishment of agencies in areas where the Standard had hitherto been unrepresented and the sparing use of special agreements and allowances to reinforce the activities of agents in towns of considerable growth potential.[28] Reliance, however, on this last approach was scarcely justified in terms of the meagre returns which it yielded. In the majority of instances cash and rental inducements had little effect in galvanising the office's representatives into action, leaving the board with the unenviable choice of terminating or revising its allowances, dismissing the agent, or doing both simultaneously.[29] In the light of these trends there was almost an element of inevitability about the decision, taken in 1862, to contain the spread of 'the practice of making the [new] Agents any allowances beyond the usual Commission'.[30] Implicit in that verdict was a recognition of the overriding importance of other techniques in advancing the Standard's position in the whole-life market and an acknowledgment of the relative failure of this experiment not merely in England but also in those Scottish and Irish cities where it had been put to the test.

Yet even in failure the use of these procedures on a United Kingdom basis raises the question as to how far the controls exercised over the burgeoning agency system conformed to a monolithic model in the constituent parts of the nation. Outwardly, of course, the common ties were strong: in Scotland, England and Ireland a uniform scale of commission payment was in force throughout the period under examination. Despite this major continuity in policy, however, it is also possible to discern the existence of significant departures in Scottish and Irish administrative practice from the English model. Quite apart from the fact that their mechanism of control was centred upon Edinburgh rather than London, the actual process of inspection and agency extension was somewhat differently ordered. As late as 1863 Scotland and Ireland possessed not one full-time inspector between them, whereas England at the same juncture had two such officials. Both countries were therefore to some extent dependent upon their chief officers' agreeing to act as unpaid overseers of their agency networks in addition to coping with their other duties. In Thomson's words, 'it is not the practice to visit regularly the Agencies in Scotland but that he or some other official of the Company took advantage of any convenient opportunity that presented itself to see certain of the Agents'.[31] But such a policy always had serious drawbacks. Firstly, since neither Thomson nor Smylie — until 1863 the Standard's Resident Secretary in Ireland — could afford to be away from their respective headquarters for any length of time, their prospects of securing new representatives through direct contact was correspondingly reduced. Secondly it was impossible to maintain 'that constant or continual inspection' of existing agents which was one of the distinguishing characteristics of the Standard's proceedings in England.[32]

None the less it is possible to exaggerate the actual harm which was inflicted upon the office's business prospects by the weaknesses inherent in this *modus operandi*, since in Ireland and Scotland the field work of the salaried officials was supplemented by the decisions taken by the long established Agency Committee in Edinburgh. The record of this particular body in the post-1850 era was certainly not free from blemishes. For instance, consistently disappointing returns from such major centres as Belfast and Glasgow produced several detailed analyses of the nature of their problems but strikingly little in the way of significant reform.[33] Again, complaints from smaller urban areas about agents 'not [being] inclined to canvass for proposals' were as likely to result in the recruitment of additional representatives as in the dismissal of the lethargic or uninterested.[34] Whenever, therefore, black spots were to be located in the Irish and Scottish networks they were less a reflection of the inability of Thomson and Smylie to devote more than a small proportion of their time to inspection, and more a commentary upon the refusal of the Agency Committee to act with despatch.

In terms, however, of the totality of the work undertaken by the committee, such shortcomings must be kept in perspective. For most of the vital decisions affecting the development of the agency system were taken by its members. It was they who deliberately restrained the size of the company's undertaking in post-Famine Ireland until the contours of the Irish economy had assumed a more definite shape. Conversely, once convinced that Irish land was again a safe outlet for the office's funds, they went to considerable trouble in the post-1855 years to carry through a well conceived strategy of expansion.[35] In that period they encouraged Smylie to foster a connection with Thomas Ringland, manager of the Ulster Bank in Belfast and from February 1860 the Standard's third agent in that city, in the expectation that considerable gains could flow from such a connection. By early 1862 the wisdom of the move was clearly demonstrated when no fewer than sixteen of the office's Irish appointments had been recruited from the ranks of representatives of that financial institution.[36] In short, it can be concluded that in an Irish context the degree of success which attended the supervisory role of the Agency Committee outweighed its shortcomings.

On the other hand, as I have argued elsewhere, the corresponding Scottish balance sheet of the committee's labours was much nearer a state of equilibrium.[37] In particular it can be indicted both for its continuing failure to tap effectively the whole-life market in Glasgow and its general unwillingness to recruit a full-time inspector to deal exclusively with the question of agency revision. Other areas of its activities were, however, better attuned to market requirements. Among other things it sanctioned an extension of the local board system to Greenock (1852) and Paisley (1856); attempted to stimulate existing local boards at Inverness and Aberdeen into action whenever the size of their annual returns did not match up to its expectations; and, in the late 1850s, tried to raise the office's standing in the Highlands.[38] But because the prospects of generating a substantial volume of new business within Highland society was always limited, such gains as accrued from this source could not effectively compensate for its disappointing performance in the heartland of the west-central belt.

It is reasonable to conclude that the continuous interaction between those endogenous variables which have so far been discussed exercised a profound influence over time upon the contours of the Standard's new premium income. Yet at the same time this list should not be regarded as exhaustive. Above all it excludes three specifically internal forces which affected the office's overall rate of growth. Firstly it does not take into account the repercussions, at the local level, of any disruption of its ties with banks, although this factor was put forward as a partial explanation for poor results from Glasgow in the early 1850s. For whereas £96,800 of new business had been won in 1847, £49,300 in 1848 and £32,500 in the following year principally through 'sum [sic] large transactions which were brought through one of the Banks', the level of annual returns in the ensuing quinquennium, when this tie had been severed, was on trend markedly below these figures, even taking into account the contribution made by that city's spreading network of sub-agencies.[49] Secondly it overlooks the 'braking' effect on the rate of growth of premium income produced by the company's insistence upon insuring only 'first class' lives. Thirdly, it ignores some of the drawbacks inherent in the design of the original tontine plan which were highlighted in Thomson's reports to the 1855, 1860 and 1865 investigation committees. Prominent among these deficiencies was the fact that while 'the existing Scheme of Division [of profits] ...

holds out considerable advantages to those who assure early in life and have the prospect of longevity', its high premiums, 'more especially at the earlier age', tended to act as a disincentive to many who sought life cover at the start of their professional career.[40] In addition, although the bulk of the quinquennial profits was allocated to policy-holders, the manager had to grapple with the problem posed by secularly declining reversionary bonuses. Whereas a bonus of £1 5s per cent per annum had been declared at the first three Investigations, the figure fell to £1 1s in 1850, 18s in 1855 and 16s in 1860. The implications of this pattern were obvious enough. In Thomson's words:

it is to be feared that the repeated diminution in the rate of benefit, may influence the amount of business transacted by the Company, but the Institution has now attained so high a position in public estimation, that I do not dread anything like an important reaction. At the same time it is to be anticipated, and it is right the Directors should have the facts fully before them.[41]

Thomson was equally correct to acknowledge that 'the mode of Division [of profits], was 'a source of much anxiety, knowing its tendency',[42] since by the 1850s the Equal Scheme of the Scottish Widows' Fund was producing a higher rate of return to its more recent with-profits policy-holders than the tontine plan of the Standard. Yet while this factor had a decelerating effect upon the office's performance in the ordinary life market — a fact acknowledged in 1865, when the office introduced its own Equal policy — its overall impact depended not merely on the overall nature of the Standard's services to its assurers *vis-à-vis* those of its rivals but also on the operation of those external forces which aided or retarded the growth of the life industry on a national scale.

## IV  The market environment

On balance exogenous factors worked strongly in favour of the major offices throughout the years of the mid-Victorian boom. In this sphere perhaps the most important development was a sustained shift in income distribution in British society during 1851–71 in favour of the middle class. One aspect of this process was a sharp rise in the number of middle-class taxpayers: in percentage terms, they increased at a faster rate than the general population. But, inextricably associated with this change, increasing wealth also manifested itself in significant alterations in their pattern of expenditure. As Banks has demonstrated, the search for status came to involve heavy outlays on furnishings, servants and entertaining. But conspicuous consumption on this scale did not exclude the fulfilment of more mundane obligations to the family.[43] Prominent among them was the sealing of a whole-life policy, either in connection with a marriage settlement or to provide for wife and children in the event of the death of the head of the household. In other words, life insurance in this period was more strongly entrenched than hitherto among the income tax-paying classes, a change which was abetted by the 1853 budgetary concession of allowing insurance premiums to be regarded as a tax-deductible expense.

That the Standard derived considerable benefits from this trend can be amply demonstrated from its surviving records. Examining policies in force at the time of its 1860 Investigation in terms of £100 'bands', over 20% of the individual proposals — 2,339 out of 10,797 — were for sums of between £400 and £500, a further 1,359 for between £900 and £1,000, while some 1,317 covered the spectrum between £200 and £300, only 358 policies accounting for the whole spread between £500 and £900.[44] Relating these data to the company's scale of premiums, it can be reasonably claimed that the vast majority of policies between £200 and £1,000 were protecting middle-class taxpayers. But middle-class growth was not merely restricted to such groups. The post-1850 period was also marked by a parallel development in the ranks of a lower middle class which embraced the shopocracy, commercial clerks and schoolteachers.[45] And if within the ranks of this heterogenous class overall gains were more modest, some of these gains were still to be recorded at the lowest level within the records of the insurance companies. Thus in 1860 2,406 whole-life policies were still in force with the Standard for sums of under £100 and an additional 1,837 for between £100 and £200.[46] Given the annual premium required to meet this level of obligation — at the age of thirty the premium on a £100 participating policy was £2 10s 7d, at thirty-five £2 16s 11d — it is equally valid to conclude that the company was a gainer from the broadening of those occupations which collectively formed the domain of the *petite bourgeoisie*.

Two other exogenous influences conducive to growth remain to be considered. In a limited sense the return of a measure of prosperity to Ireland led to a reappraisal of the attitudes of some offices towards investing part of their funds in the form of loans on the security of Irish land. In the Standard's case the embargo which it had placed upon such transactions at the start of the Famine was only slowly lifted. But after 1855, assured that the workings of the 'Incumbered Estates Court' had 'made all real Property in Ireland much more eligible as Security for loans in as much as the means for enforcing payment is now so simple and summary', it was decided to sanction a cautious resumption of the company's lending activities in the 'sister isle'.[47] But such a commitment was in its turn bound to increase the size of the Standard's life business in Ireland, since the terms for such transactions usually included a clause which compelled the borrower to insure his life for a stipulated sum with the company. Lastly the state of the economy during 1850–64 was another factor working in favour of life offices. Throughout that decade and a half a sustained buoyancy in the general level of economic activity, only temporarily interrupted by the 1857–58 financial crisis and by regional difficulties posed by the 'Cotton Famine' of 1861–65, generated a climate of confidence which was reflected in a sharp rise nationally in the volume of whole-life business.

How far each company exploited these trends to its own advantage depended upon its responsiveness to market opportunity. While, however, most contemporaries would have endorsed that conclusion, they at the same time argued that increasing competition between the principal companies and the rapid proliferation of new offices in the wake of the Joint Stock Act of 1844 placed severe limitations on the growth prospects of the individual office.

For instance, it was believed that the flotation of 'bubble' companies in the late 1840s and early 1850s would, if unchecked, be ultimately attended with grave consequences for the life assurance world generally. In January 1856 the *Post Magazine* succinctly summed up these fears when it surveyed the subsequent performance of offices whose origins could be traced back to the 1844 statute. Of 228 companies which, according to its own calculations, had been formally registered,

130 have ceased to exist, some have transferred their connections to other Companies, some have become amalgamated with other offices, and the large remainder are struggling on, living from hand to mouth, and squandering year after year thousands and tens of thousands of pounds which the policyholders from whom the money has been drawn, have foolishly expected would be laid up for the benefit of their families.[48]

In reality, however, such attacks tended to exaggerate the instability and overall effect of the 'bubble' companies; for in the post-1850 era they were merely one component in creating an atmosphere of intensified competition in the search for new business.

Of more immediate significance was the heightened rivalry between the older offices as they tried to obtain something approximating to national coverage of the main centres of population. This pattern was clearly discernible by the late 1840s in parts of Scotland[49] but there can be little doubt that after 1850 England rather than Scotland was to be the scene of the principal struggle to secure good lives. The nature of this process can be illustrated in microcosmic form in Manchester, where the number of accredited agents rose from 300 in January 1855 to 417 in October 1857, 'some Offices being represented by at least a dozen agents'.[50] In many respects this experience was to be repeated elsewhere. By the early 1850s the Standard itself had more than one representative in Leeds, Sheffield, Birmingham and Leicester, among other places. Nevertheless it must be borne in mind what this trend denoted; for, despite Bentham's denunciation of 'excessive competition' in England,[51] the spreading agency network sprang from a justifiably optimistic assessment of a fast developing market.

V *Finale*

By the early 1860s, however, Thomson was acutely aware that, notwithstanding the excellent results achieved in 1862–64, the Standard could not guarantee to sustain such a rate of progress with its existing tontine plan.

His response, therefore, to competitive pressures within the market entailed a revival of the take-over strategy which had served the office well in the mid-1840s and the speedy implementation of a new participating plan. During the course of 1864–66 the directorate, convinced of the validity of this reasoning, was to endorse both these ploys. In 1864–65 it sought to extend its hold on the lucrative English market by absorbing, and utilising the existing agents of, the London-based Minerva and Victoria companies. With its acquisition of the Colonial Life Assurance Company of Edinburgh in 1865, an office with which the Standard had always had strong links, it made its first major step towards securing 'good lives' among white settlers in the Empire. Equally important, Thomson was able to persuade the 1865 Investigation Committee to adopt an 'Equal Scheme' which combined the attractions of lower premiums and a more immediate return from profits to policy-holders than its tontine counterpart.[52]

The wisdom of this last move was amply vindicated in the ensuing quinquennium. On the one hand, as Table 3 illustrates, there took place a serious erosion in the value of new contracts sealed under the tontine scheme. On the other hand, the Equal plan did not quite manage to attract sufficient custom to affect this loss. Nevertheless, by 1869–70 it was already generating a greater volume of business than its older rival, and it was clear that the

Table 3. *New United Kingdom with-profits business of the Standard Life Assurance Company*

|  | Tontine scheme | Equal scheme |
|---|---|---|
| 1860–61 | £388,480 | – |
| 1861–62 | £371,385 | – |
| 1862–63 | £536,370 | – |
| 1863–64 | £664,428 6s 6d | – |
| 1864–65 | £830,435 | – |
| Total | £2,791,098 6s 6d | |
| 1865–66 | £488,085 13s 2d | £113,920 |
| 1866–67 | £376,255 10s 0d | £180,200 |
| 1867–68 | £323,939 19s 6d | £252,910 |
| 1868–69 | £258,825 | £180,140 |
| 1869–70 | £228,635 | £290,785 17s 2d |
| Total | £1,675,741 2s 8d | £1,017,955 17s 2d |

*Source.* Tontine and Equal Schemes, Comparative Amount of Assurances, 1860–70, in Investigation Box No. 6. Too much weight cannot be placed upon the precise accuracy of these data, since they differ markedly from the data embodied in Table 1, particularly for 1860–62. Part of that difference stems from the fact that Table 1 incorporates without-profits policies. On the other hand Table 3, unlike that table, probably includes proposals which either lapsed in their first year or upon which the first premium was not paid. Table 3, however, clearly indicates the general trend.

trend was bound to continue. Indeed, as Thomson percipiently remarked when analysing the respective performance of the two plans in 1866–67, the Standard's hold on the United Kingdom market would have been severely shaken — it had already been loosened [see Table 3] — 'if no equal Scheme had existed', since 'very few of the policies effected under it would have gone to the Tontine Scheme'.[53] By 1870 disillusionment with the tontine policy was total when it was acknowledged that it was 'a most exhausting system operating as a heavy drag upon profits' and likely to deter potential assurers through 'a falling Bonus which is unavoidable'.[54] In short, unlike some of its rivals, the Standard, largely through the proddings of Thomson, in the mid-1860s moved in new directions in order, hopefully, to retain its share of a highly competitive domestic market and to tap a burgeoning overseas demand for life cover.

### Notes

1  J. H. Treble, 'The performance of the Standard Life Assurance Company in the ordinary market for life insurance 1825–50'. *Scottish Economic and Social History*, V, 1985 (forthcoming).
2  *Report [of the Investigation], 1850*, p. 18. All references to the Standard's records are taken from the voluminous collection in head office, Edinburgh, and its depository at Peebles.
3  *Investigation Report, 1861*, p. 7.
4  Treble, *'Performance of Standard Life, 1825–50'*.
5  See Table 1.
6  B. Supple, *The Royal Exchange Assurance*, Cambridge, 1970, pp. 130–45, 169–84.
7  *Annual Report, 1865*.
8  London Committee Minute Book, VI, 6 March 1862.
9  On the basis of the 'tontine' scheme see n. 52 below.
10  Report to the Board of Directors by the Investigation Committee on the Suggestions of the Manager, March 1851 (Deed Box No. 2, 1850 Investigation).
11  *Report [of the Investigation], 1855*, pp. 11–12.
12  *Investigation Report, 1861*, pp. 14–15.
13  *Report [of the Investigation], 1855*, p. 9.
14  *Ibid.*, p. 7.
15  Report by the Board of Directors to the Special General Meeting of Proprietors, 9 May 1861 (Deed Box No. 4, 1860 Investigation).
16  Number of Select Assurance Certificates issued since February 1851 (Deed Box No. 3, 1855 Investigation); Number of Policies admitted to the Select Class (Deed Box No. 4, 1860 Investigation).
17  *Annual Report, 1864*, p. 3.
18  *Report [of the Investigation], 1855*, p. 15.
19  London Committee Minute Book, VI, 6 March 1862.
20  *Post Magazine and Insurance Monitor*, 15 June 1861.
21  Private Minute Book, II, 12 February 1855.
22  Committee Minute Book, II, 16 March 1852.
23  Private Minute Book, II, 12 February 1855.
24  Committee Minute Book, III, 14 October 1856; Sederunt Book, XV, 13 February 1857.

25 Committee Minute Book, II, 24 July 1849.
26 Committee Minute Book, III, 5 March 1858.
27 London Committee Minute Book, VI, 6 March 1862; Sederunt Book, XIV, 2 May 1856.
28 Sederunt Book, XIV, 2 May 1856.
29 London Committee Minute Book, VI, 6 March 1862.
30 *Ibid.* This decision, however, was subsequently abrogated.
31 Committee Minute Book, IV, 28 May 1863.
32 *Ibid.*, 19 January 1863.
33 On Glasgow see Sederunt Book, XIV, 22 September 1856.
34 Committee Minute Book, III, 14 October 1858.
35 *Ibid.*, 22 September 1857, 17 December 1858; Private Minute Book, II, 22 September 1857, 14 March 1859; Sederunt Book, XVI, 26 July, 2 August 1859.
36 Sederunt Book, XVIII, 31 March 1862.
37 J. H. Treble, 'The performance of the Standard Life Assurance Company in the ordinary life market in Scotland, 1850–75', in J. Butt and J. T. Ward, eds., *Scottish Themes*, Edinburgh, 1976, pp. 135–40.
38 Sederunt Book, XII, 25 October 1852; XV, 9 December 1856; Committee Minute Book, III, 14 October 1858.
39 Sederunt Book, XIV, 22 September 1856.
40 Minutes connected with the Investigation at 15 November 1855, 17 April 1856 (Deed Box No. 3, 1855 Investigation).
41 *Ibid.*
42 *Ibid.*
43 J. A. Banks, *Parenthood and Prosperity*, London, 1954.
44 Investigation 1860, IX, Final Results (Deed Box No. 4, 1860 Investigation). The figures quoted relate to the aggregate of with and without-profits policies which were still in force in 1860. The policies not accounted for in the text were those for over £1,000.
45 J. F. C. Harrison, *The Early Victorians, 1832–51*, London, 1971, pp. 103–4.
46 See n. 44.
47 Sederunt Book, XIII, 16 April 1855.
48 *Post Magazine and Insurance Monitor*, 5 January 1856.
49 Committee Minute Book, II, 10 July 1849.
50 *Post Magazine and Insurance Monitor*, 24 October 1857.
51 Sederunt Book, XIV, 2 May 1856.
52 Minutes of the 1865–6 Investigation Committee, 27 April 1866 (Deed Box No. 5, 1865 Investigation).

Under the terms of the tontine scheme a with-profits policy-holder, at each quinquennial declaration of profits, received the appropriate annual bonuses for each year his insurance contract had been in force. Thus at the end of the first five years a sum equivalent to five annual bonuses would be added to the value of the policy; after a further five years the value of the policy would be increased by another ten annual bonuses; and after another quinquennium had elapsed, by another fifteen annual bonuses. Such a method of distributing profits meant, over time, a secular fall in the size of the annual bonuses and a corresponding decline in the attractiveness of such a scheme to new investors.

Under the terms of the equal scheme, the number of annual bonuses which were added to the value of a policy at the end of each quinquennial division of profits related exclusively to the number of years that a policy had been in force between each division of profits. No matter, therefore, how long a policy had been in force, no individual, at the end of a given quinquennium, would receive an addition to his policy in excess of five annual bonuses.

53  Private Letter Book No. 2, W. T. Thomson to W. Bentham, 3 July 1868
54  Preliminary Report by the Joint Actuaries to the 1870 Investigation Committee (Deed Box No. 6).

*Acknowledgement*

This paper is part of a broader project on the insurance industry in Scotland which has been undertaken in conjunction with my colleague, Professor John Butt.

CHARLES A. JONES

# Competition and structural change in the Buenos Aires fire insurance market: the local board of agents, 1875−1921

## I *Dramatis personae*

Until recently the historical literature on multinational corporations reflected the post-1945 dominance of United States manufacturing concerns. When European historians began to contribute the emphasis on manufacturing persisted, even though the earliest British multinationals had typically been financial or commercial in origin. The effect has been to obscure one of the more fascinating chapters in the evolution of international business. British overseas banks and insurance companies did not expand in an economic vacuum, as manufacturers of new products often appeared to do. Instead they represented new administrative systems for performing tasks which were *already* being carried out with varying degrees of efficiency by some combination of intra-firm and market transactions. Thus, by the third quarter of the nineteenth century, the British fire insurance industry was already world-wide in scope, and Argentina, as a rising field for British trade and investment, was already known to many companies. The subsequent history of the industry was therefore less one of spatial expansion than of continued administrative and structural adjustment to changing political and market circumstances. In large part, it is also the history of the crisis and decline (or more rarely the transformation) of an older institutional form, the general international merchant house, which had served the British during the earlier nineteenth century.

Such houses were prominent in the first phase of British fire insurance in Argentina as agents of the major companies. By 1868 the London Assurance Corporation, the London and Lancashire, and the Royal, all had agencies in the city, as did L'Union, the Basle, of Switzerland, the German Gladbach and the Providencia from nearby Uruguay.[1] In the early 1870s high continental wool prices and a bouyant capital market in London brought prosperity to Argentina and attracted more companies. The Sun appointed a young firm of commission agents, Rooke Parry and Co., to act for them in 1874.[2] By the following year the Lancashire, the Liverpool and London and Globe, the

Imperial, and the Alliance had entered the market, though the Royal had withdrawn, as the Alliance and the Sun were soon to do, in the face of the new tax legislation of 1875.[3] The agents of those firms which were not deterred by this legislation banded together that same year to form a Local Board or association to pursue common interests and regulate the market. This chapter, substantially based on the records of the board, provides an account of the problems of business policy encountered by fire insurance firms in Argentina during the following fifty years.

Figures are scarce, but the Argentine market appears to have been very small in these early years. Prior to appointing a local agent the Sun earned a total underwriting profit of a mere £4,394 on Argentine risks through its London, Liverpool and Glasgow offices between 1859 and 1874.[4] Over the period 1856 to 1866 profits earned by the Buenos Aires agency of the London Assurance totalled £2,455, less than a quarter of the earnings of its agencies in Calcutta, Batavia, Hong Kong and other Eastern centres. Yet by the mid-1870s the same agency was yielding profits averaging £24,000 per annum on risks of about £800,000.[5] This must have been exceptional, for the average gross premium income of agencies in the admittedly more crowded Buenos Aires market of the 1900s was below £20,000, with only a handful of agencies — three in 1900, six or seven in 1906 — exceeding that figure.[6] Viewed in relation to their business as a whole, Latin American premiums were of marginal importance for all but a handful of British companies.[7]

The relatively small sums involved make it clear why British companies preferred an agency system to the creation of branch offices with salaried employees in Buenos Aires or, for that matter, elsewhere in Latin America before 1914.[8] Many entrusted their business to established commercial firms for whom fire insurance was just one of a wide range of business activities. Some preferred a specialist, perhaps a man with experience in the insurance department of one of the major houses. Whereas the former might attract business by the inertia of established influence the latter might devote a smaller but more adaptable and vigorous energy to expanding the business. One of the older local import-export houses, Moore and Tudor, acted for three companies: the Queen, the Guardian, and the London and Lancashire. Similarly, by 1885, Congreve and Co. held the agencies of the Norwich Union and the Royal, while Mantels and Pfeiffs acted for the Imperial and the German Transatlantica insurance companies. By contrast, when the Alliance re-entered the Argentine market in 1895 they chose as agent Robert Ramsay, a man of modest means, who at the time was on the point of leaving the employment of Bates Stokes and Co., for whom he had managed the agency of the North British and Mercantile, to set up on his own.[9] Many of the British companies preferred firms with British-born partners, which were in any case still predominant up to the 1880s, but others, including the London Assurance, the Imperial, the

Northern, the Fire Insurance Association, and the Commercial Union, appointed German firms.[10] The distinction was not yet felt to be of any serious consequence.

The terms on which agents were appointed varied little. Early in 1885 the Commercial Union transferred its agency to Moller and Co., agreeing to allow a 10% commission plus 5% brokerage, wherever payable, and a further 5% on the net annual profits of the agency.[11] E. Roger Owen of the Alliance, who visited Buenos Aires a few weeks later, confirms this, and goes on to list the terms of every agency in the city. The rule was 15% commission plus 5% on profits, the only exceptions being the London Assurance and the North British and Mercantile, the latter paying its agents, Bates Stokes and Co., 10% commission, 10% on profits and a further 2½% on business obtained through brokers. The North British looks to have been paying over the odds. Yet Bates Stokes, as one of the leading firms in Argentina, may well have influenced sufficient business to justify the high percentage on profits, while Robert Ramsay, their insurance manager, was competent enough to attract poachers; the Alliance had their eye on him in 1885. The disparity between the London Assurance and the rest was, however, merely technical. That most contracts gave the agent a simple 15% commission instead of 10% plus 5% on business obtained through brokers is simply a reflection of the fact that more and more business was passing through the hands of brokers. By 1885 there were only three specialist insurance brokers, but a veritable host of general brokers who dabbled in commodities, exchange and real estate as well as insurance. These, like the specialists, charged 5% on all insurances they introduced to agents. Owen remarked, 'the business is getting more into the hands of brokers every year', and before very long this was to cause trouble for the Local Board of Agents of foreign insurance companies.[12]

By the 1880s, then, the agents of foreign insurance companies and the brokers they dealt with formed a heterogeneous group more or less representative of the cosmopolitan commercial community of Buenos Aires. There were, however, some important exceptions. Thomas Armstrong, Samuel B. Hale, Edward Lumb and James Drabble, all of whom had been leading figures in the foreign trade of Buenos Aires since the 1820s and had gone some way towards settling themselves in Argentina by marriage and the acquisition of land, chose not to represent established foreign firms.[13] Instead they combined in 1865 with leading Argentine and Italian-born businessmen to form a locally registered insurance company, La Estrella (the Star), with an initial paid-up capital of $ *fuertes* 100,000 (£20,402) and an authorised nominal capital of $ *fuertes* 4 million (£816,080). Twenty years later E. Roger Owen of the Alliance, reporting on the Argentine market, found the Estrella well entrenched, 'an old and sound office doing a safe business ... they take the best risks at slightly lower rates than the English companies'.[14] From the beginning the Estrella made a point of the fact that its funds were invested locally, contributing directly to national development. This would later be used in the lobbies of Congress to support the appeal for protective legislation discriminating in favour of Argentine-based companies. Shorn of nationalist rhetoric, it amounted to little more than that the resources of the company acted as a pool to finance the pet schemes of its directors.

II *The context of policy-making: secular structural change*

From this brief survey of the participants it should be clear that during the half-century following the direct entry of British insurance companies into the Argentine market the competitive process was called upon to resolve three quite distinct, though interconnected, structural problems.

The first of these had to do with the expansion of the British insurance companies. How might they best deal with Argentina? A substantial amount of business could be done without straying more than a few hundred yards from the Bank of England. By 1890 roughly £70 million had been invested on the London stock exchange in shares of British-registered companies doing business in Argentina and Uruguay. All these companies were controlled by boards of directors sitting in London. Furthermore, the senior figures in those complex networks of partnerships which controlled so much of South American international trade lived, for the most part, in Liverpool and London. Why should not these firms insure their property in Argentina with local London or Liverpool offices?

The emphasis and repetition of appeals by the Local Board of Agents against this practice are themselves evidence of its existence, though it is clear that a significant part of the property of the London-based Argentine railway and utility companies was insured in Buenos Aires.[15] This was less true of the bonded warehouses. The Sun noted, about 1868, that the Imperial had not tried to build up a large agency in Montevideo, 'as they are generally full in London even to £100,000 in the Custom House at Monte Video'.[16] However, there were many firms in Argentina which had no direct access to British insurance offices. When establishing its own agency in Buenos Aires in 1874, the Sun expected that wholesale dealers of the second rank would provide the bulk of their business. The leading firms kept most of their goods in bond until purchased and might have close connections with British or European financial centres which led them to insure there, but the smaller French, Basque and Spanish wholesalers kept stocks in their own warehouses and had no European branches.[17] Eleven years later Owen of the Alliance drew the line a little lower than this by accepting the very best town-centre Italian retail general stores, distinguished from their suburban and provincial equivalents by the absence of that combustible conjunction, still to be met with in rural Ireland, of kerosene and a bar.[18].

The reason that local agents could not compete with home offices for the top-class business of the Anglo-Argentine companies and the international trading houses and were driven back into smaller wholesalers, major retailers, and private houses, was not simply a matter of custom, influence and proximity. The fact was that Buenos Aires agents could not compete on price. The Sun found that because of the tax differential between Britain and Argentina any clients who currently paid premiums for property in Argentina would have to pay higher charges to absorb the *patente* or licence fee if they were to pay premiums to a *profitable* Sun agency in Buenos Aires.[19] It was this line of thought that led the Sun to withdraw from Argentina in 1876 and it may well have deterred others from entry. The solution devised by those who persevered was indeed to make a surcharge on premiums of $1 for every $5,000 insured. By 1885 Owen was to find that 'many of the offices, notably the North British and Mercantile and the London Assurance made a profit out of this item'.[20] But this was a profit achieved at the cost of a market restricted to those captive clients who lacked easy access to cheaper markets, and the persistent tax differential inevitably became a bone of contention between agencies and home offices and between those companies which had local agencies and those which did not.[21] The latter, of course, benefited almost as much as Argentine-registered companies from any outbursts of nationalist sentiment, since, as the *Review of the River Plate* noted in 1898, the effect of increasing the tax on offices of foreign insurance companies in Buenos Aires was to increase the value of Argentine risks insured abroad.[22] The Local Board of Agents resolved as early as 1886 to request the home offices 'not to accept insurances on risks in this Republic except through their respective Agents and thus avoid the trouble constantly arising from the differences in tariffs and the difficulties caused by the custom in Europe of allowing commission to insurers'. This appeal can have had little effect, for the Board observed in 1913 that many firms in Buenos Aires refused to insure there, 'stating that they can obtain in London or Paris lower rates and better conditions'. Accordingly the Board, by this date reconstituted as the Argentine Fire Insurance Association, appealed to the Fire Offices Committee (Foreign) in London to adopt a resolution 'to the effect that the companies of those centres should always consult the tariff adopted by the companies in Argentina when they are insuring risks radicated in this country'.[23]

In short, the agency system was always unsatisfactory. Tax legislation put the agent at a disadvantage in competition with home offices for top-quality business. Locally registered companies had a substantial tax advantage and the buoyant if unreliable profits of a more adventurous investment policy to support them, especially in their drive for provincial business.[24] The agents themselves often found the rewards from insurance insufficient to divert more than a fraction of their attention from other business interests.[25] The last problem might be overcome by setting up a full branch with a full-time manager, but this would still leave home competition and local taxation untouched. So for half a century the agency system operated as an unsatisfactory interim solution to the problem of corporate adaptation which was to be solved only in the present century by the full multinationalisation of the leading British insurance companies.

The second prevailing structural problem in the Argentine insurance market lay in the changing system of international trade. As communications and transport improved and better financial facilities became available the grip of the great trading houses of the mid-nineteenth century was loosened. Once direct telegraphic communication between Buenos Aires and London was initiated in 1876 it became far easier for large textile firms to send out buyers to circumvent the major houses and save the commission formerly paid to them for buying and shipping the Argentine clip. Equally, it became possible for travelling salesmen from major manufacturing firms in Europe to circumvent the importing services provided by the established houses. Salaried men coming out as buyers or salesmen built up personal contacts with banks, retailers and the consignees who acted as middlemen between farmer and port, and were encouraged, after a season or two, to venture into business on their own account. This swelled the class of commercial jacks-of-all-trades, mostly calling themselves brokers, who were to emerge as such a distruptive force in the local insurance market (not to mention the booming stock market) from the mid-1880s.

This was not the worst of it. The commercial giants might have withstood such ant-like nibbling at the margin of their business, but they were faced at the same time with a much more serious problem of under-utilised capacity. The great strength of the major houses had been their ability to hold stocks. Now, thanks to the telegraph, the time elapsing between order and receipt of goods was halved, and inventory financing costs were consequently reduced.[26] Moreover, with relatively cheap bank finance available, the gearing of the international houses could be effectively increased if some part of the trade were conducted on bank credit. The established houses could not simply expand their trade; there was not sufficient demand. What, then, were they to do with their money?

A search began for fields of activity with substantial barriers to entry which would keep at bay the stream of hopeful small men brought in by the new liner services week after week. Frequently new and capital-intensive technology provided the solution: elevators in the grain trade, refrigerated shipping, canning, or extract production in the meat trade, baling equipment for fibres, drilling equipment and tankers in oil helped transform a select few of the multitude of nineteenth-century trading houses into multinational corporations such as Bunge y Born, Cargill, Armour, Liebig, Ralli, Dalgety or Shell.[27] A second alternative was to seek the protection of the State, expressed either in protective tariff, taxation or monetary policies or in sheer purchasing power. This path was the obvious one for arms-related heavy industry and helps account for the absence of steel and aircraft manufacturers from lists of leading multinationals today. The third tactic was to rely on personal connections and capital itself as the barrier to entry by diversifying into banking and kindred activities, not least insurance.

Many firms pursued more than one of these strategies. Ernesto Tornquist and Co., for example, diversified out of a general import-export trade to become one of the leading banks in Argentina. Simultaneously the firm invested heavily in the development of a sugar industry in the northern province of Tucuman, protected from local competitors by its ability to command the latest technology and from foreign competitors by State subsidies.[28] Here, all three strategies were in play: technology, capital and State. Lumb Wanklyn and Co., a firm of comparable age and standing to Tornquist's, opted more emphatically for the second and third strategies. They raised capital in London to convert their existing foreign exchange business into a fully fledged bank.[29] The participation of Lumb Wanklyn in the Estrella insurance company obviously represented another aspect of this diversification into high commerce, but it was distinguished from the Mercantile bank by the fact that the Estrella, as a locally registered company, stood to gain from a partnership with the Argentine State.

This digression through the perturbations of international trade in the third quarter of the nineteenth century helps explain the emergence of the Estrella and the ubiquitous brokers. The firms which acted as local agents for British insurance companies stood, for the most part, between the large, quasi-Argentine backers of the Estrella and the small, profoundly cosmopolitan brokers. Many were suffering in some degree from the same sorts of pressures that were driving bigger firms to diversify, but they had a less clear appreciation of the solutions and smaller means to pursue them. For some firms, then, accepting the agency of a foreign insurance company was a stumbling and insufficient gesture towards diversification, to be overtaken ultimately by failure. For others, it was one energetic thrust among others, ultimately to be abandoned in favour of some more promising, controllable and secluded venture. For many agents, as for the companies they represented, the agency system was unsatisfactory, temporary and marginal.

Like those already considered, the third structural problem of the Argentine insurance market had to do with the future evolution of an economic institution. The Argentine State had set off after 1852 on an emphatically and explicitly liberal tack. The constitution of 1854 was closely modelled on that of the United States of America. It appeared to insist on equal treatment of individuals and firms in the country regardless of nationality. The federal government seemed to believe that it had only to secure law and order, and economic development would ensue. It was not until the mid-1870s that this optimism received its first check. Recognising that the economic problems of the country were the outcome of fluctuations in world markets over which they themselves had no control, many Argentines lept to the conclusion that foreign capitalists *could* control these markets and were therefore responsible for the recession. The mercantilist strand was woven back into Argentine history and made manifest in growing State intervention in the economy.

In short, the history of the fire insurance market in Buenos Aires may be resolved into three central questions. How would British insurance companies solve the problem of world-wide operation? How would established merchant houses surmount new competitive pressures born of the revolution in transport and communications? How would the liberal State respond to pressures for protection from the instability of world markets? And at the intersection of the three stood a single institution, the Local Board of Agents of Fire Insurance Companies.

III *The making of policy: competition, co-operation and taxation*

The local Board had been founded in 1875 with seven member firms representing eight British insurance companies. The election as founding chairman of F. W. Moore of Moore and Tudor, agents for the Queen and the Lancashire, together with the use of Moore and Tudor's offices for early meetings, suggests that this leading Anglo-Argentine house may have been the prime mover. The immediate problem which had brought the agents together was a government proposal that every insurance agency should pay a *patente* or licence fee: a fixed sum bearing no relation to the volume of business transacted. Representations to the Minister of Finance led to some reduction of the tax, but, more important, the agents came to an agreement about how to pass on the tax to the insured in a way that would avoid any disruption of the market.

What began as an *ad hoc* committee soon institutionalised itself. One basic function was the provision of common services. In 1891 an inspector of customs warehouses was appointed; the following year an inspector of electrical light installations. Just as vital as this centralisation of risk inspection was the retention, in 1894, of Lucio V. Lopez, one of the top corporation lawyers of his day, on a retainer of £400 per annum to represent the agents in their dealings with government.

The Board aimed from its inception to achieve an orderly fire insurance market by the ultimate inclusion of all companies operating in Argentina under a single common tariff and set of regulations, insulated against competition from overseas by the strength of the London Fire Offices Committee and against division of interest within the Argentine market by non-discriminatory taxation and liberal insurance legislation. This objective was never achieved, though hotly pursued for almost half a century. The reasons for failure are apparent from the minutes of the Local Board of Agents, which are complete from late 1886. Competition from overseas offices without representation in Argentina, already noted, was a persistent problem provoking repeated appeals for support to the F.O.C. in London. Though this may have been allayed to some degree by the F.O.C. (Foreign) resolution of 23 April 1914 imposing a surcharge of 15% on all Argentine business placed in England, it was certainly not a practice against which any effective direct action could be taken in Buenos Aires, and, accordingly, it does not figure largely in the minutes.[30] Much more prominent were surface manifestations of the second and third of the three structural problems identified in section II. Despite repeated attempts, the local agents were never able to dominate local non-tariff companies or brokers to their own satisfaction. Despite a carefully fought rearguard action, they were unable to reverse a general tendency towards State intervention which manifested itself, in the insurance market, in discriminatory legislation and, later, in direct competition from the National Mortgage Bank (Banco Hipotecario Nacional).

The Buenos Aires tariff, first circulated less than three months after the first meeting of the Local Board, was under constant attack from at least the mid-1880s. The assault took several forms. There were from time to time breaches of the tariff or the regulations by member firms or their head offices, dealt with by reprimands, fines or, in extreme cases, suspension of reinsurance and co-insurance.[31] In September 1901, on order from head office, the Royal withdrew from the Board in protest at the high brokerage being paid in Buenos Aires, not to return until 1906. By and large, though, the agents of British companies remained united in their support of their tariff.

Agents of firms based in continental Europe were less loyal to the cartel. Like locally registered companies, they had always tended to accept risks at rates fractionally lower than the tariff. However, this competition became especially severe and troublesome to the Board in the depressed post-Baring Crisis market of the early 1890s. The main offenders were German: the Aachen and Munich, the Hamburg and Magdeburg, and above all the Transatlantica. Heavy undercutting on rates for grain led to a threat to suspend co-insurance arrangements late in 1892. The Board had by then already taken arms against Steinhaus of the Transatlantica, whom they clearly saw as the chief offender. When he refused to come to heel and abide by the tariff the Board reacted forcefully, writing to their London principals to request authority to ostracise the Transatlantica by suspending co-insurance facilities. Permission was given, and from December 1893 the Local Board resolved to have nothing more to do with the German company. Realising that the refusal of co-insurance would make it impossible to accept any but the smallest risks, Steinhaus gave way immediately, and the following month the secretary of the Local Board was able to report receipt of a letter from the Transatlantica promising future adherence to the tariff and applying for membership.

Aside from this, the chief challenges to the tariff from agents of British and European companies arose from exploitation of loopholes in the regulations. Norton, representing the Norwich Union, developed a way of offering very substantial discounts after the financial crash of 1890 by allowing clients to pay premiums in heavily depreciated paper currency though the policy was written in gold. Further falls in the value of paper later in the year doubtless made this scheme inexpedient. In 1899 unnamed member companies were censured by the Board for allowing credit to insurers on the payment of premiums.

Locally registered non-tariff offices like the Estrella, even more than the German companies, were inclined to undercut for two very good reasons. First, they had, as will be seen, a margin of State protection against the local agents of foreign companies. Second, they tended to regard underwriting as a loss-leader activity, the prime function of which was to assure a flow of investible funds. This rate-cutting tendency was evident from the start, but became especially evident in the dull 1890s. Early in 1896 the Local Board noted that Argentine companies were going in for long-term insurance at reduced rates in a big way. Retaliatory measures taken by the Board, far from subduing the local competitors, seem to have helped bring on a full-scale rate war, with both sides reducing premiums on all classes of risk by 20%.

A more insidious form of competition between locally registered firms and foreign agents was possible only because of the strong position of brokers in the Buenos Aires market. By 1887 the Estrella, along with the German offices and one or two British firms, had already fallen into the habit of paying high commissions to brokers in order to secure business. The terms of local agencies as noted by Owen in 1885 implied a standard brokerage of 5%.[32] This figure was plainly being grossly exceeded, and in retaliation the Board authorised its members, in 1891, to pay 20% on non-hazardous business with the exception of certain named industries (10%) and the customs warehouses (7½%). Further means of tying brokers to a particular company were the extension of credit in the form of accepting delayed payment of premiums, and the payment, by a company on behalf of a broker, of the *patente* or licence fee.

The chief problem was that although this sacrifice of some part of premium income to the broker was consistent in principle with the maintenance of a uniform tariff, in practice it was not. Time and time again the Board found that brokers were returning commissions to the insured. One firm, Freijoo and Co., were outlawed by the Local Board in 1891 for returning 10% of premiums to the insured. The practice was so prevalent by 1893 that the Board demanded that all brokers sign a declaration binding themselves to renounce it in future, a requirement which remained in force for over a year.

Variations of this abuse were the appointment by companies of sub-agents (who might be brokers or even the insured themselves) or by brokers of sub-brokers (the insured) in an effort to disguise excessive commissions, the return of commissions, or both, and also the granting of credit by companies to brokers.

Plainly part of the problem lay in the strength of the brokers. Francis Chevallier Boutell of the River Plate Trust Loan and Agency Company, agents for the Royal Exchange, remarked in 1896 that 'all the big policies, such as the Great Southern Railway, etc., are and have been for years in the hands of certain brokers who have their arrangements for placing'.[33] Yet one suspects that in the early 1890s it was less the major brokers than the larger number of general brokers who were returning commissions and acting, in effect, as a screen for more or less deliberate rate-cutting by Argentine insurance companies. There is support for this view in the fact that the response of the Local Board to the brokerage abuses of the late 1880s and early 1890s was to negotiate with the Argentine *companies* (not the brokers) through their association, the Comité de Aseguradores Argentinos. Following the conclusion of an agreement between the Board and the Comité in 1895, order appears to have been restored to the market, for a time at least.

Indeed, in spite of substantial differences of interest, the Local Board and the Comité co-operated more and more closely to secure an orderly market and to moderate proposed legislation. In 1889 negotiations began to bring the non-tariff companies into line with the tariff. By 1895 some progress had been made, even on the vexed question of brokerage, and the Board confidently voiced its intention 'to make one tariff, so that all can work under it in the Argentine Republic'. Up to this time a degree of unity had been obtained on brokerage only through the effective surrender by the Local Board in 1891, when it had brought its rates into line with those of the local companies. The agreement of 1895 represented an improvement from the point of view of the Local Board, as the local companies bound themselves to pay no more than 15% of net premium to brokers. By a subsequent agreement, in 1901, the Comité and the Local Board moved even closer on brokerage, and by this time the Comité had arrived at the opinion that although

they did not think that the time had yet arrived for the formation of a united Board, as proposed by the Local Board sub-committee ... [they] were of the opinion that a permanent arrangement could be arrived at for regulating in a uniform manner the operations of all the companies forming part of the two Boards by the appointment of a committee of five members from each Board, with ample powers for treating upon and resolving everything relating to regulation, tariff, and brokerages, uniform for all companies of both committees, and to intervene in any breaches of the tariff that might occur.[34]

Co-operation on the basis of the agreement of 1901 appears to have worked well enough for ten years. However, in 1911, as the pre-war boom gathered pace, members of the Comité and the Local Board all found themselves under particular pressure from eager newcomers. Brokerages began once again to creep up, and the recent good relations between foreign and Argentine companies were eroded to the point where the joint tariff was suspended. As always, the Local Board placed order ahead of dignity and immediately sought the permission of the F.O.C. to cut rates and raise brokerages to whatever extent might be necessary in order to restore the effective united Argentine and foreign cartel. Negotiations continued, enlivened by the temporary withdrawal from the Comité of three hard-line companies: the Estrella, the America and the Continental. Some sort of *modus vivendi* appears to have been found by 1915, which endured, informally, until 1921, when the Local Board and the Comité both dissolved and reformed as the Argentine Fire Insurance Association and the Associación de Ageguradores

Argentinos respectively, the two being closely linked, as in the past, by a series of joint committees.

Why was full and sustained co-operation between Argentine and foreign insurance companies so elusive? The answer is only partly to do with the ubiquitous brokers and the natural antagonism of newcomers towards cartels. A further difficulty arose from government policy. For even when, as was generally the case after 1895, the differentials in tariffs and regulations between Argentine and foreign companies was small and carefully monitored, it remained true that the costs of locally registered companies were lowered relative to those of their overseas competitors by discriminatory tax legislation. In the long term such protection seemed bound to have a damaging effect on the profitability and market share of overseas companies using either the agency or the branch system of organisation for their international business.

A great deal of the attention of the Local Board was devoted to tax legislation. It had been the allegedly discriminatory *patente* law of 1875 that first brought the Board into existence. Far more serious, however, was the legislation of 1890. Against a background of xenophobia brought on by the collapse of the London foreign loans market, the national Finance Minister, Vicente Fidel López, had little difficulty in pushing through substantial increases in the taxes levied on insurance companies. The *patente* was to be raised to between $5,000 and $10,000 paper, but in addition a system of deposits was introduced, ranging from $50,000 to $100,000 according to the size of the agency, and, furthermore, a tax of 7% on premiums was proposed. National companies were also to be taxed, but on net profits, not premium income. However, they were not to be required to make any deposit, and were to pay smaller *patentes*.[35]

Naturally the Local Board reacted strongly against this explicitly nationalist legislation. Indeed, in 1891 a substantial minority favoured withdrawal. Year after year — for these taxes came up for annual review by Congress in the Finance Bill — the distinguished legal representative of the foreign companies fought to narrow the tax differential between foreign and Argentine companies, to restrict the sums which foreign companies were obliged to deposit, and to ensure that these deposits continued to be denominated in gold pesos, proof against depreciation. However, the Board was unable to shake the principle of discrimination, try as it might. Even when the generally liberal and anglophile executive could be squared, as in 1898, Congress remained resolute in what one liberal Buenos Aires daily newspaper called 'a morbid, incongruous, little-minded policy which has raised discord amongst national industries and arranged them all against foreign capital'.[36]

The truth was that Argentine companies were the more effective lobbyists, having on their boards of directors some of the leading legislators of the day. Not only were they able to secure a margin of protection against foreign agencies (a protection which was only effective, incidentally, to the extent that the F.O.C. or market imperfections restrained London offices from taking Argentine business direct), but in addition they were able to use the threat of further legislation as a deterrent against any aggressive use of the undoubtedly stronger market power of the foreigners. At one point in 1904 Francis Chevallier Boutell, manager of the firm which held the agency of the Royal Exchange, was on the point of urging an all-out war to drive the national companies out of business. He admitted ruefully, however, that such a confrontation might only serve to push government into offering even stronger protection to the national industry.[37]

## IV  The end of the agency system

The history of fire insurance in Buenos Aires is deceptive. A superficial reading of the minutes of the Local Board would seem to show a British-led cartel, established in 1875, in steady retreat before an alliance of local capital and local State. Yet though this is an accurate enough picture of events from the point of view of the great majority of local commercial houses that acted as agents, it does not represent the position of the insurance industry as a whole. In short, the history of the Local Board savours much more of the marginalisation of British commercial houses in Buenos Aires than of British insurance companies. That was to come much later, in the first Peronist period, when the proportion of total reinsurance premium paid by companies operating in Buenos Aires that left the country, a proportion reckoned to be in the region of 50% in the early 1940s, was reduced by more than half through the operations of the Instituto Mixto Argentino de Reaseguros, a joint private and State-owned reinsurance institute established in 1947, and its wholly State-owned successor, the Instituto Nacional de Reaseguros.

In the meantime British insurance companies searched for ways to overcome the increasingly evident weaknesses of the agency system. To open a full branch, as did the London and Lancashire, the Royal, the Sun, and the Northern, in 1890, 1912, 1914 and 1916 respectively, was only half an answer. It got over the lack of motivation to expand business which had plagued the agency system, but it did not appreciably improve the tax position. Only local registration could do that. Accordingly, the London and Lancashire acquired two local firms, La Buenos Aires in 1898, and La Azulena shortly afterwards.[38] Later, La Buenos Aires passed into the hands of a consortium comprising the Phoenix, the Union and the Royal Exchange, for whom it was managed by Leng Roberts and Co. in close co-operation with Tornquist's.[39] The branch manager of the Sun, aware that it might not be possible for every foreign company operating in Argentina to follow this strategy, deplored the consortium solution in terms which betray a degree of envy:

The influence of foreign insurance companies generally [he suggested] may be undermined by ... the tendency to form a sort of trust, such as the Leng Roberts combine, which combine is so constituted as to run equally with either the foreign or national element in the country, and to give the agent double voting powers in both the foreign and national fire insurance associations, thus conferring a much stronger power on a mere [managing] agency ... than is conferred on the direct local branch management of a company.

Deplore it as he might, Truzzell was bound to admit that 'a company established on these lines would be able to command a large and profitable business'.[40]

So it appeared by the beginning of the 1920s that the three questions formulated in section II had been answered; insurance companies, like any other twentieth-century multinationals, had started to opt for equity control of locally registered companies as their preferred form of international organisation; general mercantile houses had either failed or diversified, each into its own specialism; and the Argentine State, despite the continued if intermittent emission of liberal rhetoric, had embarked in practice on the route to increased intervention in the economy.

## Notes

1 Records of the Sun Insurance Office (Sun), 63 Threadneedle Street, London E.C. 2., Foreign Notebook (F.N.), Buenos Aires, etc., p. 37, E. V. Francis, *London and Lancashire History*, London, 1962, p. 135. Until 1875 the London and Lancashire had a single agent covering Argentina and Uruguay. In that year Saunders and Co. of Buenos Aires were given a separate Argentine agency.

2 P. G. M. Dickson, *The Sun Insurance Office, 1710–1960. The history of two and a half centuries of British Insurance*, London, 1960.

3 Association of Foreign Insurance Companies in Argentina (AFICA), San Martin 201, Buenos Aires. The records of the Association comprise a pamphlet, 'The Argentine Fire Insurance Association, 1875–1921', privately printed, Buenos Aires, 1921, and printed minutes from 1886. Where no other source is given, information throughout this paper is derived from these records.

4 Sun, F.N., Buenos Aires, etc., p. 201.

5 Guildhall Library (G.L.), MS. 18,827, London Assurance Corporation, summaries of foreign business.

6 Sun, F.N., Buenos Aires 1, p. 240; *Review of the River Plate*, 1 September 1911, p. 597.

7 E. Liveing, *A Century of Insurance. The Commercial Union Assurance Group, 1861–1961*, London, 1961, p. 45, indicates that the whole of Latin America and the West Indies accounted for about 2% of the Commercial Union's premium income in the 1880s. Even the Phoenix, which had a considerable Latin American business, found Argentina difficult, making a mere £4,050 profit from that market during the decade 1890–99, followed by a loss of £20,004 in the subsequent quinquennium. Records of the Phoenix Assurance Company Ltd, Phoenix House, King William Street, London, E.C. 4, Foreign Agents' Annual Results, Vols. 3 and 4 (c. 9).

8 On the more general experience of British insurance in Latin America see C. A. Jones, 'Insurance companies', in D. C. M. Platt, ed., *Business Imperialism, 1840–1930. An inquiry based on British experience in Latin America*, Oxford, 1977, pp. 53–74.

9 G.L., MS. 18,506. Alliance Assurance Co. Ltd, Report from E. Roger Owen relating to fire insurance in various towns.

10 *Ibid.*

128  The business of insurance

11   G.L., MS. 14,027, Commercial Union Assurance Co. Ltd, Foreign Fire Committee Minute Book, 1885–87, p. 109, 17 June 1885.
12   G.L., MS. 18,506.
13   Sun, F.N., Buenos Aires, p. 37. In 1868 the Sun approached Lumb Wanklyn and Co. asking if they would act as agents. Lumb Wanklyn felt bound to decline because of their interest in the local Estrella company. They passed the inquiry to the Estrella, whose manager offered to take the agency, but the Sun declined.
14   G.L., MS. 18,506.
15   Sun, F.N., Buenos Aires 1, p. 230 (1918).
16   Sun, F.N., Buenos Aires, etc., p. 71.
17   Sun, F.N., Buenos Aires 2, 1874, Establishment Report, p. 29.
18   G.L., MS. 18,506.
19   Sun, F.N., Buenos Aires 2.
20   G.L., MS. 18,506. P. G. M. Dickson, *The Sun Insurance Office*. By 1884 'It had been established that the licence tax on foreign insurance companies should in practice be paid by the insured'.
21   Complaints of home office poaching and undercutting are frequent. The local board of agents in Lima, Peru, complained repeatedly between 1866 and 1869 that London offices were undercutting the Lima tariff via their Hamburg connections. The Sun noted, 'No one confessed but Imperial suspected.' Sun, F.N., Peru 1.
22   *Review of the River Plate*, reprinted in *South American Journal*, 29 October 1898.
23   *Ibid.*, 1 April 1913.
24   Sun, F.N., Buenos Aires I. H. S. Whiting, visiting Buenos Aires to report on the proposal to convert the agency into a full branch, reported in his letter of 22 May 1914 to the manager of the Sun in London that the local companies made very little on underwriting but reckoned to make good profits from their investments in real estate. He had also seen unpublished balance sheets for 1908/9 for some local companies which showed that they were rapidly developing a profitable business in the provinces. It was difficult for foreign companies to match this because each provincial government would demand a *patente* (p. 133).
25   *Ibid.* Whiting's report reveals the frustration of head office at the obstinate refusal of their agent, A. J. David, to try to expand their business. This appears to have been more a matter of inclination than ability, since Whiting observed that he had been 'particularly struck with the enormous number of friends Mr. David has secured; we scarcely enter any train or town — no matter in how distant a part of the Republic — without Mr. David's coming across some of them'.
26   This argument is advanced a little less briefly in C. A. Jones, '"Business imperialism", and Argentina, 1875–1900. A theoretical note', *J. Lat. Amer. Stud.*, 12, 2, p. 439ff.
27   An interesting example of the link between technology and concentration is given by M. Vicziany, 'Bombay merchants and structural changes, 1850–1880', in K. N. Chaudhuri and Clive Dewey, eds., *Economy and Society*, 1979.
28   Archives of the Bank of London and South America, University College Library, Gower Street, London W.C. 1. Records of the London and River Plate Bank, D. 35, 4 January 1894, 28 May 1897 and 12 May 1899.
29   C. A. Jones, 'Commercial banks and mortgage companies', in D. C. M. Platt, ed., *Business Imperialism*, p. 41, and C. A. Jones, 'Great capitalists and the direction of British overseas investment in the late nineteenth century. The case of Argentina', *Bus. Hist.* XXII, 2 July 1980, p. 158.
30   Competition from companies not registered in Argentina, or not affiliated to the F.O.C. in London, or both, appears to have become especially serious at the peak of the pre-war boom. Lloyd's is mentioned specifically.

31 Fines were instituted in 1890. In 1896 it was resolved that after breaking the tariff a company would be required to wait a year before insuring the property in question, even at the tariff rate.
32 G.L., MS. 18,506.
33 Archives of Mandatos y Agencias del Rió de la Plata, seen by the author in 1971 before their destruction in 1976. Microform publication of notes on these archives is under consideration.
34 AFICA, Minutes, 2 September 1901.
35 Sun, F.N., Buenos Aires 2, pp. 230 and 233.
36 *El Diario*, quoted in *South American Journal*, 31 December 1898. *South American Journal*, 19 November 1898.
37 Archives of Mandatos y Agencias del Rió de la Plata, River Plate Trust Loan and Agency Co. Ltd, Boutell to Anderson, 12 August 1904 (now destroyed).
38 E. V. Francis, *London and Lancashire History*, p. 136.
39 Sun, F.N., Buenos Aires 1, p. 262, 31 January 1920.
40 *Ibid.*

OLIVER M. WESTALL

# David and Goliath: The Fire Offices Committee and non-tariff competition, 1898–1907

I *Introduction*

One of the most subtle of the last generation of industrial historians wrote:

Without a familiarity with the inner history of firms and industries it is impossible to discuss monopoly and competition with exactness or move out of the sphere of generalisation ... and the weakness of British historical writing ... is nowhere more apparent.[1]

This study is an attempt to recount an episode in the 'inner history' of one of the most sophisticated and long-standing of all British pricing agreements — the Fire Offices Committee. The history of this organisation has been recounted elsewhere. From 1868, with less formal roots stretching back to the 1790s, the F.O.C. exercised an overwhelmingly important role in the fixing of premium rates in British fire insurance, attracting the allegiance of the great majority of companies in that market.[2]

The object of this reconstruction is to focus on the premium rate-fixing aspect of the organisation's activities; to explain the way in which it operated; and to assess the extent to which it could control market levels. The method used is to observe this great Goliath in operation at a time when it was subject to competitive pressure as the result of a reduction in costs. This poses one of the critical questions to be asked of a collusive market. Was the reduction passed on to the consumer through lower premium rates, or was the combination able to retain the benefit for its members in higher profits? In investigating this issue historically it is hoped that the F.O.C.'s methods will become apparent and its competitive strength seen with 'exactness' rather than within the 'sphere of generalisation' in which it is often assumed that businessmen have only to agree together in order to carry price arrangements successfully. It will become apparent that insurance companies operating outside the F.O.C. play an important role in the story. Non-tariff competition occurred sporadically throughout the nineteenth century and became an increasingly significant feature of twentieth-century fire insurance. The study therefore also tries to explain the rationale of this type of company.[3]

It should be made clear that, in concentrating on rate-fixing, some important aspects of the F.O.C.'s role are ignored. Arguments can be advanced that it increased consumer welfare by providing security and stability among fire insurers and by supporting a range of technical and other services concerned with the reduction of fire loss. These are not considered here, in order to concentrate on the central question of its market power.

## II  The Fire Offices Committee

The origins of the F.O.C. lay in the modest but significant degree of concentration of business in the accounts of the large fire insurance companies.[4] Unfortunately it is impossible to measure this for the British market alone, let alone the regional markets in which rates were formed, because company accounts included the large foreign revenue. However, information is available for the London market and an attempt can be made to suggest the distribution of business for three other important markets. This evidence indicates two things: a striking consistency in market structure, with seven, eight or nine companies taking half the business; yet while the same large companies appear in this dominant group, there are marked differences in their ranking in each market.[5]

In consequence the British fire business was dominated by a group of up to a dozen large companies. This gave them all an interest in market stability, but this in itself does not suggest the most acute potential for oligopolistic interaction in premium rate formation. The real force behind this came from the special positions individual companies had achieved in particular markets, based on a large market share and high profitability, which they were usually determined to defend. The special links companies such as the Sun had in London, the Phoenix in Lancashire or the Royal in Liverpool made them acutely sensitive to a loss of business which they saw as central to their revenue and profitability.

The costs of such a defence could be high. There were few constraints on the expansion of an aggressive concern; the financial leeway created by the receipt of premiums before claims were met could prolong premium rate warfare. The most likely outcome was a general reduction in rates with little change in market shares after a period of below-cost underwriting. Furthermore the lower level of rates yielded no benefits for the companies, because by the late nineteenth century the practice of fire insurance was so widespread as to make the aggregate demand schedule very inelastic. There was therefore little prospect of compensation from additional business.[6]

In these circumstances the larger companies were under a powerful incentive to accept the constraint of overall rate control in order to protect both the general level of rates and their market share. While they may have often attempted to evade the letter of F.O.C. regulation, their adherence to its spirit was not in doubt.

For this reason collusive arrangements might have remained implicit and informal, if it had not been for three further aspects of the business. Firstly, as industrial and commercial premises become larger, more integrated and complex, it was no longer possible to ascertain an appropriate premium rate *en bloc*. Only with elaborate and specific regulations governing the premium rate on each component of a risk was it possible to ensure the companies quoted the same premium for the whole.

Secondly, as premium rates came under control, competitive effort moved elsewhere. The F.O.C. could not hope to prevent this; indeed, in some cases it made no effort to control such consequences, most importantly in the case of the proliferation of marketing methods in the forty years before 1914.[7] However, some such activity was both potentially dangerous to market stability and only controllable through formal methods, as in the case of the level of commission rates paid to agents.

Thirdly, and of greatest importance, there was the problem that not all companies shared the oligopolistic position of the larger companies. The difficulty arose from the wide dispersion of company size, sustained in the long run by the absence of overall scale economies.[8] In principle smaller firms could benefit from rate-cutting. It enabled them to pick up business more successfully. The effect of their activity would be so marginal that it would not be worth while for a large concern to retaliate with a rate reduction that would lose it revenue across business it would in any case retain. Yet there would be a steady haemorrhage of business that could gradually tax the market shares of the larger companies and, if amplified by a large number of small companies, eventually force a rate reduction.

Furthermore, if rate regulation created a more stable and profitable market, this carried with it the seed of new entry. There were no scale barriers to entry and, while there were marketing barriers, important sectors of the market were sensitive to premium rate reductions alone. Continuous entry occurred and, while there was a high mortality rate, a significant number of new companies became established. Seventeen of the sixty-one fire companies operating in 1899 had been established since 1890 and the tenth largest company in that year had only been formed in 1886.[9] The large companies had to face the fact that in its natural state their control over the market was weak.

For these reasons the F.O.C. became a highly formal organisation directing itself towards the two tasks of effective rate and commission control and the creation of an industrial discipline that would inhibit entry and prevent insurers operating outside its auspices. A formidable bureaucracy of committees was established, composed of representatives of the companies and served by a professional and clerical staff. Furthermore, the F.O.C. represented the business to government and administered other services of mutual benefit to the companies.[10]

The thrust and significance of competitive control can best be understood by distinguishing between the non-hazardous and hazardous fire insurance markets. The former, consisting of residential and small-scale commercial property, was characterised by low premium rates and small sums insured. With the modest resulting premiums, policy-holders were willing to accept cover from a convenient source; the sums involved were too small for it to be worth while investing time and effort in acquiring information on alternative premium rates, especially as even large proportionate variations could not produce more than tiny absolute savings. The bulk of the business therefore passed through the hands of the professional men who managed the affairs of the propertied classes. They commanded the market, and the price for their business was the cost of cultivating them and the commission they received.

For these reasons the non-hazardous market did not create serious problems for the F.O.C. A minimum premium rate was set but there was little scope in discounting it. The emphasis of control fell on commission rates. Yet this created no difficulty either, even though some non-tariff companies did offer higher commissions. This was because the economies of scale which arose in servicing a large number of small agents created one of the principal marketing barriers to the entry of smaller firms. Stability was therefore largely achieved in this market by a reliance on the implicit pressures which restrained the larger companies from escalating commission rates.

The real work of the F.O.C. was done in the hazardous market. This consisted of the large-scale industrial and commercial risks which generated large premiums because of high sums insured and high premium rates. Businessmen policy-holders were therefore inclined to look for the lowest rate consonant with security, and the potential savings available supported, through large commissions, the services of the specialist broker who placed business advantageously. Individual demand schedules were highly elastic and information flows efficient.

In response to the possibility of fierce competition which was thus engendered, the F.O.C. mobilised a complex system of control. Premium rates were based on the classification of risks into distinct groups or 'tariffs' in which — *a priori* — loss experience was considered similar. By 1903 some seventy-three tariffs were administered, fifty-three applying to premises in particular trades and industries and the remainder to geographical areas. Within each, loss experience from all F.O.C. members was collated. Then the application of specific rates or discounts for different components of a risk, different methods of construction or other circumstances was specified in detail. Committees were established to supervise each tariff; there were clear procedures for settling disputes, with an independent lawyer as chairman of the whole organisation. When insurance men referred to tariff 'legislation' they meant it.[11]

The F.O.C. imposed its control on the market and inhibited entry in two ways: it created absolute cost advantages for its members and it pursued a carefully considered rating policy.

The first advantage was that all F.O.C.-generated information, especially on underwriting, was considered strictly confidential. Tariff rates, based on the collected experience of the offices, provided a uniquely reliable guide to rating which no independent company could afford to ignore. Thus, in so far as secrecy was maintained, non-tariff companies had no basis on which to quote or discount rates. Furthermore, denied access to the claims experience itself, they were unable to select which classes were currently profitable or not at current tariff rates.

The second advantage was that tariff members were allowed to offer reinsurance facilities only to fellow members. Reinsurance, whereby a proportion of a risk was passed on to another company, meant that it became unnecessary to turn away profitable business simply because its scale made it too great a liability to carry without the risk of disproportionate fluctuations in the accepting company's account. If such facilities were restricted, then a new company would find it difficult to provide the market with adequate acceptance facilities to become competitive. The disappearance of reinsurance connections would lead to the total collapse of a company's marketing strategy. As long as F.O.C. members monopolised reinsurance capacity there was no possibility that non-tariff companies could write more than a tiny business and it would be impossible for a large company to leave the organisation.[12]

Rating policy also implicitly filtered entry and expansion. While the methods involved were ostensibly cloaked in mystery, they were widely believed to be based on a target loss ratio that would amount to 55% of the anticipated premium income in any class; 35% was allowed to cover expenses and commission to agents, leaving an expectation of an underwriting profit of 10%.[13] Leaving on one side the accuracy of this perception, the publicising of such a conventional approach performed two important functions.

Firstly it suggested that rating procedures were a purely technical matter of an almost scientific nature, with a reasonable service charge paid to the companies that undertook such an onerous public obligation. Such an approach helped to forestall public criticism of rate levels and was used to suggest, sometimes explicitly, that any company undercutting tariff rates must necessarily be underwriting on unsound lines. Secondly, if potential entrants or aggressive rate discounters believed that tariff procedures operated as has been described, this gave them serious cause for consideration. If only a modest underwriting margin was available, based on the F.O.C.'s statistics, then success depended on finding some special basis for undercutting tariff rates.

Quite apart from the positive attempts made by the F.O.C. to control entry, the competitive strength of its principal members was a crucial element in its success. Most of them were sustained by a reputation for long established reputable operation and large reserves, both important in a business where security of indemnity was crucial. They already controlled agencies throughout the country through which virtually all existing business passed. While always susceptible to competitive pressures in the hazardous market, these connections were cemented by goodwill of a strength that required a powerful solvent. These advantages had all been strengthened by the evolution of marketing methods in the forty years before 1914.[14] Fuelled by the redirection of competitive effort as the F.O.C. established premium rate control, the escalation of branch office organisations imposed substantial overhead costs which were far more easily carried by larger concerns. Similar scale economies applied to advertising expenditure. Thus the raising of the ante through higher selling costs significantly inhibited smaller companies, and it was deeply significant that the F.O.C. made no effort to control such development. As long as it helped to protect the F.O.C., the inelastic aggregate demand schedule meant that such extra costs would ultimately be met by the policy-holder. The constant costs in relation to scale described earlier depended upon smaller companies finding alternative marketing methods that were usually limited in scope.

In these ways the F.O.C. dominated the British fire insurance market. Its members could not contemplate leaving it, for, quite apart from their interest in market stability, such a move would make underwriting impossible because of the loss of reinsurance facilities. Any small or new company faced a formidable combination of institutional and competitive difficulties that made growth problematic.

III  *The rationale for non-tariff companies*

Despite this, some companies were forced to operate outside the F.O.C. For them the advantages of membership were outweighed by one overwhelming disadvantage. The market strength of the large companies, based on their interrelated advantages of size, reputation and existing connections through branches and agents, meant that it was practically impossible for a small or young company to attract business if it did not cut rates. By forbidding this course to its members, the F.O.C. forced such companies intent on growth to operate outside the tariff.

Given this necessity, how was it possible for companies to overcome the formidable obstacles to non-tariff operation erected by the F.O.C.? Access to tariff rates was crucial, for the margins within which non-tariff underwriters operated were too fine to allow for error. These were easily established in the non-hazardous market, where company publicity material quoted premium rates for what were homogeneous classes. However, as has been argued above, rate discounting in this market was unimportant.

The real opportunities for rate discounting existed in the hazardous market where individual demand schedules were so elastic. Here, even when total premiums paid were known, it might be very difficult for an underwriter to deduce the rates paid on the separate components of a complex risk, in order to form a basis for future quotations.

In practice, rating information was obtained in four ways. The most important leakage of tariff confidentiality came through the recruitment of staff by non-tariff companies. They made it their business to staff underwriting departments with clerks who could bring fresh tariff experience with them. Brokers would often divulge tariff information in order to obtain more competitive quotations for their clients, though wise non-tariff underwriters would always exercise discretion in their assessment of its reliability. Tariff rates might also be revealed in the documentation provided when a non-tariff company obtained a share on a co-insurance schedule with a tariff company. Finally, there were the exchanges which took place between non-tariff underwriters, the gossip of 'friends' in the business and occasional references in the insurance press. In practice it was usually possible for non-tariff companies to obtain a fair idea of the rates they had to discount. However, the actual profitability of individual classes remained far more speculative.[15]

Reinsurance was a more complicated problem which could not be dealt with on the same informal basis, for it involved enforceable contracts. Barred from obtaining assistance from any of the British tariff companies, this requirement for successful underwriting certainly posed the biggest problem for non-tariff underwriters. Even the facilities of the large Continental reinsurance companies were unavailable, for F.O.C. members passed on a substantial business to them, making it a condition that they did not deal with British non-tariff offices. Some reinsurance was effected between British non-tariff companies, but their small size and number meant that such resources were very limited. In any case, the more reputable non-tariff underwriters were often apprehensive about the methods and financial security of some of their contemporaries. A reinsurance treaty could easily provide another company with a shopping list of risks for its inspectors to canvass.[16]

However, from the later years of the nineteenth century the tariff monopoly of reinsurance was eroded by Lloyd's. Led by the great Cuthbert Heath, who provided the Hand in Hand with reinsurance in 1885, Lloyd's brokers began to place the reinsurance business of more reputable non-tariff companies. In solving the major problem of reinsurance, this provided the main foundation of successful non-tariff underwriting from that date.[17] Yet this facility was delicate and limited. Any difficulty with an underwriting syndicate would almost certainly lead to the withdrawal of all Lloyd's support and thus destroy a company. Most non-tariff underwriters were therefore beholden to their Lloyd's connections. Furthermore, at this date the acceptance capacity for such business at Lloyd's was restricted and far too small to allow a company to grow to the scale of a large tariff office. As a result, until other sources of reinsurance developed, non-tariff underwriting was inevitably restricted to a number of small offices.

In these ways the difficulties of access to rating information and reinsurance cover could, in some measure, be overcome. However, the whole essence of non-tariff underwriting lay in one final problem. How was it possible to discount tariff rates when they were supposedly set on the basis of providing reasonable profits on costs established by the information at the disposal of the F.O.C.?

The answer lay in what underwriters termed 'selection'.[18] Opportunities for this arose if the F.O.C. was slow to adjust its rates for a particular tariff in line with current loss experience. Alternatively, a particular sub-group of risks within a class might be identified as enjoying a better than average loss experience for the class as a whole.[19]

Selection was not unique to non-tariff underwriters. All underwriters tried to improve their underwriting results by such methods, and tariff companies were in a better position to do it because of their access to F.O.C. statistics. However, the non-tariff underwriter's critical advantage was that, having identified a favourable group, he could then attract it by lower premium rates, relying on the high elasticity of demand in the hazardous market to create an adequate response.

In the closing decades of the nineteenth century this responsiveness was increased by institutional change. Large insurance brokers, operating on a regional or national basis, assumed an increasing importance in the placing of hazardous insurance. They became enthusiastic supporters of non-tariff companies, for these provided the opportunity for them to reduce premium rates and thus attract policy-holders. Through them small companies could obtain a substantial premium income without the need for a large-scale marketing organisation, thus circumventing a critical element in the market power of the large companies. Controlling brokers and the large commissions they demanded became one of the intractable problems facing the F.O.C. after 1890.[20]

Of course, the problem inherent in selection was that, in principle, it was essentially a short-run opportunity. Eventually the tariff could be adjusted to take account of any imperfections, leaving no scope for non-tariff discounting. Yet the tariffs never reached this equilibrium.

This was because in the first place it was extremely difficult for the tariff documents, complex as they were, to reflect all the possibilities for rate adjustments. Physical differences between risks might be comprehended, but the 'moral hazard' — all the non-material circumstances surrounding hazard such as the likelihood of arson, the quality of management or the precise type of business being transacted — was far harder to capture. Such distinctions were always susceptible to perceptive selection.

Secondly, tariff rates always lagged behind loss experience. This was inevitable, for significant changes in the latter could be detected only retrospectively as statistics became available. Even then it was sometimes difficult for the F.O.C. to reduce rates. Once a rate was cut it would be difficult to raise it again without incurring the displeasure of agents and policy-holders, who might then turn to non-tariff competitors. There were always some tariff members whose experience in a particular class was unrepresentatively bad and would therefore wish to retain a higher rate. The more successful a non-tariff incursion was in collecting more favourable risks, the less tariff evidence would reflect an improvement in experience.

Finally, tariff rates might not move with experience simply because F.O.C. members believed that they could carry them successfully against competition on most business because of their market strength and all the restrictions on non-tariff competition described in the previous section. If this was so, it was irrational for them to cut premium rates across the board in order to stem a marginal loss of business. The more powerful the tariff companies believed themselves to be, the greater the margin they would allow to open up between costs and premiums, allowing scope for non-tariff companies.

For all these reasons non-tariff underwriting was possible. David could take a shot at Goliath. Opportunities were greatest when the conditions for selection were especially favourable. Such an occasion arose in the years immediately after 1898, when a major improvement in fire hazard was not matched by commensurate reductions in tariff rates, even though the F.O.C. itself had been the principal instrument in the risk improvement.

## IV  Fire risk improvement and the F.O.C., 1898–1907

Attempts to introduce automatic fire extinguishing apparatus had been made from the middle of the nineteenth century and a variety of models were sold in Britain from 1870. However, really effective protection became available only in 1885 when Mather and Platt purchased the British rights to manufacture the American 'Grinnell' sprinkler. Its impact on the fire insurance market was profound. Initially the F.O.C. refused to allow any special concession for risks protected by the new apparatus. It was left to the Mutual, a Manchester-based non-tariff company, to introduce discounts, initially of 20% and then 30%. This was so successful that business in the market where the device was of greatest value — Lancashire cotton mills — was sufficiently disrupted for the Cotton Mills Tariff to collapse in 1888, and a free market operated for a few years during which sprinkler discounts rose to 80% off the normal premium rate.

Eventually the Cotton Mills Tariff was re-established in 1892 with a premium rate half its original level and a 60% discount available for fully sprinklered risks. Some of the non-tariff companies joined the tariff, while the remainder were gradually bought out by tariff companies. Through the 1890s sprinkler protection gradually spread, encouraged by discounts that were available in twenty-six tariffs by 1898. As early as 1894 sixty-eight flour mills had been protected, by the following year thirty-six woodworking risks and by 1901 two-thirds of the spinning sector of the cotton industry.[21]

However, there was an underlying problem in these apparent improvements. While the F.O.C. had issued regulations governing technical aspects of sprinkler installation, these had not prevented the continued use of outmoded devices, the deterioration of equipment and the construction of systems that had inadequate water supplies. The technicians of fire insurance had not learned the need for regular and intensive inspection. As a result a gradual rise in losses on sprinklered cotton mills occurred where the equipment had been longest installed. This reached a climax in 1898, when five total losses occurred. In 1900 the general manager of the Equitable reported that his company's loss ratio on cotton fireproof mills had been 500%.[22]

The F.O.C. was quick to respond to the situation. Tariff rates on sprinklered cotton mills were raised from 2s 6d per cent to 6s per cent. Beyond this the committee tried to rectify the problems that seemed to be the cause of the losses. In December 1898 it decided that its experts should examine several of the older types of sprinkler. In the following year a new edition of its sprinkler regulations was introduced which approved only three of the available models and introduced far more stringent requirements governing the approval of installations.[23]

The imposition of these new regulations on new risks might have led to a gradual improvement in risk experience, but the F.O.C. had been so shaken by the events of 1898 that it decided to institute a complete revision of all the sprinklered risks its members insured, in order to make certain that the new regulations applied across the market. During the following few years a committee of experts examined all the 866 risks where sprinklers had been installed prior to 1898. The need for the new regulations is indicated by the fact that only 148 were regarded as adequate; the success of the inspection is measured by the 400 or more risks where modifications had been undertaken and approved by early 1903; twenty-one settled for partial improvement and smaller discounts, while ninety-three were to be brought up to standard before the renewal of their policies.[24]

In retrospect, the effect of these changes on the competitive environment can be seen clearly. A sudden improvement had been created in some 60% of all sprinklered risks. In addition the new regulations meant that, as sprinkler protection spread, as it did quickly in the following years, the quality of protection would be higher than before 1898. Yet no commensurate reduction in premium rates was made to allow for this improvement. In the most important sprinkler-protected market, cotton mills, rates were actually 140% higher. An ideal opportunity for selection had been created. The margin available is not known, as the tariff loss statistics are unavailable, but a report by the fire manager of the Commercial Union to his board in 1905 stated that loss ratios on all sprinklered risks, calculated over the whole of the previous ten years, had shown that '... a material reduction in the rates was justified ...' and that loss ratios on individual classes had fallen as low as 10%. The loss ratio on the company's agency premium income, in which much sprinkler business was concentrated, fell from 66% in 1898 to an average of 33% for the years from 1901 to 1905. When it is remembered that this was in place of a conventional 55% loss ratio, the scope for rate discounting will be appreciated.[25]

Quite apart from the scope for discounting, sprinkler-protected risks had other advantages for non-tariff underwriters. They were easily identified and accessible from both an underwriting and a marketing point of view. Several of the larger firms of brokers had taken an early interest in them and could immediately offer an ample supply. Though sprinkler manufacturers protested their innocence, lists of their installations circulated and their publicity regularly featured recently protected risks. As a last resort, company representatives had only to look for the distinctive red alarm gong outside a property which indicated sprinkler protection.

The opportunity was also a growing one. In the years after 1900 the problems of adapting sprinkler protection for the special requirements of particular trades were increasingly overcome. In each case this gave non-tariff companies a chance to collect business before the innovation was reflected in the relevant tariff.

Finally, sprinklered risks reduced the non-tariff company's reinsurance problem. The main effect of such protection was not to eliminate the risk of a fire breaking out, but of almost eliminating the possibility of total loss. As reinsurance is principally concerned with reducing the variability of loss experience, this reduction in the likely maximum loss possible on a risk meant that underwriters were able to retain a far higher proportion of their gross acceptances — to the extent of double or more than the amount retained on an unprotected risk. This enabled the non-tariff companies to expand their underwriting in relation to any given reinsurance facilities and contemplate accepting far larger risks than had previously been possible. Taking all these circumstances into account, it is not surprising that non-tariff underwriting grew vigorously after 1898.

## V  Non-tariff expansion, 1898–1907

Table 1 indicates that between 1898 and 1905 the net fire premium income obtained by non-tariff companies rose from £111,000 to £501,000; from an estimated $1 \cdot 8\%$ of the British home fire insurance market to $6 \cdot 6\%$. After a fall in 1906, when a large non-tariff company was forced into the F.O.C. in order to obtain reinsurance, it rose again in 1907 to £410,000 or $5 \cdot 4\%$. These measures of market share are not precise, but probably suggest the minimum level of competitive impact. While they are exaggerated by the impossibility of distinguishing foreign revenue in company accounts, this was almost certainly a modest component of non-tariff business at the time. In any case, it would certainly be more than compensated by the amount of reinsurance business passed on to Lloyd's by these companies and the direct fire business written in the fire market on a non-tariff basis by Lloyd's brokers. Some idea of the significance of the size of the non-tariff business may be suggested by comparing it with other companies. In 1900 the net home fire premium income of the Commercial Union was £343,000 and that of the Royal

Table 1. *British non-tariff fire insurance companies: net fire premium income, 1898–1907*[26]

| Year | £'000 | Estimated share of British domestic fire market (%) |
|---|---|---|
| 1898 | 111 | 1·8 |
| 1899 | 144 | 2·1 |
| 1900 | 141 | 2·0 |
| 1901 | 165 | 2·3 |
| 1902 | 224 | 3·1 |
| 1903 | 302 | 3·8 |
| 1904 | 368 | 4·8 |
| 1905 | 501 | 6·6 |
| 1906 | 292 | 3·9 |
| 1907 | 410 | 5·4 |

Exchange Assurance £219,000. In aggregate, therefore, the non-tariff growth was equivalent to the sudden emergence of a very large tariff company.[27]

Unfortunately it is difficult to focus clearly on the components of this premium income. Of course, it was not all obtained from sprinkler-protected risks. There were other opportunities for profitable non-tariff underwriting, and any company wishing to build a significant agency organisation had to be prepared to write a fairly general business. Yet it is possible to show that the sprinkler-protected market was a major motive for the formation of several of the companies involved, that many sought such business avidly, and that it was of disproportionate importance in securing the growth that took place.

Twenty-five companies took part in the incursion between 1898 and 1907; eight of them were in operation in the earlier year and the rest entered the market subsequently.[28] Those of principal interest fall into two groups. Several had close links with brokers at Lloyd's or in the provinces. The Fine Art and General was linked with C. E. Heath and in the 1890s began to write a far wider industrial and mercantile business than is implied by its title. Although a Glasgow business, the National of Great Britain also had Lloyd's connections. It was one of the most austere sprinkler specialists, working closely with Scottish brokers to collect an enviably select business whose loss ratio averaged as low as 32·8% over the years 1898–1907. The Textile Mutual was probably formed by Manchester brokers, explicitly publicising its intention of writing a specialised sprinkler business, mainly in the cotton trade.[29] Brokers were well aware of the profitability of sprinklered business. The disappearance of earlier non-tariff companies had deprived them of an opportunity for expanding the market for their services. In addition, Lloyd's brokers could obtain reinsurance business to place. It is hardly surprising that they should have helped to reconstitute an element of the market that was so important to their survival.

The other group's origins are suggested by the names of some of the companies: the Bolton Cotton Trade Mutual, the National British and Irish Millers, the Leather Trades and General; they were formed by trade groups, sometimes even a formal trade association. Some, like the Bolton concern, were long established mutual companies with a geographically restricted membership which had no interest in expansion. Writing exclusively cotton risks in Bolton, however, it could not help but benefit from the discontent at the tariff charges, and its average claims ratio of 33% between 1898 and 1907 signalled the profitability of such underwriting to others.[30]

Others had been formed more recently, for businessmen's reaction to the F.O.C.'s treatment of sprinklers formed a potent source of non-tariff underwriting. The National British and Irish Millers was founded in 1896. Grain-mill risks had been one of the first classes to follow cotton mills in the installation of sprinklers, and it was widely believed that no such protected mill had been lost. When the last of the earlier generation of non-tariff companies was purchased in 1895, the millers' trade association stimulated the formation of a mutual company to offer discounted rates. It soon began to specialise in sprinklered risks only. Similarly, the Leather Trades and General was formed by trade interests in 1899 to offer sprinkler-protected tanneries a discount refused by the F.O.C.[31] The Birmingham Mutual provided a variation on the sprinkler theme. Established under the chairmanship of a member of the ubiquitous Chamberlain family, to serve local trades, it made discounts for automatic fire alarms the initial focus of its marketing strategy. These were for technical reasons more appropriate for fire protection in the metal and engineering trades, yet the F.O.C. was unwilling to provide the modest discount offered by the Birmingham Mutual.

Although they began on a limited basis, relying on trade support and a mutual financial structure, these companies were quick to realise the opportunities for a wider business. In 1903 the Birmingham Mutual changed its name to the Central and began to develop a more diversified business, emphasising both automatic alarm and sprinkler discounts. It eventually became the largest non-tariff company, with a net premium income of £154,000 in 1905.[32]

In the same way the National British and Irish Millers and the Leather Trades and General eventually looked beyond their own trade markets. From an early stage they had accepted some risks, but in 1905 the latter raised additional funds in order to extend its business over a wider area, '... especially cultivating the insurance of risks which are protected by an approved installation of sprinklers ...'. In addition it changed its name to the more generally appealing North Western. In the following year the National British and Irish Millers undertook a similar step by eliminating its mutual basis. As a result, both enjoyed an expansion in business which, though modest, remained extremely profitable.[33]

It is difficult to penetrate the external surface of all these companies' activities to obtain a picture of their methods and opportunities. However, the records of one, the Provincial, enable some picture to be formed of its operations in the sprinkler market. This is of particular interest because the owners of the company consulted several other non-tariff company managers at the start of their business, and relied heavily on their advice in planning development.[34]

Founded in Bolton by a successful cotton spinner, there could be no question that the Provincial's management realised the opportunities for sprinkler discounts in the cotton trade. The business was obtained in several ways. Some risks came as a result of direct approaches by the company. These might be made on the cotton exchange in Manchester, through circulating prospectuses to lists of sprinkler-protected businesses or by direct approach by the company's representatives to mills or company offices. A discount was offered on sprinklered risks of up to 50% below the tariff rate (already subject to a sprinkler discount of 60%) in the early years. Later it fell to 20%. This compared with the company's normal approach of offering a 10% discount below the tariff rate on classes of business it considered desirable.

The large brokers were another important source of business and some could provide it on a very large scale. In principle, the Provincial tried to restrict its acceptances from this source to sprinklered business, though this was not always possible. London-based brokers supplied sprinklered risks from the south of England, but far more was provided from the Manchester and Leeds firms whose connections stretched through their industrial hinterland. A. W. Bain and Sons of Leeds provide an interesting case. They had been involved in the sprinkler market since its inception, at one stage even starting their own company to write sprinklered risks. They had moved their main offices from Belfast to Leeds to exploit the potential of the growing sprinkler protection of woollen and worsted mills, before this was appropriately recognised by the F.O.C. At the same time they cultivated other classes of risk that were receiving sprinkler protection for the first time, such as drapers, one of the most hazardous of the ordinary retail trades, and printers, where large quantities of paper handled at high speed created a major hazard. Above all, they placed the insurance business of some of the largest British companies with sprinkler protection, such as Joseph Rank and Lever Brothers.

Through this source the Provincial received as much sprinklered business as it was willing to take. Yet a high price had to be paid for such revenue. Brokers with such business at the Bains received glittering commission way beyond the tariff-regulated 12½% for large brokers. The Provincial paid them 25% on all sprinklered risks, with a 10% overriding commission on profit. It is a measure of the scope for discounting that the Provincial, which was an almost excessively conservative company, could cut rates by 50%, pay these commissions and still regard the business as worth having.

Part of the momentum behind the sprinklered market came from the opportunities it provided not just for companies to expand but for new brokers to become established. The Provincial was fortunate in establishing an early link with A. R. Stenhouse.[35] He had recognised the opportunities for sprinkler underwriting when working in the United States and had returned to Glasgow to establish a brokerage concern, specialising in the business. Supported by the Provincial and other small non-tariff companies, he began to offer them a select Scottish sprinklered business on which he was paid a modest 20% commission.

Finally, sprinklered risks were available through reinsurance. From its formation the Provincial had accepted such business from the Leather Trades and General, the National British and Irish Millers and the National of Great Britain, thus obtaining a share in their highly specialised underwriting.

By such means the non-tariff share of the fire market increased. What effect did this have on the tariff offices and how did they respond?

## VI  The response of the Fire Offices Committee

It is important to be clear what was at stake for the tariff companies in handling the non-tariff threat. If the F.O.C. could retain control of the market, there was no motive for it to reduce premium rates on risks where demand was inelastic for tariff companies as a whole. Sprinkler discounts ate up premium income when they were applied to the classes of business which, through size and hazard, provided the staple income of all companies. Furthermore, the problem threatened to become cumulative, for larger discounts encouraged the spread of sprinkler protection and therefore further discounts and loss of revenue.[36]

In the face of this, administrative costs would not fall proportionately. Policies required the same processing; the competitive pressure actually raised the costs of marketing. It was also now recognised that if sprinkler protection was to be effective it would require regular, expensive inspection. Lower premiums had other implications as well; short-term reserves would fall commensurately, reducing investment income; staff remunerated by commission would suffer a fall in their income.

These were the high costs of additional and spreading discounts. It is not difficult to understand the reasons for the reports current around 1900 that tariff companies were discouraging the installation of sprinklers as 'not worth while', or the need for a tariff official to refute suggestions that the F.O.C. was 'hostile to sprinklers'. It was certainly widely believed in the business.[37]

Given these strong commercial reasons for the preservation of modest discounts among its members, it is reasonable to suppose that the F.O.C. would not make further concessions willingly, that it would seek to retain its control over the market, and would capitulate only in the face of alternative consequences that appeared even more dangerous to the interests of its members.

Before 1903 the non-tariff companies remained a barely perceived problem. Competition among the larger companies relaxed as the result of a series of amalgamations, and it was possible to regard the few companies offering special sprinkler discounts as limited in importance and isolated to narrow, specialised markets.

Yet, despite this, it did not take much to provoke some adjustments. In 1902, three years after the formation of the Leather Trades and General, the F.O.C. granted special sprinkler discounts to tanneries for the first time, although the new company had collected a net premium income of only £5,500. In the same year a similar move was made to counter competition from the National British and Irish Millers, by increasing the sprinkler discount for grain mills from 30% to 40%. In fact these adjustments were too marginal to affect the two companies' progress, but they suggest a degree of sensitivity to relatively minor incursions.[38]

Such local skirmishes became increasingly irrelevant as non-tariff companies began to realise their opportunities and their business assumed a more general character. In 1903 there was evidence of the companies suffering from more serious losses of business. By 1904 non-tariff business had grown to £368,000 or 4·8% of the home market. The business of both the Royal Exchange Assurance and the Commercial Union fell, in the latter case because non-tariff competition meant that '... we have lost a large amount of premium income rather than accept business at what we have deemed unremunerative rates'.[38]

These pressures were sufficient to provoke the first major concession by the F.O.C. The Commercial Union fire manager explained the link, referring to:

... the action taken by the associated offices as a consequence of this competition on tariff rated risks. The experience of the Offices for the last ten years having been ascertained, it was found that a material reduction was justified in some cases, notably ... on sprinklered risks ...

The link between non-tariff pressure and the reductions is quite explicit.

Twenty-eight tariffs, covering nearly all the classes of risk where sprinklers were appropriate, were amended by raising the sprinkler discounts. The typical change was to raise them from 25% to 35%, though some variations occurred. The important exception was the Cotton Mill Tariff, where the already high 60% discount was not changed. The companies still remembered the big losses in 1898. None the less, such a general revision was a significant step towards recognising the progress of risk improvement, and a painful cut in revenue. The Commercial Union's average premium rate on business fell by nearly 7% from 1903 to 1905, when the full effect of the reduction would have been operative. As the company's fire manager ruefully admitted, '... through competition we have not only lost business but have had to reduce our rates on a good deal of that which we have retained'.[39]

If the F.O.C. members thought that this step was sufficient to eliminate non-tariff competition they were mistaken. After all, it amounted to no more than 13·3% reduction in the actual rate paid, and the non-tariff companies had been successfully quoting at 50% below the previous tariff rate. In any event, their business continued to expand, to reach £501,000, or 6·6 of the home market in 1905. However, the F.O.C. appears to have decided that it was time to try other ways of reducing competitive pressure.

The first direction in which it turned was to the sensitive area of reinsurance. If the F.O.C. monopoly here could be re-established, then the foundation of the non-tariff activity would be destroyed. An inducement had to be found to persuade Lloyd's to cut off reinsurance from the non-tariff companies and to stop writing direct fire business. Negotiations were begun with major Lloyd's brokers in 1905, and over the following year the outline of a deal emerged. The proposal was that tariff companies would for the first time, offer a substantial fire reinsurance business to Lloyd's, dealing through F.O.C.-recognised 'tariff brokers' who would commit themselves to accept all the tariff regulations and rates and pass business only to underwriters who did the same. They would therefore no longer be able to deal with any non-tariff company or write direct fire business. It was, in effect, a bid to persuade Lloyd's to join the F.O.C. C. E. Heath, the doyen of Lloyd's, believed that four-fifths of the underwriters would join the scheme and this would make the institution worthless to non-tariff companies. The critical question was the price tag; how much business would the tariff companies provide? It was at this point that negotiations became protracted towards the end of 1906. Lloyd's required a guarantee of a minimum annual premium business of £250,000; initially the F.O.C. members agreed that this was possible, but when it came to the point, early in 1907, a subscription list obtained only £160,000, and thus negotiations were suspended.[40]

At the same time as these negotiations were proceeding, other developments were suggesting an alternative solution for the F.O.C. Some of the structural limits on non-tariff underwriting were beginning to take effect. The first of these was the purchase of companies. This was a traditional way of eliminating non-tariff-company competition and, indeed, some companies were deliberately set up with this in mind. They would collect a select business together that formed an attractive purchase for a tariff office. In 1905 the Textile Mutual was bought by the Royal and in the following year three more small non-tariff companies were picked up by other tariff companies.[41]

The really dramatic break came with the accession of the Central to the F.O.C. at the beginning of 1906. The company had grown quickly to become the largest non-tariff concern and had run into the problem that it was exhausting its reinsurance facilities. Entry to the F.O.C. would resolve the difficulty. For the F.O.C. the prospect of drawing into membership the largest and most aggressive of its non-tariff competitors was obviously attractive. A deal was struck. The Central entered the F.O.C. with the guarantee of a reinsurance treaty from a tariff company and that the tariffs would quickly incorporate its special automatic fire alarm discount. In return, the Central would quote tariff rates on all renewals, and its reinsurance treaties with other non-tariff companies would be terminated. Within a year the automatic alarm discounts had been introduced and the Central had been purchased by the Liverpool London and Globe.[42]

With the non-tariff market cut back to £292,000, or 3·9% of the market in 1906 as a result of these changes, the F.O.C. members must have felt that the problem would become more manageable. However, the difficulty proved more persistent. The business of the remaining companies grew, rapidly sustained, no doubt, by the risks that had become accustomed to non-tariff rating with the former non-tariff offices, and were now open to approaches that would retain this benefit. Furthermore, the two principal trade-based companies had only recently reconstituted themselves to underwrite a more general business; they were thus well placed to attract a more diversified portfolio of acceptances. Equally important, however, was a group of six new companies, led by the British Crown, which grew particularly fast. Its prospectus described the motive for formation quite explicitly — '... experience of recent years goes to show that non-tariff companies, carefully managed, prove renumerative to shareholders ...' — and pointed out that the loss ratios of the non-tariff companies were some ten percentage points below the tariff average.[43] This vigorous response to the opportunities in the market was critical, for it demonstrated that the F.O.C. would find no solution to the problem of non-tariff competition under current conditions of profitability through the purchase of companies or their accession to the tariff. Their place would simply be taken by others, for entry was easy and the opportunities of non-tariff underwriting were now well known in the business community. Furthermore, the only alternative solution, that of cutting off reinsurance, had to be ruled out, at least temporarily, when negotiations with Lloyd's broke down early in 1907.

The vitality of the non-tariff companies, new and old, was demonstrated by a more rapid annual growth rate in their business between 1906 and 1907 than in any other two years in the period examined; in the latter year premium had grown back to £365,000, or 5·4% of the market. The pressures this created were described in familiar terms by the Commercial Union fire manager: 'During the year a number of small non-tariff companies were formed and their competition, together with an increased activity on the part of Lloyd's, has led to a very general demand for a reduction of rates.'[44]

The picture is clear. The tariff companies were continuing to lose business to the interlopers. For the reasons described above there was no immediate prospect of any end to this erosion through the re-establishment of control over the market. It was therefore not simply a matter of the loss of current business, but the threat of a continued loss into the future. The 1904 sprinkler discount revisions had been inadequate for the competitive conditions, however equitably they may have been based on loss experience. Indeed, they demonstrated how irrelevant loss experience was as a guide to rating in a quickly changing market.

From May 1907 substantial and far more sophisticated new sprinkler discounts were gradually introduced to thirty-seven tariffs. They were more subtle in the distinctions they made between the various forms of protection. In 1906, under pressure from the Commercial Union fire manager, detailed regulations discriminating between various standards of sprinkler protection had been devised and introduced on a limited basis. These were now applied to virtually all the tariffs where sprinkler discounts were relevant. For the very highest standard of protection, discounts were now available up to 50% on many tariffs, in place of the previous normal maximum of 35%; when the Cotton Mills Tariff was amended in line with the new appoach in 1908, the maximum discount for this standard was raised to 70%. At the same time, the competition that had taken so many risks with lower-quality protection away from tariff offices was dealt with. Different discounts were also available for three lower standards of efficiency, reaching down to 20% for systems with only one water supply.[45]

Thus the F.O.C. introduced a series of discounts for sprinklers that reflected more adequately the magnitude and the variability of reduced loss experience that sprinkler protection provided. Of course, it is not suggested that the new arrangements reflected this perfectly. Scope for the discounting of sprinklered risks remained, but it was on a far smaller scale and limited to special circumstances in particular markets. The discounts established in 1907 remained broadly operative until the first world war and beyond. Although non-tariff competition continued, it had to broaden its strategy if it was to remain viable, for the bonanza days of sprinkler underwriting had disappeared. It had fulfilled its role of forcing the F.O.C. to provide a more equitable structure of premium rates.[46]

## VII  Conclusion

Thus, despite the apparently formidable strength of the F.O.C., its members were forced to adjust their premium rates in the face of falling claims costs provided by the spread of improved sprinkler protection. They did not do so willingly or promptly, yet eventually rates fell substantially and began to reflect the varying levels of protection provided by different systems. This adjustment took place because of the competitive realities of the hazardous fire insurance market. The strength developed by the F.O.C. in the third quarter of the nineteenth century stimulated the emergence of Lloyd's as a reinsurance market and the rise of brokers as effective market intermediaries. This made it impossible to prevent the growth of a small but potent non-tariff sector whenever uncompetitive premium rates created opportunities for rate discounting. Indeed, the vigour of this entry is a tribute to the entrepreneurial dynamism of the economy.

Tariff companies were extremely sensitive to such incursions, even when modest in scale. While direct evidence as to why this was so is hard to come by, it is not difficult to suggest a reasonable explanation, though further research is required to establish it solidly. When a non-tariff raid occurred, one tariff company, or a small group, was affected with particular intensity because of the distribution of its business. In such circumstances the F.O.C. would usually act promptly, for, if it did not, those affected might be forced to consider leaving the tariff. This was a far more serious threat to all tariff companies, for even if only one significant member left the F.O.C. the oligopolistic structure of market meant that there would almost certainly be a slide into premium rate warfare. The costs of this had been imprinted on the minds of all tariff underwriters by such episodes as the competitive consequences of the Tooley Street fire and the collapse of the Cotton Mills Tariff around 1890, and they were determined to avoid it at all costs.[47]

In short, while F.O.C. members were always happy to take advantage of any temporary opportunity to profit from the high rates that their organisation might be able to set, this was a subsidiary objective to that of creating stability in market shares and long-term profitability. Given the competitive conditions of the market and within the F.O.C., attempts to secure permanent and significant monopoly gains could interfere with this aim. The emphasis in the business on conventional 'cost-plus' rate fixing and 'reasonable' profits was not window-dressing but a recognition of what was necessary to secure existing tariff members' best interests. The F.O.C. survived so successfully only because it was sufficiently flexible to recognise this and act accordingly.

Of course, this study has concentrated on the hazardous fire insurance market where the F.O.C. concentrated the overwhelming weight of its sophisticated and complex system of rate control. Yet this took the form it did because of the essentially weak and unstable competitive structure, which the organisation tried to ameliorate for its members. The non-hazardous fire insurance market has not been investigated here, but it provides an instructive contrast. With only the sketchiest regulation, which required little enforcement, the large tariff companies were able to avoid rate competition almost entirely. Instead, they redirected their efforts into the branch and inspectorate organisations which made it so hard for small companies to compete successfully. It is another reminder of the important insight that the more formal the institutional arrangements surrounding collusive agreements, the more evidence they generate and the more distinct their profile in the historical record, yet the weaker they are likely to be. It is when businessmen do not need to come to complicated arrangements that the consumer has most cause to worry.

## Notes

1  W. H. B. Court, *British Economic History, 1870–1914: Commentary and Documents*, Cambridge, 1965, p. 244.

2  On the early history and development of the control of competition in fire insurance see Barry Supple, *The Royal Exchange Assurance. A History of British Insurance, 1720–1970*, Cambridge, 1970, pp. 127–30, 217 and 282; Hugh A. L. Cockerell, 'Combination in British fire insurance' in F. Reichert-Facilides, F. Rittner and J. Sasse, eds., *Festschrift für Reiner Schmidt*, Karlsrühe, 1976; P. G. M. Dickson, *The Sun Insurance Office, 1710–1960*, London, 1960, pp. 149–60. Dickson examined the question raised in this study at pp. 149–60, and my contribution may be regarded as an attempt to test his general remarks.

3  The main challenges to the effectiveness of rating agreements in the second half of the nineteenth century occurred when the associated offices attempted to raise premium rates after the Tooley Street fire in 1861 and when they were slow to recognise the effectiveness of sprinkler operation in cutting fire loss in the cotton trade in the late 1880s. On the latter see p. 138 below. The Monopolies Commission report, *Fire Insurance, Report on the Supply of Fire Insurance*, H.M.S.O., 1972, suggested that by 1968 the tariff share of the fire insurance market had fallen to 63%.

4  My account of the activities of the organisation is based on an examination of the records of the F.O.C., along with Hugh A. L. Cockerell, 'Combination'; D. Deuchar, 'The necessity for a tariff organisation in connection with fire insurance business', *Journal of Federation of Insurance Institutes*, VI, 1903, and F. J. Kingsley, 'Tariff legislation and risk improvement', *Journal of the Federation of Insurance Institutes*, III, 1900, both provide valuable contemporary material.

5  Specialisation within the British market is extremely difficult to assess because all the company accounts contain foreign business — some two-thirds of the aggregate business. However, clues can be obtained from two sources: the returns made under the Metropolitan Fire Brigade Act, 1865, reported in the *Post Magazine Almanack* (*P.M.A.*) each year, indicate the *gross acceptances* obtained by each company within the metropolitan district of London. The *Policy Holder* (*P.H.*) regularly and precisely reported the same information in relation to fire losses on a risk-by-risk basis. There is no space here to elaborate the problems faced in using this material. However, for what it is worth, it suggests a considerable variation in the degree of specialisation and one that fits with an intuitive understanding of the probable distribution of company business. The five largest companies, in order of size, in the four markets investigated are as follows: (1) Metropolitan London, 1903: Sun, Alliance, Royal, Phoenix, Law. (2) Glasgow industrial and mercantile, 1895–1900: North British and Mercantile, Royal, Northern, Scottish Union, Commercial Union. (3) Lancashire cotton trade, excluding Liverpool, 1896–98: Phoenix, Palatine, Manchester, Equitable, Royal. (4) Yorkshire wool and worsted trade, 1896–98: Royal, Liverpool, London and Globe, Scottish Union, Caledonian, Palatine.

6  Supple, *R.E.A.*, pp. 211–12.

7  *Ibid.*, pp. 284–93.

8  An analysis of management expenses as a percentage of net premium income in relation to the scale of net premium income for 1899 indicates no systematic pattern. See also Supple, *R.E.A.*, p. 294.

9  *P.M.A.*, 1901; the tenth largest company was the Palatine.

10  A comprehensive sketch of these developments is provided by Cockerell, 'Combination', pp. 868–71.

11  Deuchar, 'Tariff organisation', p. lviii; he also reported that in 1902 all the F.O.C.'s senior officials were barristers; the description of the tariff documents themselves is drawn from my own experience of examining them at first hand.

12  Supple, *R.E.A.*, p. 282.

## The Fire Offices Committee 151

13 These rather precise figures as to the 'target' loss ratio were quoted by the managing director of the Provincial Insurance Company, a small non-tariff company, in an analysis he wrote of his company's opportunities. As the company's archives are not available for inspection, I will not provide detailed citation, merely referring to 'Provincial'.

14 Supple, *R.E.A.*, pp. 284–93.

15 Provincial.

16 It is probable that some companies, such as the Fine Art and General, continued to obtain foreign reinsurance, but smaller concerns, without C. E. Heath's powerful patronage, found it impossible to obtain access to reputable Continental reinsurance companies. When the Provincial was established, its managers were strongly advised not to reinsure with certain non-tariff companies for this reason.

17 D. E. W. Gibb, *Lloyd's of London: A Study in Individualism*, London, 1957, p. 163, describes the genesis of this business; its significance is emphasised by Cockerell, 'Combination', pp. 869–70. See p. 146 below for the importance of reinsurance for non-tariff companies.

18 'Selection' is a well known fire insurance technique; however, I owe my emphasis on its special importance for the non-tariff company to an analysis written by the managing director of the Provincial. He wrote, 'Given intelligent and experienced underwriting it is possible to offer a discount of 10 per cent off the tariff rates and even provide for an extra commission of 5 per cent to overcome the inertia of brokers and agents. This is where selection comes in, in selecting the classes of risk to cut and the particular cases of those classes which are rated by the tariff unfairly and will stand a lower rate.' Provincial.

19 Examples might make this a little clearer. When tariff rates overcharged sprinkler-protected cotton mills in the 1900–07 period, it became possible for non-tariff companies to discount rates for virtually all risks in that class. In addition, extra discounts could be offered by underwriters who were aware, for example, that bales of very fine cotton, which were tightly packed, suffered far less damage from sprinkler operation and could therefore usually be salvaged.

20 The absence of any substantial history of insurance brokers is a major gap in our understanding of the development of the business. Quite apart from the Lloyd's brokers, about whom something is known through the history of that institution, there are the large provincial brokers such as A. W. Bain and A. R. Stenhouse who were great powers in the fire insurance market. S. D. Chapman's study in this book makes an important contribution in this area.

21 On the introduction of sprinkler protection see R. Northwood, *Fire Extinguishment and Fire Alarm Systems*, London, 1928, pp. 24–7, and Kingsley, *op. cit.*, pp. 251–2. On the spread of sprinkler protection see *Sprinkler Bulletin (S.B.)*, December 1894, March 1895 and June 1901. The twenty-six tariffs in which sprinkler discounts were available were listed in *P.H.*, December 1898.

22 The best account of the crisis is provided in the files of the *P.H.*; see especially December 1898. *S.B.* reported the Equitable's loss ratio.

23 F.O.C., Cotton Mills (England and Ireland) Tariff, November 1898; F.O.C. Fire Extinguishing Sub-committee Minutes, December 1898 and June 1899.

24 F.O.C., Fire Extinguishing Sub-committee, Sub-sub-committee appointed January 1900, Minutes of Meetings held July 1901, October 1902 and February 1899.

25 Guildhall Library, London, Department of Manuscripts, (G.L.) MS. 14026, Commercial Union Assurance Company Ltd, Fire Committee Minute Book, Vol. 28, April 1905. The loss ratios have been calculated from the annual accounts of home fire business provided in this source.

26 The non-tariff net fire premium income has been compiled from *P.M.A. Acc.*, which also lists F.O.C. membership each year. The estimate of the size of the home fire insurance market on which the non-tariff percentage share is based is crude. There

is no clear evidence on the distribution of home and foreign business and therefore any estimate must be rough-and-ready. Contemporaries assumed that the home fire market was about one-third of the total fire premium income obtained. Deuchar, 'Tariff organisation', p. lv, appears to have used this rule in his estimate of £7,227,000 for the home fire market in 1902. However, it seems worthwhile trying to do a little better than this. Annual fluctuations in the average premium rate obtained were sufficiently large to make a significant difference in the scale of premium income and these would be completely masked in the aggregate of all the companies' international business. K. Maywald's 'Fire insurance and the capital coefficient in Great Britain, 1866–1952', *Economic History Review*, Second Series, IX, 2, 1956, provides an estimate of British insurable assets in his table 2 (p. 94). If we can assume that the degree of underinsurance was stable, then this can provide a good proxy for the gross sums assured, or movements in that statistic. Average premium rates obtained on sums insured are not easily available, especially from companies with a sufficient spread of business to make their business representative. However, an annual series is provided by the Commercial Union Fire Committee Minute Books in the Guildhall library. Applying this average premium rate to the gross sums assured suggested by Maywald, it is possible to obtain the estimate of home fire premium income suggested below. If the degree of underinsurance is stable and movements in the Commercial Union's average premium rate reflect movement in the market as a whole — two reasonable assumptions — then movements in this estimate should be reasonably reliable. Because we cannot know the absolute degree of underinsurance and how the level of the Commercial Union's average premium rate compared with the overall market level, it is impossible to be so sanguine about the absolute level of the estimate. However, it cannot be too far out. Deuchar's estimate of £7,227,000 for 1902, made by a man who was in the best position to know through his intimate knowledge of the business, is matched in this estimate by a figure of £7,238,000 — only 0·15% higher. This happy coincidence provides some reasonable support for the absolute level of the estimate as well.

*Estimated British home fire premium income, 1898–1907* (£'000)

| | | | |
|---|---|---|---|
| 1898 | 6312 | 1903 | 7855 |
| 1899 | 6758 | 1904 | 7677 |
| 1900 | 6990 | 1905 | 7619 |
| 1901 | 7072 | 1906 | 7482 |
| 1902 | 7238 | 1907 | 7567* |

*Unfortunately, the series of average premium rates obtained on the Commercial Union's home fire business is broken by a gap in 1907. Literary evidence from the same source suggests that it fell, but in the absence of clear statistical evidence I have assumed that it remained at the level of 1906. This therefore means that the 1907 estimate is probably slightly inflated, but I pushed it up in order to be sure that the non-tariff share was an underestimae. A final problem in calculating the non-tariff share of business lies in our ignorance of how much foreign business they underwrote. They were certainly not entirely restricted to the home market, but the evidence suggests that foreign revenue was relatively insignificant; see Deuchar, 'Tariff organisation', p. lv.

27 G.L., MS. 14,026, Commercial Union Fire Committee Minute Book, Vol. 26; MS. 16,248, Royal Exchange Assurance, Fire Manager, Special Report Book, Vol. 1.

28 *P.M.A.*, see 'Synopsis of the published Revenue Accounts of the Fire Insurance Companies ...', *passim (P.M.A. Acc.)*.

29 C. E. Heath was a director of the Fine Art and General; Claude Hay, M.P., claimed in his entry in *Who's Who* to be the company's founder. The National of Great Britain was chaired by Lord Kinnoul, Hay's father; reports on the company's select business may be found in the *Post Magazine (P.M.)*, May 1897 and September

1905. The Textile Mutual's formation and objectives were reported in *P.H.*, May 1902.
30  *P.M.A. Acc.*
31  *P.M.*, September 1896 and November 1902; *S.B.*, December 1899; *P.H.*, June 1903.
32  *P.H.*, January 1902; premium income from *P.M.A. Acc.*
33  *P.H.*, May 1905.
34  The Provincial and the Cornhill are the only two that have remained in independent existence, and the latter took only a small part in the incursion in its later stages. Where other company records have survived they are too incomplete to be helpful. The Guildhall Library, Department of Manuscripts, has two small collections in its magnificent insurance archives: some Fine Art and General documents (MS. 14,044) and some Central documents (MS. 11,689). All subsequent discussion of the Provincial's development is based on the private papers of the company. S. H. Scott and F. C. Scott, Personal Account, *Some Recollections of Fifty Years of the Provincial Insurance Company*, Kendal, 1953, and Oliver M. Westall, *A Family Policy. A Brief History of the First 75 Years of the Provincial Insurance Company*, Kendal, 1978; both provide brief accounts of the company's development.
35  This business was to grow into the well known concern with the name of its founder.
36  The problem implicit in this discussion is explored in a detailed and formal way in N. Doherty, *Insurance Pricing and Loss Prevention*, Farnborough, 1976.
37  *S.B.*, June 1899; Kingsley, *op. cit.*, p. 353; the Provincial managers were told by the general manager of another small non-tariff company that sprinklers were '... discouraged by Tariff Offices on purely business grounds ... Insurers pay the premiums therefore it does not concern them to get lower rates, the profit on each being the same ...' Provincial.
38  F.O.C., General Meeting, April 1902, March 1906; *P.M.A. Acc.*
39  G.L., MS. 14,026, Commercial Union, Fire Committee Minute Book, Vol. 28, April 1905.
40  F.O.C. Home Sub-committee Minute Books 4 and 5 provide the details of this negotiation. Significantly, the committee concerned changed its name, starting as the 'Non-tariff Competition Sub-committee' and finishing as 'Membership of Lloyd's Committee'.
41  *P.M.A.*, 1907.
42  G.L., MS. 11,689, Central Insurance Company, Minutes of Special Committees, January 1906, records the negotiations; a public report is provided in *P.H.*, January 1906; F.O.C. Home Sub-committee Minute Books 4 and 5 record the story from that organisation's point of view, beginning in October 1905.
43  *Times New Issues*, Vol. 33, 1907, 25 March 1907.
44  G.L., MS. 14,026, Commercial Union Fire Committee Minute Book, Vol. 29.
45  F.O.C., Special General Meeting, May 1907; the new discounts were gradually introduced to a wider range of tariffs in the following year or so.
46  The story of non-tariff operation in the years after 1907 is another and complicated problem. While the success of the non-tariff companies before 1907 must have contributed to it, this later entry was interwoven with the rapid expansion in the accident insurance market and the consequences of the very sharp increase in the concentration of business which had occurred by 1907.
47  Supple, *R.E.A.*, p. 217, for an account of the competitive consequences of the Tooley Street fire. He goes on to quote Deuchar, 'Tariff organisation', who argued that the effect of the new entry at that time had imprinted on the collective mind of the F.O.C. the danger of raising rates inequitably. The sprinkler episode must have jogged their memory.

## Acknowledgements

I would like to acknowledge the generous support of the Provincial Insurance Company in the preparation of this chapter and thank the company for the access it has provided to its business archives. In addition I would like to thank the Secretary of the Fire Offices Committee for permission to examine the records of his organisation and the Keeper of Manuscripts at the Guildhall Library for his expert assistance in studying some of the many insurance company records in his care.

JOHN BUTT

# Life assurance in war and depression: the Standard Life Assurance Company and its environment, 1914–39

## I  *Introduction*

Although there had been intermittent indications before 1914 that the world economy was about to succumb to violence, the scale of dislocation to the international financial system, based, as it was, on sterling and gold, which occurred as a consequence of the first world war was impossible to predict. Increasing militancy was also a feature of relationships within the United Kingdom: in particular, the Home Rule crisis in Ireland deepened with the approach of the war, and civil order, as the Easter Rising of 1916 later made clear, was in peril. Class antagonisms multiplied as war-induced inflation proceeded. Syndicalist ideas had already penetrated the trade union movement, and before the war there had been dalliance with the concept of a general strike duly but imperfectly realised in practice in 1926. Women, organised by a middle-class cadre, had assaulted the citadels of male chauvinism, which gradually began to collapse after 1918.

Insurance companies on the outbreak of the war were faced with a range of difficulties. Those underwriting property and fire risks had most at stake in the event of riots, civil disorder and bombardment of urban centres; life offices were presented with an entirely different range of problems. No doubt, general insecurity deterred potential policy-holders from undertaking long-term commitments, but of far greater significance was the substantial increase in mortality risk which temporarily destroyed the mathematical basis of pre-war actuarial practice. No actuary could have assessed the extent of impending mortality on the Somme, or among the poppy-dotted fields of Flanders or on the sandy slopes and beaches of Gallipoli. For existing policy-holders the life offices agreed not to charge extra premiums, but new proposals immediately produced the problem of determining 'war risks'.[1] Higher premiums, even taking account of inflation, were likely to deter would-be policy holders, and the slow growth of new life business during the war attests to this consequence. International life companies, such as Standard Life, which had extensive business in Belgium and the enemy State of Hungary, had particular difficulties.

If the Armistice ended problems associated directly with the conflict, it inaugurated others no less substantial for the industry. Britain had dominated the pre-war international payments system; the gold standard was really John Bull's watch and chain whereby the world's commercial structure was carefully regulated. The war had destroyed this mechanism, and the gold standard had vanished, although not entirely without trace. However, when the peace came there was no real possibility of resuming pre-war financial relationships. Britain and Europe were both relatively weaker; the United States had emerged as the world's greatest creditor nation and yet was reluctant to undertake the full range of international responsibilities that this new role enjoined. Rapid changes in parity exchange levels were always likely in this environment, further complicated by problems of international indebtedness which the war had compounded. Stable capital movements were unlikely in these circumstances; companies with international business outside the United States encountered increasing difficulty in making remittances homewards; economic nationalism predominated in the post-war world — even in the British Empire — with devastating effects on world trade.

Because world trade could not grow in any sustained fashion, Britain's economy remained weak throughout the 1920s, despite the temporary return to the gold standard in 1925, worsened sharply in the years immediately following the Wall Street crash of 1929, and recovered only patchily on a regional basis after 1933. Despite this apparently unpropitious economic environment the insurance industry expanded greatly and diversified widely. Thoughtful management and conscientious effort enabled many companies to increase their income from underwriting and from investment.

Legal constraints and State intervention, both at home and abroad, were natural products both of neo-mercantilism and of the growth of new technology. Road Traffic Acts clearly influenced the development of the motor insurance market, for instance, but in Britain it was the operations of 'fringe companies' in the industrial life insurance sector that led to a series of measures beginning with the Industrial Assurance Act of 1923. Of course, State intervention was not new, but especially overseas it was much more discriminatory than in the past. Some countries favoured native offices because of the importance of preventing outflows of capital, and, in general, British companies found that making remittances home became more difficult and occasionally impossible. Sometimes foreign governments insisted that offices should increase the size of funds kept on deposit; sometimes they raised taxation levels. Fiscal policy in Britain also encouraged high taxpayers from 1924 onward to seek to offset commitments to the Inland Revenue by taking out single-premium policies upon which the authorities granted an allowance, particularly since these were often the basis of loans, the interest upon which also attracted favourable treatment from the Inland Revenue. The purpose of this chapter is to examine a number of themes with particular reference to Standard Life Assurance Company, the response to war, the growth of the life market, particularly the growth of group business at home, and changes in investment policy.

## II. *The response to war and its aftermath*

As a result of the war, new life business fell both at home and abroad, particularly in the period up to 1916 (sums assured from £59 million in 1913 to £44 million in 1916); recovery even then was partly a consequence of inflation. Standard Life mirrored these developments. New premium income fell abruptly in 1915 and remained at about two-thirds the level of 1914 until the last year of the war, when there was a marked recovery, as indicated in Table 1.[2]

Table 1. *Standard Life Assurance Company's ordinary life business, 1914–1920*

| Year | New policies | Net sum assured (£ million) | Premium income (£) | |
|---|---|---|---|---|
| | | | New | Total |
| 1914 | 3,095 | 1·713 | 76,857 | 997,992 |
| 1915 | 1,935 | 1·050 | 49,850 | 940,799 |
| 1916 | 1,512 | 1·081 | 52,404 | 892,075 |
| 1917 | 1,789 | 0·903 | 50,546 | 872,508 |
| 1918 | 1,901 | 1·170 | 63,227 | 932,325 |
| 1919 | 3,031 | 1·960 | 104,520 | 919,545 |
| 1920 | 3,623 | 2·511 | 118,286 | 954,591 |

*Source.* Standard Life Annual Reports, 1914–20.

Leonard Dickson, manager of the Standard, was Chairman of the Scottish Life Offices Association throughout the war, and in his correspondence the early optimism about a speedy conclusion to hostilities soon gave way to a grim prediction that 1917 or 1918 might see an end to the war. The Scottish Offices decided to charge extra premiums according to risk for new policies; surrender values were to remain the same; loan interest charges to policyholders were to follow Bank rate.[3]

Standard Life limited its maximum war risk on a single life to £2,000 in September 1914, and above that figure reassurance was undertaken.[4] As war mortality experience became known, companies devised war risk schedules which were often very elaborate and graded according to the type and location of military service. Generally, premium rates rose; this acted against the writing of new business.[5]

Difficulties arose over war claims where the assured was reported missing but there was no firm proof of death. The Standard's board considered such cases individually. In only one instance did the directors decline to pay the executors on the evidence submitted; instead, a bank deposit was established until more satisfactory proof of death was forthcoming.[6] Once an interval of a year had passed, the board agreed to pay, subject to an agreement by the beneficiary that the company would not lose by making a settlement.

Since life offices were compelled by statutes of 1870 and 1909 to conduct investigations into their operations and to declare the results to the Board of Trade, there was much agitation within the industry as to whether these provisions should be dropped for the duration of the war. Some English managers favoured government legislation to indemnify the life offices, but the managers of the Edinburgh-based companies preferred to leave the offices free to make their own decisions. Two meetings at the Board of Trade on 8 and 23 October 1914 were attended by Dickson, in his capacity as chairman of the Scottish Life Offices, Marks, who was chairman of the Life Offices Association in England, and Thompson of the Prudential, representing the industrial assurance offices. While the English offices, according to Marks and Thompson, could not agree, some Scottish companies were already declaring bonuses.

The possible courses of action open to the government were outlined in a memorandum prepared by Dickson. The Board of Trade could require companies to value their assets and liabilities but dispense with the certificate required under the terms of the 1909 Act. If a valuation and a certificate were required, most companies would write down their assets on a massive scale, and there was a danger that the weaker offices would go to the wall. The worth of stock exchange securities was particularly difficult to assess in wartime, but at any investigation it might be reasonable to give them a book value. Another possibility was to delay by Act of Parliament any investigation until 31 December in the year after the war ended. Bonuses and dividends — in the case of proprietary companies — could be maintained but not increased. This would prevent unfair competition in a market which was temporarily shrinking. Finally, it was also possible for the government to permit companies to postpone valuations. Thus any office able to meet the terms of the 1909 Act could go ahead and declare dividends and bonuses. In practice, the Board of Trade accepted this last option in December 1914 and also allowed life offices to value their assets at the level prevailing at 31 December 1913 for the purpose of making statutory returns; assets acquired since that date were to be entered at not more than cost price.[7]

For most offices the main difficulty was the shortage of suitable staff, for accounting procedures depended upon both skill and experience.[8] The Standard at the quinquennial investigation of 1915 valued assets by the time-honoured method of taking the market value or the ledger value, whichever was the lower. Special writing-down provisions of £163,843 were relatively modest considering that the company's total funds exceeded £14 million. The directors cautiously decided not to fix a permanent bonus for participating policies as they would normally have done but ensured that every appropriate policy becoming a claim before the next investigation was allotted an intermediate bonus of £1 per cent for every year since 1910.[9] Despite the fact there was a rise in sums assured in 1917 to £52 million and a more definite recovery to £68 million in 1918, most life offices continued to pass their bonuses, unlike the Standard.[10]

Yet the effects of mortality experience during the war proved to be less significant than most companies had feared. For there were many policyholders over the age of military service in 1914, and for new proposals higher rates were of course charged. None the less, the net extra loss on policies maturing but not charged extra premiums was about £13·6 million, a clear indication of the extent of wartime mortality.[11] However, companies offset this actuarial loss against the rise in income from investment. Table 2 indicates the particular experience of Standard Life over the period 1909 to 1920, to set war claims in a slightly wider perspective. There was clearly a sharp rise in the three years 1914, 1915 and 1916, but 1917 and 1918 cost the office less than some pre-war years. The annual average claim for the five years 1914–18 was £737,205, compared with £679,101 for the preceding five years. Thus there is little evidence that efficient management could not deal with the problems which life offices faced.

Table 2. *Claims by death met by Standard Life Assurance Company, 1909–20*

| Year | Amount (£) |
|---|---|
| 1909 | 731,857 |
| 1910 | 666,895 |
| 1911 | 713,876 |
| 1912 | 651,955 |
| 1913 | 630,924 |
| 1914 | 746,964 |
| 1915 | 820,276 |
| 1916 | 763,883 |
| 1917 | 698,544 |
| 1918 | 656,349 |
| 1919 | 673,111 |
| 1920 | 665,406 |

*Source.* Annual Reports, 1909–20.

Abroad, however, multinational companies faced different hazards, notably in enemy-held territory. The Austrian government imposed loans on the branches of British companies within its territories. Gresham Life, for instance, repudiated these once the war was over, and successfully applied for reparations.[12] Standard Life's branches in Belgium and Hungary were well established by 1914 and their experience provides valuable insights. In Hungary investments estimated at £47,647 were at risk as well as existing premium income, modest sums relative to the company's total assets. Despite the fact that Hungary was an enemy, the branch in Budapest was not entirely isolated. Charles Szilagyi, the agent, managed to use the telegraph at the American consulate and sought by telegram, redirected via The Hague agent, powers to revive policies and to continue the loan side of the business; these head office in Edinburgh refused.[13] Szilagyi coped excellently with the difficulties of conducting business in a country that was ravaged by inflation, and his loyalty greatly reduced the possibility of losses. Full accounts were not available from the first year of the war, but he managed in March 1917 to send a statement regarding funds and investments via Van Reeth at The Hague.[14] After the war Thomas Darling, who had spent six months in Budapest before 1914, was sent to Hungary, but conditions were most unsettled. In March 1919 Bela Kun established a short-lived communist State which disintegrated into total disorder and the imposition of martial law by the Roumanian army. During this period Szilagyi was 'dismissed', and a workers' committee of three clerks made itself responsible for management. One, Feber, assumed full powers, doubled staff salaries and allowed the company's bank balances to be replaced with government paper. Thus Darling entered a hostile environment of hyperinflation, with general disregard for law and order.

Although Charles Szilagyi was reinstated, the neo-mercantilist attitudes of the post-war Hungarian government, in particular its insistence on forced loans later cancelled by tax payments, encouraged the Standard to close down its Budapest branch. An agreement was made in Paris on 11 April 1921 with the Hungarian government to transfer the business to a native office of their choosing. Policy-holders received the full sums assured no matter what the terms of their original policies, and this was possible without loss to the company because of the scale of local inflation. Bank accounts in Budapest were kept open until 1924, and loyal staff were paid during the period while they were seeking alternative employment. Szilagyi continued to manage the Standard's property in Budapest till it was sold in 1927, and thereafter became a company pensioner.[15]

The closure in Hungary was merely part of a withdrawal from Europe which developed during the war. Belgian business never recovered from the German occupation, and in 1919 arrangements were made with Lloyd's Bank and the National Provincial to collect premiums and mortgage interest.[16] The Copenhagen branch had been closed before the war, and withdrawal from Scandinavia followed. In 1916 the Standard's board decided to discontinue the Stockholm agency before the Swedish insurance law of 1917, which prescribed a deposit in State bonds to cover all liabilities, became effective. No new business was, therefore, taken in Sweden from 1917, but about 5,000 policies were in force, and Soderberg, the local agent, was retained on commission to handle these.[17] Disengagement continued in the inter-war period.

Yet, for the life insurance industry in general, the war marked an unfortunate intermission in overseas life business closely following the domestic pattern. Sums insured abroad fell from £8·6 million in 1913 to £4·3 million in 1916 and then rose to £5·4 million in 1918 and £10·3 million in 1919.[18] However, British companies were increasingly subject to pressure in Europe, and much overseas new business arose elsewhere, a trend which the war probably accelerated.

## III  The growth of the life market

Table 3 summarises the basic data relating to the ordinary life business of British offices between the wars. Total premium income increased by over 220% by 1939, the only significant falls occurring during the Great Depression years, 1930–32, with the trough reached in 1931. New premium income was less consistent in its behaviour: the early 1920s were significantly worse than any other period, although the check to progress in 1931 and 1932 is perceptible. However, in raw money terms, the amount of new business achieved in 1920, measured by premium income, was not exceeded until 1934. Total sums assured moved steadily upwards, increasing on average between 1922 and 1937 by nearly 12% per annum; growth was markedly slower between 1922 and 1928 than in the nine years following. The difficulties in obtaining business in the 1920s are made most obvious by comparing the new sums assured on a year-by-year basis: not until 1927 was the figure of 1920 exceeded, and the depression of 1921–23 was even more significant than the downturn in 1931–32.

Industrial assurance companies also did good business between the wars, their premium income increasing from £25·3 million in 1919 to £59·8 million in 1939 (i.e. 236% over the period). These companies had been originally founded to meet the needs for insurance of the 'industrial classes', i.e. working men and lower middle classes, and therefore based their policy options on the principle of small generally weekly, and occasionally monthly, collection of premiums. Thus ordinary life offices did not really affect the expansion of industrial assurance between the wars, and one can only conclude that all sections of the community were interested in providing security (and/or savings) for their families. Common prudence encouraged thrift among many groups in society; social and occupational changes, most notably the evolution of a 'salariat', aided the expansion of demand for life insurance, as did the course of rising real wages for those who retained employment.

But life insurance is not simply a demand-led industry; policies had to be created to suit the market at various levels and energetically sold, particularly in the 1920s. The long trend away from whole-life without-profits policies towards endowment and with-profits policies continued. More expensive they might be, but such policies guarded savings better from the ravages of inflation, and as incomes rose, longevity increased and tax relief was granted,

Table 3. *British office ordinary life business, 1919–39*

| Year | Ordinary life (£ million) | | | | New sums in comparison with previous year (%) |
| --- | --- | --- | --- | --- | --- |
| | U.K. premiums | | Sums assured | | |
| | Total | New | Total | New | |
| 1919 | 37·8 | 6·1 | n.a. | 131·5 | +79·2 |
| 1920 | 41·9 | 6·6 | n.a. | 146·5 | +11·5 |
| 1921 | 44·1 | 4·6 | n.a. | 109·2 | −25·5 |
| 1922 | 45·6 | 4·5 | 1,144 | 106·3 | −2·7 |
| 1923 | 46·8 | 4·5 | 1,182 | 111·8 | +5·1 |
| 1924 | 51·5 | 4·9 | 1,209 | 123·7 | +10·7 |
| 1925 | 57·9 | 4·9 | 1,291 | 130·2 | +5·3 |
| 1926 | 58·5 | 4·9 | 1,353 | 128·9 | −1·0 |
| 1927 | 63·9 | 5·5 | 1,398 | 147·8 | +14·7 |
| 1928 | 68·2 | 5·8 | 1,439 | 160 | +8·1 |
| 1929 | 69·8 | 5·8 | 1,492 | 162 | +1·2 |
| 1930 | 66·8 | 6·0 | 1,591 | 166 | +2·5 |
| 1931 | 65·3 | 5·7 | 1,668 | 161 | −3 |
| 1932 | 67·9 | 5·5 | 1,706 | 164 | +1·9 |
| 1933 | 71·4 | 6·0 | 1,759 | 183 | +11·6 |
| 1934 | 71·5 | 6·7 | 1,809 | 208 | +13·7 |
| 1935 | 74·3 | 7·3 | 1,936 | 224 | +7·7 |
| 1936 | 77·3 | 7·7 | 2,061 | 243 | +8·5 |
| 1937 | 80·5 | 7·9 | 2,139 | 261 | +7·4 |
| 1938 | 83·9 | 7·6 | n.a. | n.a. | n.a. |
| 1939 | 84·1 | 5·7 | n.a. | n.a. | n.a. |

Sources. Supple, p. 427, Table 18.1; *The Economist*, 1929, p. 918, and 1939, 15 July.

they became relatively more attractive to those who wanted to provide for retirement and dependants. Between 1900, when with-profits policies took about 20% of the life market, and 1916, when they account for about 38%,[19] the tone was set, and most policy improvements between the wars were variants of this type of contract. By 1937 with-profits contracts accounted for over two-thirds of all policies, a trend which was reversed only during the second world war.[20]

The field men of Standard Life were given new policies to sell in 1919. Several assurance plans were available to women 'without charging any extra premium on account of sex'; Victory Bonds could be purchased on annual instalments, an excellent means of providing for death duties; the Public Schools Policy was devised to combine 'provision for the most expensive years of a child's education with protection in the event of the parent's death — a policy particularly adapted to the needs of the present day'. Annuity rates were revised upwards and were highly competitive.[21]

Stewart Macnaghten[22] (1873–1952), after experience with the Equity and

Law in London and the Old Equitable, became the Standard's chief actuary in 1912 and, after Leonard Dickson's death in 1919, its manager. Macnaghten's conviction was that specialist life offices could survive in competition with the new composite companies only if they maintained an up-to-date and comprehensive range of schemes to sell on competitive terms. His new policies were eclectic; he was prepared to be an innovator without necessarily being an inventor. During the course of 1921–22 the Acme policy was introduced (Standard was already operating it in Canada as the 'Perfect' policy), and this had many novel features as far as the United Kingdom market was concerned. Its principal characteristics might be summarised as a list of guarantees: the policy was payable at death but premiums were paid for a maximum of twenty years; surrender and paid-up policy values were both guaranteed; at the end of twenty years a guaranteed bonus of 50% of the sum assured was added, and the policy then participated in all further bonuses; a policy-holder who became permanently disabled was freed from the payment of premiums and was due an annual sum equal to 10% of the sum assured, the full sum still being payable at death.[23] This type of policy, although not cheap, was relatively popular and on that account was soon copied by other offices. This led the Standard in 1924 to reduce its premiums for the Acme policy and to improve its terms, including the provision that, in the event of the death of the assured within twenty years, the policy automatically became a with-profits contract.[24]

During 1923 two new schemes were issued. The 'Family Provision' policy was, as its name implies, intended to offset future family expenditure such as death duties or marriage settlements and sold at low non-profit participating rates. Another whole-life without-profits policy was specially intended for businessmen under the age of forty. This 'Business Man's' policy contained the important proviso that at the option of the assured it could be converted later into an endowment or any form of whole-life policy then available.[25]

Many other companies were also inventive or innovative. Allied Assurance in 1924 added disability benefits to certain life policies to cover loss of income during serious illness.[26] The Royal Exchange introduced 'Bachelor Policies', short-term endowment assurances convertible to whole-life contracts.[27] Thus the bachelor could celebrate the end to wild oats by converting his endowment policy on his marriage! Many companies were offering policies to pay for the education of children by 1925, as advertisements in *The Economist* and other financial journals make clear. A number of companies formulated contracts to offset death duties, notably the Phoenix.

Macnaghten of the Standard also recognised the significance of competitive but steady bonus rates as a magnet for new business;[28] by 1927 bonuses were being declared annually, and the compound reversionary bonus was maintained up to 1938 at £2 2s per cent.[29] In 1925 he had also pioneered the mutualisation of the old proprietary company, paying off the shareholders with £675,000 drawn from the company's inner reserves; this hardly rippled the surface of the company's financial strength and won very favourable publicity.[30] The move forestalled any likely take-over and drew the fangs from the charge that profits were going to shareholders rather than policyholders.

New schemes were also launched in the late 1920s. In August 1928 the Minimum Premium Cash Bonus type of policy began. This had a lower rate of premium than many non-profit policies of other companies — but the Minimum Premium contract had the right to participate in profits. Participation took the form of an annual cash bonus which could be used *inter alia* to reduce the following year's premium.[31] According to *The Economist*, 'the Standard Life Assurance Company's new form of policy combines the maximum cover with the cheapest contract'.[32] It certainly sold to young men who required the greatest immediate cover with the lowest premium rate.[33] Endowment assurance plans, tailored to the needs of particular individuals, who often paid varying single premiums, were also sold on an increasing scale in the late 1920s and 1930s. This type of business grew remarkably after 1924, Equity and Law, London Life and the National Provident also being heavily involved, but some life offices did not like it, and one or two actually discouraged it in the early years.[34] The Standard's new life business increased from just over £1 million (new sums assured) in 1925 to slightly below £5 million in 1938. This particular company defied the maxim that 'The day of the purely specialist office has nearly ended' by excellent salesmanship founded on sound organisation and inspirational leadership. It was ahead of the trend in devising new participating policies, which the market sought. By the investigation of 1929 with-profits policy-holders of all types accounted for nearly 72% of total new business.[35]

The Standard was one of the companies which pioneered staff schemes or group business (as it became generally known) in Britain during the 1920s. Pension funds had been in existence for many years, and as early as 1860 a Mission Society had provided a scheme for its employees. Just before the first world war the Standard had accepted responsibility for managing the London County and Westminster Bank staff scheme (1911) and taken over the liabilities of the Glasgow Faculty of Procurators Widows' Fund, an annuity scheme, in exchange for a cash payment of £46,000 (1913).[36] The Royal Exchange from 1909 also began to look for group business. From ordinary life business group schemes gradually evolved as employers and employees realised the advantages of using the specialist facilities of insurance companies. The advantages of such business to a life office were considerable. As distinct from individuals effecting ordinary policies (the essence of 'pure' life business), where the office has constantly to replace old business with new, once a pension scheme is placed with a company it is usually not necessary to think of its termination. Employees come and go, but the group scheme normally survives and grows, if the business is well selected. Every new group scheme is, therefore, an absolute addition to the company's business.

The implications for the growth of premium income and of investible funds are so obvious as not to require further comment.

Pension business of this type was also considerably influenced — as it still is — by the attitudes of the State.[37] During and immediately after the first war favourable but sometimes ambiguous tax legislation — the Income Tax Acts of 1916 and 1918 and the Finance Act of 1921 — took account of payments made by enlightened employers and their employees for pensions. Already in 1921 individual policies were being tailored by the Standard's specialist policy section to meet the differing requirements of a few firms, and a number of apparently satisfactory schemes were written. However, insurance company schemes at that time were at a disadvantage, more apparent than real, when compared with privately managed pension funds, because the latter initially seemed cheaper in consequence of the fact that they made allowance in advance for the release of reserves expected as a result of withdrawals from the service. The development of group schemes of the modern type on a 'single premium' or 'current cost' basis more than adequately disposed of this superficial competitive disadvantage.

At first premiums for pension schemes were based on a system of level payments; this method resulted in a reserve being created in the early period which could be used in later years to offset any shortfall in premiums. Under the 'current cost' system, however, premiums were restricted simply to cover the cost of each year's benefits. In practice the employer paid very little for young employees, and among these the withdrawal rate was likely to be highest. Thus the initial premium for a group scheme could be kept to the minimum.

Despite the fact that pension business was certainly growing in the 1920s, competition for it was by no means excessive. It is not enough to explain this by reference to the 'traditional conservatism' of insurance firms which favoured the policy of allowing others to discover the difficulties in group business — and the solutions for these problems. Almost certainly, the development of a quantity of group business necessitated the creation of a specialised section of staff to deal with its administration, and this acted as a deterrent to many offices.[38]

Group assurance schemes, such as those for university teachers and the Royal Exchange's business on behalf of the Musician's Union (1921), preceded group pension business, but both had their origins in the United States. The Equitable Life Assurance Company of America in 1912 issued the first group life assurance in respect of the employees of a large industrial firm, and its example was quickly followed by other American companies. Because of the Great War group life assurance schemes were not issued in Britain until 1918, and there are a number of claimants for the title of originator in this country. Compared with the United States, this business grew relatively slowly in Britain, and progress was fitful because of the depressed state of important sectors of the economy.[39]

Pride of place probably ought to go to the Metropolitan Life Assurance Company of America, which established an active group office in London. Many schemes were written by this company, but in 1934, before deciding to withdraw, it transferred the business to the Legal and General. This office was one of four companies before 1934 which made a speciality of group pensions — the Eagle Star, the Prudential and the Standard being the other three. When other companies entered the field in the late 1930s and, more important, after 1945, they were initially at a disadvantage because the four main underwriters had assimilated the technical lessons of administering group business, which became more complex as time passed.

The Standard had particular reason for entering the field. Once Macnaghten and his board had decided on mutualisation early in the 1920s, the special advantages of group business for a mutual company became the basis for a well reasoned strategy. Macnaghten believed that it would enable the Standard to entrench itself firmly in the business community and at the same time serve the national interest by administering pension schemes successfully. He thought it vital for the office to reduce its expense ratio (running at about 20% in the early 1920s), a general problem for specialist life companies, and he visualised that group business would bring substantial and permanent additions to the premium income account at relatively low cost, thereby easing this problem. Assuming that adequate premiums were charged, group life assurance and pension business had the additional advantage that it would not involve the Standard in paying high rates of reversionary bonus and consequently placed no real burden on the funds. There were long-term benefits also — at least, so the board and Macnaghten thought. Additional life business might come from employees of firms with group schemes; the name of the office would be more widely broadcast; indeed, it was optimistically believed that so great would be the respect accruing from the growth of group business that the payment of commission on new life contracts would become unnecessary. If these hopes, in the event, proved illusory, they at least reveal the existence of a coherent strategy in which group business had an important role.

First mention of the group schemes on any scale occurred during 1924, when Vickers Ltd and Metropolitan-Vickers Electrical Company already had life and pension funds managed by the Standard.[40] In the following year the office quoted terms for a large number of pension schemes.[41] The installation of data-processing equipment at head office in 1927 — the birth of what became known as the Powers Department — provided the technical facilities for a great extension of this new business. In the following two years staff pension business was written for Gestetner, Pullar's, Barclay Perkins and Portland Cement.[42] To allow common commission rates for this new business and to avoid competitive rate-cutting the Standard, the Legal and General and the Prudential agreed a tariff of premium rates in 1928 and continued to meet regularly. In 1931 they were joined by the Eagle Star and some other companies, many of which did not transact pension business at that time. The first Group Pension Agreement, with the signatory offices adopting general tariff rates and specifying common policy clauses, was signed in 1932. As interest rates fell in the 1930s, premiums had to be increased, and the common action of what was called originally 'the Inner Circle' took in more and more companies.

A specialist life office, Standard Life clearly did well in group pension business, although composite companies with their connections with industrial companies and commercial firms through fire and accident underwriting activities might have been expected to perform better. Of the companies active in group business, the Standard had the advantage of being the only mutual office. Employers intending to establish pension schemes were often persuaded of the wisdom of paying the extra premium for the right of participating in profits. Even though the economy was severely depressed in the early 1930s, some sectors were sufficiently prosperous to allow group business to grow — brewing, electrical engineering, the motor-car industry and the confectionery trades, for example. Schemes were not always confined to salaried staff, and the Standard accepted any employees of twenty-five years or more. The company's inspectors were given sound enough advice: to concentrate their efforts on prosperous firms and to provide voluminous information. Booklets, relating to other companies' schemes were available for potential clients to see; sometimes it was sufficient merely to give a list of firms with pension funds managed by the Standard.[43]

The place of the London City branch was critical, for much pension business came from the metropolis, where the growing group of insurance brokers tended to concentrate. R. H. Mackay, from 1932 the company's first pensions inspector in London, believed that 'the best tactics were to concentrate on brokers and brewers'. The former had the money, and it was a reasonable, indeed a telling, argument that they should possess their own pension schemes if they hoped to sell group business to clients. For without a pension scheme for their own employees, Mackay convinced many of them, they were in a position of weakness.[44] The wisdom of this approach — indeed, the cunning simplicity of it — was immediately apparent. Firms of brokers expanded in harmony with the development of the Standard's group business, and they commonly recommended the company to their clients. Regarding the brewers, Mackay was also correct; they could certainly afford to provide pensions, and the Standard arranged tailor-made schemes for them.

These two sectors were not the only ones to provide business. Joseph Terry and Sons, the family chocolate firm with over a thousand employees in 1931, took out a pension scheme for all their workers, but before 1945 the alliance of white-collar and blue-collar in a common scheme was exceptional. Paton and Baldwin's group scheme was written in 1934, this textile firm widening still further the Standard's clientele. All firms with pensions schemes were

168    *The business of insurance*

visited regularly by the office's inspectorate, often fortnightly. Undoubtedly, additional life business was written because of this assiduous attention.[45]

Good data for 'schemes' business for companies before 1939 do not at present exist for the whole industry, but as Supple pointed out, the official category of 'other classes' of life business grew from 7% of sums assured in 1922 to 15% in 1937.[46] A basis had been laid for post-war expansion, but the figures for Standard Life — first separated in 1930 — are given in Table 4.

Table 4.   *Standard Life's new group business*

| Year | Sums assured (£) |
|---|---|
| 1930 | 57,000 |
| 1931 | 262,000 |
| 1932 | 86,000 |
| 1933 | 351,000 |
| 1934 | 1,760,000 |
| 1935 | 468,672 |
| 1936 | 502,030 |
| 1937 | 788,800 |
| 1938 | 1,816,720 |
| 1939 | 358,150 |

*Source.* Annual Report, 1930–39.

Although British companies continued to do a large quantity of life business overseas between the wars, many offices, like the Standard, increasingly concentrated upon the market within the British Commonwealth and Empire. Transfer of liabilities in places where operations ended was achieved by differing means according to local circumstances. For all practical purposes there were four principal methods of contraction: complete transfer to another company; another office agreeing to act as agent; bankers acting as agents; ending new business but continuing to administer old. Usually such drastic action was preceded by a review of operations, including the quality of business, operating costs, and the branch's contribution to total company profits. Rarely, however, were these economic criteria the sole bases for termination. Usually there were political events or a threatening legal environment which enjoined cautious withdrawal on profitable terms. Insurance Acts designed to discriminate against British-based companies were a general hazard — even in Eire — and often they prescribed larger deposits in foreign government bonds than existing business justified.[47]

Standard Life decided to complete its withdrawal from Scandinavia in the early 1920s. No new business was transacted in Denmark after 1922, and in 1924 existing liabilities were transferred after negotiation to the Dana Insurance Company of Copenhagen.[48] The same year Norske Forenedi

Insurance Company took over the Norwegian business. Spain was the last European company to witness this process. When Ernest Noble, the office's agent in Barcelona, died in 1920 the board decided to close the branch, to decline new risks and to use bank agents to manage the existing business.[49] In Latin America in 1923 the Standard closed down in the Argentine, managing existing business from its Uruguay branch, with premiums in Buenos Aires being collected by the London and River Plate Bank.[50] In Egypt the Cairo office was closed in 1930, existing business being administered by Price Waterhouse and Co., chartered accountants.[51] Existing business in South Africa was maintained throughout the inter-war period, but new risks were declined after 1931, largely because local companies were exceedingly competitive.[52]

About 15% of all the Standard's new business had been written in India c. 1900, but in the 1920s this proportion had fallen to 10% and in 1937 constituted only 4%.[53] New companies entered the subcontinent's market between 1910 and 1920; in that decade fourteen local companies were established, many of them with apparently better premium rates and paying agents higher levels of commission. Between 1921 and 1937 a further 118 companies invaded the market, including a pirate, the Standard of India (1936), and the prospects of raising business or lowering the expense ratio receded.[54] Political unrest and the rise of a national liberation movement associated with the Congress Party made it a native virtue to take a policy with an indigenous company. Agitation for insurance legislation and discriminatory income taxes compounded the effects of a generally poor economic environment. Most British life companies in India attempted to increase their business with Europeans, but this was a self-terminating process. The Standard decided, in 1938, not to transact new business but continued to administer existing policies.[55] Expansion, however, occurred elsewhere: in the West Indies, Uruguay and particularly Canada.

## IV. *Investment and conclusion*

During the war interest rates rose around the world but most obviously in Britain. This encouraged institutional investors, particularly insurance companies, to invest in government stocks. The Treasury prepared schemes for using Canadian and American investments to finance war purchases abroad, and in November 1915 the Chancellor of the Exchequer sought the cooperation of all the offices with such assets. Since Canadian and American stocks generally stood high compared with their pre-war (and often 1890s) prices, their exchange for 5% war loan was financially advantageous — especially the sale of American railway debentures, which never again reached their wartime levels.[56] Thus most companies by 1918 held substantial amounts of government stock. For the industry as a whole 32% of assets of just over £700 million by 1920 were held in this form, compared with about 1% in 1913.[57]

In the early 1920s acquisition of government securities continued: 35% for the industry in 1922, with Standard Life in 1923 holding 49% of its assets in gilts.[58] This policy certainly paid in the later 1920s, when the ledger value of these assets appreciated.[59] No doubt Victorian actuaries such as A. H. Bailey (1861),[60] who stressed capital certainty as the principal objective of investment, would have been greatly pleased. Yet old canons were being challenged. Bailey's view presupposed that investment managers should avoid stock exchange ordinary securities because of fluctuations in their prices; H. E. Raynes challenged Bailey's view in 1928 by suggesting that offices should invest more in ordinary shares.[61] J. M. Keynes, as chairman of National Mutual, agreed with Raynes, but most companies, deterred by the Great Depression and the slump in share prices, followed Bailey's canons and began to expand their ordinary portfolio only in the late 1930s.[62] As cheap money became increasingly recognised as a continuing weapon of monetary policy, investment managers in the later 1930s began to buy particularly new issues of debentures, preference and ordinary shares in industrial firms for storing long-term. This policy was arrested by the needs of the State in the second world war, and Bailey's preference for government securities was once again reinforced as it had been after 1914. Yet by 1937 ordinary shares represented 9% of the total assets of the offices compared with under 4% in 1913.[63]

Certainly there was great variation in investment dispositions. In 1931, for instance, all the offices held 28·8% of their assets in mortgages, but nine held over 40% — the Friend's Provident, the National Provident, the Norwich Union, the Clerical and Medical, the Equity and Law, the Provident Association, the Alliance, Guardian, and Legal and General.[64] The experience of Standard Life between the Investigations of 1915 and 1938 reveals substantial changes in investment. Mortgages outside Britain represented over 22% of the Standard's assets in 1915 and just under 3% in 1938. Debentures account for nearly 14%, preference shares about 11%, and ordinary stocks only ½% in 1915; by 1938 these categories represented over 29%, over 10% and nearly 23% respectively. Collectively, in 1915 they were about 25% of assets compared with 62% in 1938.[65]

Yet for the industry as a whole it seems that invention and innovation were more apparent in the supply of policy options — life and accident, especially motor insurance[66] — than in investment practices. An apparently highly competitive industry — for there were still 456 companies writing policies in 1939[67] — was operating very effective trade associations which after the early 1920s precluded the need for more obvious forms of integration which the composite companies represented. The 'Inner Circle' which managed the development of group business so effectively simply exemplifies the extent of collaboration.

## Notes

1 Sederunt Book, XXXVI, 4 and 11 August 1914. All references, unless otherwise specified, are to the Standard Life Assurance Company's records, from the extensive collection at head office, Edinburgh, and its depository at Peebles.
2 Annual Reports, 1914 and 1915.
3 Manager's Private Letter Books VII and VIII, *passim*; Sederunt Book, XXXVI, 4 and 11 August 1914.
4 Sederunt Book, XXXVI, 22 September 1914.
5 *Ibid.*, 20 October 1914, 29 December 1914.
6 Sederunt Book, XXXVII, 22 August 1916.
7 Investigation Minutes, 1915.
8 Manager's Private Letter Book (Canada), Dickson to McGoun, 15 April 1915; Manager's Private Letter Book, VII, 7 June 1916; Supple, pp. 423 ff.
9 Investigation Report, 1916; Sederunt Book, XXXVII, 21 November 1916 and 20 November 1917.
10 S. G. Warner, 'The effect on British life assurance of the European war (1914–18)', in Sir Norman Hill, *War and Insurance*, 1927, pp. 101–68; Investigation Report, 1920.
11 Hill, *War and Insurance*, pp. 136–8.
12 *The Economist*, 12 July 1919.
13 Annual Report, 1914; Investigation, 1915; Sederunt Book, XXXVI, 22 September 1914.
14 Annual Reports, 1915–17; Sederunt Book, XXXVII, 17 April 1917.
15 Annual Report, 1918; G. A. S. Norman, *The Overseas History of the Standard Life Assurance Company*, II, pp. 243–7; Investigation Box No. 16, 1920; Sederunt Book, XXXVIII, 13 June 1922; *The Standard Newsletter*, No. 1, March 1922; No. 23, September 1927; (Private Minute Book No. 7, 20 June and 3 October 1922); Sederunt Book, XXXIX, 15 January 1924. A Hungarian life office accepted the business in 1925.
16 Annual Report, 1920; Sederunt Book, XXXVII, 31 December 1918, 28 January and 6 May 1919; Private Minute Book No. 7, 14 January 1930.
17 Sederunt Book, XXXVII, 12 December 1916; 10 April and 14 August 1917.
18 B. Supple, *The Royal Exchange Assurance*, Cambridge, 1970, p. 417n.
19 *The Economist*, 6 March 1920.
20 G. Clayton and W. T. Osborn, *Insurance Company Investment*, 1965, p. 112, table 20.
21 Annual Report, 1919.
22 The following owes much to *The Standard Quarterly*, No. 92 (March 1953) and to the *Journal of the Institute of Actuaries*, LXXIX (1953), pp. 118–19. I am also grateful to senior staff of Standard Life who served under Mr Macnaghten and allowed me to question them about his attitudes.
23 Annual Report, 1921; *The Standard Newsletter*, No. 1, March 1922; No. 3, September 1922; No. 4, December 1922; No. 7, September 1923.
24 *The Standard Newsletter*, No. 11, September 1924.
25 Annual Report, 1923; *The Standard Newsletter*, No. 8, December 1923.
26 *The Economist*, 5 January 1924.
27 *Ibid.*, 19 January 1924.
28 Manager's Report to the Investigation Committee, 1923.
29 Annual Reports, 1927–38.
30 15 and 16 Geo. V, c. xlii; Sederunt Book, XXXIX, 17 February 1925; *The Standard Newsletter*, No. 11, September 1924.
31 Annual Report, 1928.
32 *The Economist*, 27 October 1928.

33 *Ibid.*, 11 July 1925.
34 *Ibid.*, 16 October 1920.
35 Manager's Report to the Investigation Committee, 11 March 1930.
36 Sederunt Book, XXXV, 3 January 1911; XXXVI, 10 June 1913.
37 I have relied heavily in this and succeeding paragraphs upon A. R. Davidson's 'strictly private and confidential' report to the board on 28 June 1946 which, *inter alia*, summarised his view of the development of group business.
38 P. C. Reynolds, 'London office', *The Standard Quarterly*, No. 80, March 1950, pp. 292 ff; A. E. Bromfield, 'The history of staff scheme business', *ibid.*, pp. 302–4.
39 Supple, *R.E.A.*, pp. 435–6.
40 Sederunt Book, XXXIX, 18 March 1924; this association with Vickers began in 1921.
41 *The Standard Newsletter*, No. 16, December 1925.
42 *Ibid.*, No. 23, September 1927; No. 29, March 1929; No. 30, June 1929. The board authorised the purchase of 'Powers Sorting and Tabulating Machines ... to facilitate the Valuation, Bonus and Statistical work' on 17 May 1924. Sederunt Book, XL.
43 *The Standard Newsletter*, No. 36, December 1930.
44 *The Standard Review*, No. 118, Autumn 1962; No. 119, winter 1962.
45 *The Standard Quarterly*, September 1947.
46 Supple, *R.E.A.*, p. 436.
47 *The Economist*, 15 July 1939, pp. 4–5.
48 Sederunt Book, XXXVIII, 29 August 1922; 31 July and 14 August 1923; XXXIX, 5 February 1924.
49 Sederunt Book, XXVIII, 1 June 1920; Norman, II, p. 247. In 1929 liabilities in Spain were transferred to a native company, Equitativa. Annual Report, 1929.
50 Sederunt Book, XXXVIII, 14 August 1923; Norman, II, pp. 215–26; *The Standard Newsletter*, No. 9, March 1924.
51 Norman, II, pp. 239–40; Private Minute Book No. 7, 15 October 1929.
52 Norman, II, pp. 231–5; Annual Report, 1931.
53 Private Minute Book No. 7, 26 July 1938.
54 Norman, II, pp. 314 ff; Sederunt Book, XLIV, 29 September 1936; *The Standard Quarterly*, No. 62, June 1937.
55 Private Minute Book No. 7, 26 July 1938; Annual Report, 1938; Sederunt Book, XLIV, 4 January and 21 May 1938.
56 Sederunt Book, XXXVI, 20 November 1914; 1 December 1914; 16 March 1915; 29 June 1915; 24 August 1915; 7, 14 September 1915; 23, 25, 30 November 1915; Manager's Private Letter Book No. 7, Dickson to F. T. Pitman, 5 January 1916.
57 Supple, *R.E.A.*, pp. 442–3.
58 Clayton and Osborn, *Insurance Company Investment*, p. 254, appendix table 2.
59 Annual Reports, 1927–9; Investigation, 1929.
60 A. H. Bailey, 'On the principles on which the funds of life assurance societies should be invested', *Assurance Magazine*, X, 1861.
61 H. E. Raynes, 'Place of ordinary stocks and shares in the investment of life assurance funds', *Journal of the Institute of Actuaries*, LIX (1928), p. 21.
62 Clayton and Osborn, *Insurance Company Investment*, pp. 63, 168, table 37.
63 Supple, *R.E.A.*, pp. 443–4.
64 *The Economist*, July 1932, Insurance Supplement.
65 Investigations, 1915–38; Annual Reports, 1915–38.
66 Cf. Supple, *R.E.A.*, pp. 429 ff.
67 H. E. Raynes, *A History of British Insurance*, 1954 ed., p. 372.

S. D. CHAPMAN

# Hogg Robinson: the rise of a Lloyd's broker

It is well known that a large and increasing proportion of Lloyd's business is handled by a small number of brokers. The report of the Fisher Working Party on *Self-regulation at Lloyd's* (1980) provides some authoritative data on this development, disclosing that in 1978, of the total premium placed in all markets, 41% was placed by three broker groups and 68% by the leading dozen brokers. Though the activities of the giant brokers are the subject of everyday newspaper comment, their emergence from family partnerships to the present conglomerates has never been studied, mainly (it may be supposed) because this development is very recent, almost all in this century, and most of the mergers and take-overs having taken place since 1945. This chapter examines the history of one of the leading dozen firms so as to chronicle and interpret the process of amalgamation of family businesses and the assumption of an increasing range of functions. It is not possible to measure the parallel emergence of a class of professional managers distinct from the owners, but an attempt is made to indicate some of the milestones. Although Hogg Robinson has retained some of the usual kinds of formal business records (board minutes, ledgers, company reports, etc.), the most valuable part of this evidence has been drawn from retired executives and the families who owned the various small broking houses that, at one time or another, joined together to increase the size and range of the firm's activities.

The history of Lloyd's has not yet become the subject of serious research, but the first tentative ventures into the field, assembling details from published records of the leading firms, indicates some general features. These may be summarised in a simple three-phase chronology, as follows:

1. During the eighteenth and most of the nineteenth centuries the numerous family firms concentrated exclusively on marine insurance (hulls and cargoes), either as small specialists in one sector of the market or as a sideline to their mercantile or merchant banking activities. The family firms proudly maintained their individuality and contemplated liaison with a

rival only if forced to do so by the failure to produce adequate leadership in the next generation.
2. The depression in world shipping in the last quarter of the nineteenth century induced brokers to follow the companies in looking for other kinds of insurance business. Cuthbert Heath led a handful of adventurers into fire, burglary, earthquake, credit insurance, professional indemnity, householders' comprehensive and other lines, while other pioneers moved more silently into foreign markets and into business in the provincial centres, either by opening branch offices, acquiring local partners or buying up going concerns. The depression of world trade between the wars, coinciding with the appearance of new opportunities (e.g. oil, motor, aircraft), served to accelerate this process of diversification.
3. The growing sophistication of technology, concentration of investments, and the increasingly international nature of the diverse businesses that insurance broking exists to serve compelled the leading group of brokers to try to maintain a pace with their clients. The post-war years have therefore witnessed growing specialisation and professionalism and the forging of international contacts, particularly to the New York market, while the old family interests have been more or less continuously diluted.

These phases can be illustrated from the histories of all the leading Lloyd's brokers, but the sporadic way in which they developed in practice is best studied at close range. The history of the Hogg Robinson group exemplifies much of the experience of the industry, though of course, like every other firm, it retains some of the personal flavour contributed by the various founding families.

## I  Hogg and Robinson's history to 1931

The modern firm of Hogg Robinson traces its pedigree back to 1845, when Francis Hogg, a young wine merchant who had been in business nine years, and Augustus Octavius Robinson, an insurance broker and merchant, formed a partnership to develop both their mercantile and insurance interests. However, in this, as in other constituent firms of the Hogg Robinson group, family interest in insurance can be traced back beyond the founding partnership. A. O. Robinson was the son of John Robinson, who had founded a firm of insurance brokers in a house in Birchin Lane about 1800, when he was twenty-five years old. The elder Robinson became a member of Lloyd's the same year and served on the Committee many times between 1818 and 1856, so he was clearly a well known figure there.

The partnership was evidently founded on an earlier friendship, for Hogg had married Robinson's sister Frances, while Robinson had married Hogg's sister Ellen. Both the Hogg and Robinson families contained numbers of Church of England parsons and we may suspect that common religious ideology brought them together. Each of the founding partners contributed £1,000 to the initial capital, and F. H. Hogg was allowed to pay in his as he received it from the later partnership of Hogg and Edmunds. The original partnership deed also stipulated that Hogg was to receive two-thirds and Robinson one-third of the net profits, and, as the partners contributed equally to the capital, it must be supposed that Hogg contributed some other important asset. The course of development of the business suggests that this was his knowledge of overseas trade.

In the exchange of correspondence that accompanied the launching of the new firm, Hogg expressed a hope that he would be successful in selling wine to members of Lloyd's while Robinson looked for clients among Hogg's friends in the wine trade. While both these aspirations evidently enjoyed a degree of success and the two sides of the business advanced steadily, the available records show that these initial interests were not the main growth point of the successful partnership. In the London directories of the period the partners described themselves as 'Oporto Merchants' — that is, they were importing port and sherry from Portugal and Spain. Two years later they began to diversify their mercantile interests, sending vessels to Bahia (Brazil), Rio de Janeiro, Adelaide and Port Phillip (Nova Scotia). However, the interest in Australia appears to have no precedents in the partners' previous experience, but by degrees led Robinson to develop interests at the London Wool Exchange in Coleman Street, while the need of outward cargoes led him into the Baltic timber trade. When the balances were struck in June 1848 the partners had only a little over £3,000 embarked on these foreign 'Adventures', but their interest increased fairly rapidly over the next few years, reaching nearly £10,000 in the summer of 1851, almost £20,000 at the close of 1854, and £26,500 at the end of the decade.

For most of the 1850s the partners seem to have been content to concentrate on South America and Australia, the only new development being Otago in 1859. But in the 1860s they again launched out in new directions, running their first venture to Canada in 1866, to Oamuru (New Zealand) and the river Plate (Brazil) in 1868, to Demerara in 1869 and to Jamaica and to Hamburg in 1870. Nassau, Valparaiso, San Francisco, Brisbane and Wellington followed in the early 1870s. However, the bulk of their interest in shipping seems to have been attracted towards Australia and Canada.

The rapid development of the partners' business was facilitated by their first-class family and City connections. Financial support was drawn from John Robinson and Sons on a considerable scale, £4,600 at the end of 1851 and £6,500 at the close of 1860, to pick out just two examples. The other major creditor was Francis Mollison and Co., a firm of merchants in the City that may have had connections with John Robinson.

The earliest external assessment of Hogg and Robinson shows that, though their capital was initially small, they were respected and could be commended to those offering credit. In 1853 a Bank of England spokesman reported in confidence that the partners 'do a good business, their means are small, but they are prudent and may be considered safe'. Coming from such an authoritative source and referring to a very young firm, this assessment was adequate commendation. It shows that the partners were already embarked on a course that would steadily win friends and good business. So far as the broking side of the business was concerned, the partners seemed to have developed their best connections with merchants in provincial towns like Glasgow, Dundee, Belfast and Nottingham. The success of factory production of cotton, linen, wool, lace and other branches of the textile industries created world-wide export opportunities, which the exporters of the industrial regions of the Midlands, north and Scotland were not slow to exploit.

One of Hogg and Robinson's earliest and best clients were the Baxter brothers of Dundee, who were import and export merchants in the jute trade. In the second generation, W. E. Baxter (1825–90) became Liberal M.P. for the Montrose burghs (1855–85) and Secretary to the Admiralty in Gladstone's first administration. He determined to rationalise and make economies in the department and asked Francis Hogg's advice on the most efficient ways of handling Admiralty contracts. Hogg and Robinson gave their confidential views on the reliability of City firms and on the conventional procedures that governed mercantile affairs in the City. Then in April 1869 — just four months after his appointment — Baxter sought advice on the possibility of appointing a permanent Admiralty broker in the City. In reply Hogg and Robinson offered the name of a firm but added, 'If you decide to have a Broker for the Admiralty they would no doubt do their best to serve you well, but looking at the number of things the Admiralty require we doubt if any one Broker would do as well for you as an experienced City Agent who has been in the habit of shipping goods of all sorts abroad and buying them on the best terms of different houses.' Hogg failed to find a firm to satisfy the Secretary to the Admiralty and so offered the services of his own firm. Hogg and Robinson were officially appointed Shipping Agents to the Admiralty in March 1870. The appointment also brought them some insurance brokerage for troopships and other Royal Naval vessels.

Meanwhile Hogg and Robinson's mercantile interests continued to develop, particularly in Australia. In 1871 F. H. Hogg's eldest son went out to Melbourne to set up as a wine merchant and insurance agent, and then in 1880 one of A. O. Robinson's nephews was sent out to Sydney as some kind of resident agent for the firm. It seems that members of the Hogg family, following the devout leadership of Francis's father, the Rev. James Hogg, were much attached to the evangelical wing of the Church of England. In the mid-Victorian years trade and the gospel marched hand in hand, and the considerable outflow of young Hogg and Robinson talent in the next generation suggests that missionary zeal was supplying at least as much motive power as trading prospects. Unfortunately we do not know precisely what became of these Australian initiatives, but they must have offered some

## The rise of a Lloyd's broker 177

encouragement, for in 1895 a subsidiary called Hogg Robinson and Co. Pty Ltd was formed at Sydney and Melbourne. It traded in a variety of goods (wool, hides, meat, timber, wines, etc.) and ran a Lloyd's agency at Sydney. The local partners and managers were by now A. F. Robinson and W. E. ('Willy') Hogg, but the majority of the £20,000 shareholding was retained by the older generation in London in accordance with the usual mercantile practice of the period. The Australian company ran into difficulties soon after its birth, was said in 1896 to be absorbing too much capital, and in 1902 lost over £800. However, it eventually recovered and grew steadily, peaking £1,800 profit in 1916. The records are very meagre, but it seems that the other major area of development before the first world war was in Germany, or, more specifically, Hamburg. Hogg and Robinson acted as brokers for the Nord-Deutsche insurance company, insuring steamers for various voyages. They also did a lot of business for Landt und Rickersten in Hamburg, insuring cargoes and ships all over the world.

A. O. Robinson died in 1895 and F. H. Hogg about 1874, and the business passed to the control of the members of the second generation who had been selected for the succession. Unfortunately several sons lacked the business ability of their fathers, or were more interested in religion. F. G. Hogg died young and George Hogg was a liability and so retired early on a generous pension of £400 p.a. John William Robinson was a quiet, retiring, studious kind of man, worthy but not very effective in business. In 1895 John Stuart ('Jack') Robinson was still a youth at Marlborough College, but his schooldays were quickly terminated and he was hurried into the business. He worked very hard, especially after his father's death in the middle of the first world war, but was not an outstanding businessman. There is very little documentation to show the fortunes of Hogg and Robinson during these years, but it is difficult to resist the conclusion that, at best, it lived on the momentum of the first generation and the service of two devoted clerks who became partners, Blake and Grounds of the Admiralty agency. It is not surprising that the London and Australian partners drifted apart. The break-up of the Australian subsidiary at the end of the first world war, robbing the partnership of what had been its most promising hope of future growth, must have led to an absolute decline.

Evidence of lack of hereditary leadership is also seen in the recruitment of Charles E. W. Austin in 1910. Austin was a Lloyd's broker in a small way, specialising in non-marine risks and also undertaking some forwarding business. The gross commission on his enterprise does not appear to have exceeded £300 a year, and we may infer that it was a one-man business with little capital and few connections but some valuable experience. Austin was induced to merge with Hogg and Robinson by the offer of free office accommodation and clerical help in return for assistance in 'working' the insurance side of the established firm. His forwarding business was taken over by Hogg and Robinson's shipping department, but Austin was allowed to draw direct benefit from any reinsurance orders he obtained at Lloyd's or from the companies, as well as taking his £300 p.a. brokerage. It was an odd agreement, with Austin appearing to be half in and half out of Hogg and Robinson's establishment, but it seems to have worked, and by degrees Austin was drawn into full leadership. From 1916 to 1931 the business was run jointly by Jack Robinson and Charles Austin, an arrangement that kept the ship afloat until new leadership and capital could be injected.

There are no figures available to demonstrate the exact position, but it seems that Hogg and Robinson's business reached a low ebb in the 1920s, probably the lowest since the early years of the enterprise. The strength of the business, such as it was, continued to be in its connections with provincial exporters (in Nottingham, Bradford, Dundee, Manchester, Liverpool and other towns), for whom insurances were arranged at Lloyd's. The big textile warehouses in these places were in serious difficulties at this time and ready to seek any means of cutting costs, so their business was correspondingly less secure. Some business was also done through local (i.e. provincial) brokers, who would use Hogg and Robinson to gain access to Lloyd's, but there was little profit in such clients, for the Lloyd's broker was allowed only 5% for this class of service. A great deal of provincial business drifted away during the war, and other clients were lost in the post-war depression, so marine brokerage now contributed only a meagre income. Jack Robinson and Charles Austin struggled to replace these losses but in the highly competitive conditions of the period had only limited success. They managed to secure the Lloyd's business of Alfred Sasserath and Co. of Piccadilly, a firm of insurance brokers that had extensive connections within the Jewish trading community, covering furniture, furs and other lines of growing domestic consumption. E. A. Notcutt and Co., another firm of brokers, also passed on their Lloyd's 5% business. The period also saw the beginnings of marine reinsurance for the London and Lancashire Company. The government freight agency, though much contracted after the war, provided more than half the firm's income through the years of slender margins from brokerage.

II   *Ernest Capel Cure and the merger with Hogg and Robinson*

Ernest Capel Cure (1862–1945) began his career in the City in 1884 following an education at Eton and Oxford. He was the youngest son of a gentry family and so, in the familiar English tradition, had to go off to find his own fortune. There was no established family connection to join at Lloyd's, but his great-grandfather had been a member of Lloyd's from 1776 until his death in 1820 and a member of the Committee from 1797, so young Capel Cure decided to venture his talent in underwriting and insurance broking. In his youthful inexperience he lost money at underwriting and so decided to concentrate on broking. He started as a ship and insurance broker in 1893, in partnership with an older and no doubt more experienced man called F. Emanuel.

When Emanuel died in 1907 a private company was formed called E. Capel Cure and Co., the first directors being the founder and two trusted senior clerks. Capel Cure was a powerful and dominant personality and, in the manner of his day, a complete autocrat within his own business. His austere manner to clerks and juniors made everyone afraid of him, but it is fair to add that he was a very able businessman. He had been a scholar at Eton, was tall, upright, good-looking and capable of tremendous charm. After a difficult start he created a successful business, small but well known and respected.

Capel Cure's business was mainly marine insurance, particularly with grain and sugar importers. His most important client was Louis Dreyfus, an important international merchant house of French Jewish origin that imported grain, first from the Baltic and Black Sea ports, and later from North and South America. The whole firm sweated every year before the Dreyfus contract was renewed. Other outstanding clients were Czarnikow, a very large firm of sugar importers, and Mocatta and Goldsmith, the well known bullion brokers. Capel Cure was also part-time broker to the Bank of England and the Indian government and had some connections in Paris and in Hamburg. There was also a little marine business. Like other talented brokers, Capel Cure evidently did well during the first world war, and largely sustained the volume of business through the 1920s. With the fall in world commodity prices between the wars, the importers prospered and their brokers enjoyed the benefit of British advantage in the terms of trade. Capel Cure and Co. had a capital of £20,000 and paid high dividends from the first, but they moved up sharply during the war, reaching 75% in 1917, and maintaining this high plateau until 1930.

In the 1920s Capel Cure's had a staff of about thirty in their Fenchurch Street office. The principal had no sons, so his adjutants were clerks who had made their way up the business, Harold Pattison (until his death in 1927) and Percy Smith, a little man who was a marine claims settler and made himself an expert on marine clauses. He had joined the firm as an office boy in 1902, became a manager in 1911 and a director in 1914. The second generation of management was represented by E. S. Hogg, who had joined Capel Cure's from Oxford in 1921, and Pattison's son Stuart.

The initiative for the merger between E. Capel Cure and Co. and Hogg Robinson came from E. S. ('Teddy') Hogg. He was the son of John Hogg, the second generation of Heath and Hogg, a leading firm of insurance claims adjusters in the City with interests in the American market. The merger was no doubt intended to take fuller advantage of the continuously developing opportunities of the American market, and to develop branches in provincial towns in Britain. This successful development was not the immediate occasion for any change of outlook at Hogg and Robinson, for there were no longer any Hoggs in the firm. However, it evidently offered a precedent in the Hogg family experience, and taken along with other such developments in the 1920s (like the merger of leading brokers Willis Faber and Dumas) showed an acceptable way of extension of the range of interests of the business.

In 1931 Teddy Hogg had worked for Capel Cure for nearly ten years and had recently been made a manager and junior director. He had been long enough in the City to appreciate that Hogg and Robinson and Capel Cure had largely missed out on the opportunities for expanding business at home and abroad that had been exploited by the leading brokers over the previous thirty years or so. They had none of the really big accounts on which firms like Bowring's, Sedgwick Collins and Willis Faber prospered. Already in 1929 he had pressed a reluctant Capel Cure into allowing him to go to America to seek out new business. Now he urged his recalcitrant chief to merge with his family firm. Capel Cure finally agreed, on condition that young Hogg bought his preference shares for £15,000. Hogg did not have the ready money, but Hoare's Bank promptly agreed to make an advance, and Capel Cure had his cheque the same day.

The merger was effected quite smoothly. Ernest Capel Cure became chairman, Jack Robinson deputy chairman and Percy Smith and C. E. W. Austin permanent directors. E. S. Hogg and S. P. Pattison were appointed directors for two years, and all the staff, now numbering fifty, were retained at the same salaries. As we have seen, Capel Cure's were mainly marine brokers, while Hogg and Robinson were now largely non-marine, so the two firms were to a large extent complementary, a type of merger that was common at the period.

Capel Cure was now advancing in years and it was clear that any initiative for new developments had to come from elsewhere. Having visited North America, Teddy Hogg believed that the firm ought to develop new connections there. Despite the American recession, he spent two or three months looking for business in North and South America most years through the 1930s. He began with one client in Kansas City and extended his connection by means of letters of introduction to the United States managers of British companies like the London and Lancashire and the Commercial Union that Hogg Robinson had a connection with, generally through reinsurance business. In these years there was still scope for a roving entrepreneur with ideas. Hogg won the friendship of several important United States brokers; these useful connections multiplied during and after the war. E. H. Hogg also picked up good business in Latin America, particularly with the American shipping line called Grace Brothers and a firm of San Francisco insurance brokers called Cravens Dargan, both of which were active in the area. Most of the new business of these years was 'surplus line', with some hull insurance.

As a result of his transatlantic experience, Hogg persuaded Capel Cure to venture into credit insurance. The business of insuring merchants and manufacturers against bad debts was effectively pioneered by C. E. Heath from 1902, when the Excess Insurance Company was launched, and especially from 1918, when he formed the Trade Indemnity Company, but in the 1920s

## The rise of a Lloyd's broker 181

its possibilities were still only dimly recognised and little exploited. Heath's initiative was frustrated because the committee of Lloyd's panicked and banned credit insurance in 1923, and he had to turn to the tariff insurance companies for support. Several general managers were recruited to the board of the T.I.C., but it took time for them and the specially recruited technical staff to acquire understanding of this unfamiliar form of risk. Credit insurance lay on the undefined borderland between banking, insurance and the firms who specialised in providing credit ratings, and there was widespread reluctance in the City to trespass on the territory of other specialists. However, the idea of credit insurance received a considerable boost when the government launched the Export Credit Guarantees Department of the Board of Trade in 1926. Whitehall had shown up the City's conservatism, but the lesson was not lost on keen young minds.

Charles Austin had developed some interest in credit insurance following an inquiry from a connection at Bradford but in 1933 it was decided to recruit someone with experience in the field. Together Hogg and Austin managed to secure an outstandingly able man who not only made Hogg Robinson a leader in this specialised field but in time took the initiative in several other dynamic developments in the firm. After some years in the London commodity markets, John Dove had joined the Trade Indemnity in 1929 and had played a major role in developing its activities, particularly outside London. At first he concentrated on selling the idea of credit insurance to Hogg Robinson's clients. He was very successful, but soon found the field too limited, and looked for a wider clientele. At this point he ran up against the tradition that Lloyd's brokers do not advertise, and found the solution in the purchase of a near-defunct company, the Credit Insurance Association. The C.I.A. was formed in Leicester in 1912 by A. H. Swain, an insurance broker who had the agency of the Excess Insurance Company for credit insurance in the Midlands. Swain aimed to form a rival company to the Excess, but was frustrated first by World War I, then by the superior pull of the Trade Indemnity and the E.C.G.D. In 1933 Hogg Robinson acquired a controlling interest in the C.I.A., and bought it out in 1948. Up to the outbreak of war in 1939, Dove cultivated credit insurance for his Hogg Robinson clients and for the C.I.A. separately, but it is convenient to give the combined premium income, which was nearly £20,000 after only five years' enterprise.

Together E. S. Hogg and J. T. L. Dove represented the dynamic leadership of Hogg Robinson in the 1930s, while Capel Cure's former adjutant Percy Smith kept the office running smoothly. The two entrepreneurs were loyally supported by a team of young men who were steadily gaining experience translating the ideas and connections into profits. They included representatives of the next generation of Capel Cures and Robinsons, but were largely recruited from Hogg's large circle of friends in the City.

After the C.I.A., the most important initiative was the beginning of provincial offices. Of course both Hogg and Robinson and Capel Cure had

182  *The business of insurance*

had clients in the provinces for many years, and Nigel Capel Cure used to visit them in his Austin Seven, but there was no local representation. The idea was pressed on the board by Dove early in 1936 but it was not until the end of the next year that the Birmingham office, the first outside London, was opened.

A life insurance department was started in 1935, and the following year the board approved proposals for an underwriting agency at Lloyd's. Ernest Capel Cure, remembering all too well his early experiences at Lloyd's, was against the development, but a syndicate called G. N. Capel Cure and others was started in 1937. Friends, cousins, and distinguished clients composed the original list of ten names and Sturge acted as agent. Like the other new ventures, the profits were modest before the war, but the foundation was laid for the post-war take-off.

III.  *Gardner, Mountain, D'Ambrumenil and Rennie*

Robert Gardner was a small insurance broker who started in the City about 1860. He had no heirs, so in 1891 brought an able and ambitious young clerk called Frederick Hall into partnership. After thirty years in business the capital was still only £1,000, all contributed by Gardner, while Hall contracted, in the manner of the period, to 'devote his whole time and attention to the said partnership' and not to be 'directly or indirectly engaged in any other'. He was rewarded with a quarter of the profits and then, five years later, when he was still only thirty years old, with the ownership of the whole business subject to a small annuity to Mrs Gardner.

Hall evidently had little capital and needed more scope for his ambitions, so in April 1902 he joined forces with a recently formed firm of brokers called Hawley Mountain and Co. whose partners were the young sons of a wealthy hop merchant. Hall's superior experience was recognised in his appointment as first chairman of Robert Gardner Mountain and Co. The Mountain brothers evidently had capital and secured good marine business by acquiring small shareholdings in a wide variety of steamship companies in return for their insurance contracts. Most of these shipping lines were in a small way of business, but the return was reasonably secure before the first world war. Gardner Mountain also invested in tariff insurance companies to secure business, in one case on a considerable scale; in 1904 they acquired the British Dominions Marine Insurance Company for £20,000 and Edward Mountain acted as their first underwriter. Like most brokers of the period, Gardner Mountain at first specialised in a small sector of the market, in this case domestic and Scandinavian hull business. Gardner Mountain shared in the City prosperity of the first world war and early 1920s. Their dividends shot up to 200% in 1917 and remained at that level until 1923.

Onlookers may have assumed that Gardner Mountain would crown these successes in business and public service by recognition as one of the pre-eminent City brokers, but it was not quite like that. During the war the individual directors had bought many of the shipping and insurance shares from the company, and in 1921 the Mountain brothers acquired Gardner Mountain's shares in the Eagle Star and British Dominions Insurance Company. Meanwhile the committee of Lloyd's asked Edward Mountain to devote himself either to the broking partnership or the company, and he chose the latter. Fred Hall took to politics at an early age and occupied the safe Conservative seat at Dulwich for over twenty years; his interests increasingly focused at Westminster. Mountain's sudden departure brought tensions on the Gardner Mountain board to the surface and the directors divided, Hall and A. R. Collett on one side and the Mountain brothers on the other. The problem of compensation and payments was a running sore for several years, with an eminent lawyer regularly in attendance at board meetings. Needless to say, the division must have sapped the energy of the remaining directors. There were also other problems. Shipping was depressed in the 1920s, and it no longer paid to invest in shipping lines. The company's non-marine syndicate lost money on American business and there were repeated complaints that the marine syndicate reinsurances were going to Price Forbes rather than Gardner Mountain. Reading between the lines, it seems that the senior directors were too much absorbed in other matters to give adequate attention to the business.

Sir Edward Mountain sold his shares in Gardner Mountain in 1923 and Sir Frederick Hall died suddenly nine years later, so the languishing business had to look for new leadership. It was found by the usual means of a merger between personal friends, now with Barber and D'Ambrumenil, a firm that had been in the City since the 1860s as ship and insurance brokers. There was no longer any Barber in the business, but the third generation of D'Ambrumenils, Philip and Lewis, came into the new company as directors. Philip D'Ambrumenil, the first chairman of the new company, was one of the outstanding successful negotiators of marine insurances of his generation, with a formidable expertise on both the broking and underwriting sides of the business. His success probably originated with his marriage in 1921 to Gertrude Bailey, who came of a well known family of South Wales ship repairers. During the 1930s and post-war years he had most of the Welsh tramp fleets on his books, while the merger with Gardner Mountain had brought an extensive Scandinavian clientèle. After the war a large connection was built up among the Greek shipowners, and he added such prized clients as the Philippine Fleet Compania Maritina, the Australian Steam Ship Company, and Bahr Behrend and Co., the Indian government shipping agents. D'Ambrumenil's prestige was further enhanced by a post-war knighthood (awarded for his running — with Walter Hargreaves, the chairman of C. T. Bowring — of the government-sponsored War Risks Insurance Office), while in 1947 he was the first broker to become chairman of Lloyd's.

Soon after the war the company acquired additional strength from another merger, again brought about by a lack of hereditary (family) leadership. The firm of John T. Rennie originated in Aberdeen in 1849, when the founder extended his interest in stock and share broking to cover ship and insurance brokerage as well. In 1854 he built the first of a line of clippers which traded between Aberdeen and Port Natal in South Africa. He opened a London office in 1869, and an office in Durban five years later, staffed by his sons. Rennie's fleet was insured at Lloyd's through a broker, and when he died (in 1876) Rennie asked his London partner to assume responsibility for placing the hull and cargo insurances — that is, he invited him to become a London insurance broker, initially no doubt on a part-time basis. Steamers succeeded clippers from 1882 and extended the experience of the insurance broking side of the business. The fleet was sold to a Liverpool line in 1911, but the London business of Lloyd's brokers continued. The business was incorporated in 1921 as John T. Rennie Sons and Co. (Insurance) Ltd, the controlling interest in the £6,500 capital being taken by three third-generation Rennies and two Byrons. At this time the business was riding on a crest of achievement, having secured the agency for A.R.C.O.S. (the All-Russia Co-operative Society) when it opened offices in London two years after the revolution; the Russians were paying £30,000 a month in premiums at the peak of the short post-war boom in 1921. Unfortunately for Rennie's, this lucrative business was lost in 1924 when the Soviet government's agency, Ingosstrakh, placed all its insurance and reinsurance business with Willis Faber. In the period of post-war difficulties in shipping older clients had fallen away, so there was a long, uphill struggle to rebuild the business. New professional leadership gradually took control from when H. S. ('Bertie') Lawrence became manager in 1932.

In 1948 Rennie's realised that to take advantage of post-war potential for growth they would have to consider merging with another firm or try to recruit outside expertise, for Lawrence and one of his managers (Payne) were the company's only professional insurance men. Lawrence was regularly in South Africa and Payne in the United States, so someone was needed to run the London office. During the war Gardner Mountain and D'Ambrumenil had lost three of the expected heirs to the leadership; talks were initiated leading to the merger of Rennie's in July 1949.

Gardner Mountain D'Ambrumenil and Rennie took the full tide of the post-war flood of business. Gardner Mountain were one of the leading marine brokers in Lloyd's, maintaining their strength in U.K. hull business and the Scandinavian market. They had also retained a small non-marine business, mostly U.K. fire and some Australian connections. The three underwriting syndicates went from strength to strength. Rennie's brought in their South African and American connections. Sir Philip d'Ambrumenil now headed a concern with a share capital of £161,000 and a staff of about 200. New activities were soon initiated; an expert was recruited from the Sun Life to start a very successful life and pensions department, and Commercial Credits, a small credit insurance department in competition with Hogg Robinson's

C.I.A., was launched. The firm was widely recognised as one of the leading Lloyd's brokers of the post-war years. At the time of the merger in 1966, Gardner Mountain's brokerage income was about £50,000 a year, while that of Hogg Robinson and Capel Cure had recently risen to about £100,000.

## IV. *The Staple Green merger*

After the war, and particularly during the 1950s, Hogg Robinson and Capel Cure 'took off' under the energetic leadership of E. S. Hogg and John Dove. They were loyally backed by the team of 'back room' men whose experience and expertise had brought them well-merited promotion. New ventures which had been inaugurated in the 1930s now grew vigorously on all sides: international insurance and reinsurance, credit insurance, marine, life and pensions, and new offices in the provinces all flourished.

For a decade and a half after the war profits at Lloyd's came so easily that any underwriter could make good returns for his backers, while their brokers prospered on the commissions. The breakneck speed of post-war expansion led to overcapacity in the more competitive conditions of the 1960s, and the less efficient underwriters and brokers began to feel the pinch. No doubt the more perceptive Lloyd's men foresaw the doldrums of the middle 1960s, though few could have anticipated the disasters of 1965–68, when underwriters lost some £57 million. These changing economic conditions united with other circumstances, one technological and the other legal, to produce a new period of mergers in the private sector of the London insurance industry. Hogg Robinson and Capel Cure, and other constituent firms of the present Hogg Robinson group, were heavily involved in these changes, so they must be examined in a little detail.

The technical factor was the dramatic growth in the size of the major risks. The spread of air travel and the development of jumbo-jets, the rapid growth in the size of oil tankers and other ships, the continuous increase in the sophistication and scale of oil and chemical plants and other industrial fire hazards, led to an escalation of costs that small family firms could no longer cope with. This development was paralleled by a sequence of take-overs and amalgamations in industry that also served to swell the insurance policies of the top firms, and to concentrate economic power in London. The underwriters in their boxes at Lloyd's lived on specialisation in and long experience of particular types of risks, supported by the evidence of the detailed claims record of their clients. Acting alone they had little industrial experience to guide them. They needed the additional support of technical specialists such as Lloyd's surveyors or their brokers. The brokers in turn needed to be big to provide the technical specialists for their increasingly diversified range of activities.

The legal, or more strictly taxation factor, was the impact of death duties on Lloyd's underwriters and brokers. The threat of heavy death duties persuaded numerous underwrites to turn themselves into public companies or to sell their interest. There are now very few syndicates owned personally or by families or small groups of partners, and brokers have often been the buyers. When brokers were family businesses the death of a partner or share-owning manager simply resulted in the private sale of the shares to the other partners. The brokers were forced to go public when taxation and death duties reduced hereditary family wealth and hence purchasing power, while the auditors' valuations of shares distributed at death were disputed (that is, raised) by the Inland Revenue, sometimes taking them out of the reach of rising managers in the family firm.

Meanwhile, as we have already noted, brokers were increasing in size to accommodate ever-growing business risks. In 1959 J. H. Minet was the first broker to turn itself into a public company, and it was followed after a short interval by several others, C. E. Heath, Fenchurch Holdings, Bradford, and Sedgwick Collins in 1962, Staple Green, Leslie & Godwin, and Gardner Mountain in 1963. These well publicised changes brought insurance brokers into the close scrutiny of the investing public for the first time, and City stock brokers like Sheppards and Chase and W. Greenwell and Co. began to take a close interest in their performance and to publish reports on them.

The Staple Green merger originated with J. E. ('Toby') Green, one of the leading marine underwriters at Lloyd's. Green came of a shipping family; his father had sold the line to P. & O. in the period of mergers before World War I. In 1920 Toby Green joined the underwriting agency of Percy Janson, whose family had been associated with Lloyd's since 1803. Green became an underwriting member in 1925 and in due course was senior partner of Janson Green and Son. In 1963 he stood at the pinnacle of a long and successful career, the sixty-three-year-old head of one of the half-dozen or so syndicates that gives a lead to the rest of the market.

J. E. Green had two sons associated with him in his business, and as retirement approached planned to leave as much of the capital as possible to them. He approached Samuel Montagu and Co., the merchant bankers, and they advised him to amalgamate with another firm. Green spoke to his old friend Teddy Hogg (they had been at Harrow together), with whom he had enjoyed a developing business connection over the previous twenty years or so. In 1950, when Hogg had launched two new Lloyd's syndicates (one marine, the other non-marine), Toby Green had advised him on procedure and 'names' (subscribers) for his list. When the new marine syndicate was formed Green agreed to manage it for the subscribers, which included other Hogg Robinson directors. Because of this successful connection, and the social relationships that had grown round it, Green's initiative was welcomed, and the board of Hogg Robinson and Capel Cure readily agreed to merge their respective firms. In January 1963 Montagu launched a new holding company known as Staple Green, the 'Staple' referring to Staple Hall, where Hogg Robinson and Capel Cure had their headquarters. Staple acquired all the issued capital of Janson

Green, including Janeen Services, an associated company that provided supporting services, and went on to acquire, in stages, the complete interest in Hogg Robinson and Capel Cure. After various valuations and discussions the Janson companies were valued at £1·44 million and the Hogg Robinson preferred ordinary shares, representing one-third of the company's value, were sold for £1·775 million. J. E. Green became chairman of the holding company and E. S. Hogg vice-chairman. At the first meeting of the directors of Staple Green in April 1963 negotiations were already under way to acquire other companies. An interest was acquired in Stenhouse, discussions were opened with Price Forbes and two firms of Lloyd's underwriting agents were considered, but none of these came to anything.

At the beginning of 1965 H. S. Lawrence, now chairman of Gardner Mountain D'Ambrumenil and Rennie, approached Toby Green to seek his support for a merger with Staple Green. Talks between Green, Lawrence and Hogg were amicable, with no clash of interest in evidence. A merger offered the promise of a more comprehensive service to customers, with a lot of complementary rather than competing interests, especially in overseas operations and in provincial business, where Gardner Mountain had no branches. Staple Green were impressed by Gardner Mountain's marine clientèle. Gardner Mountain's underwriting agency was much bigger than Staple Green's, as they represented three leading syndicates at Lloyd's. Some conception of the size of the combining firms is offered by the 1964 profits. Hogg Robinson's were £0·54 million and Gardner Mountain's nearly £0·4 million, while the Janson companies made £0·26 million in 1963, their last full year before the launch of the holding company. A merger was agreed on the explicit understanding that a gradual fusion of interests could be achieved if spread over a period of three years, in particular the integration of the brokerage interests.

Despite this promising start, it must be frankly admitted that the merger was not an immediate success. The mutual family interests that had formed the foundation of earlier and successful mergers was clearly not present here, while Toby Green, the bridge between the two, was shortly forced to withdraw through ill-health and died early in 1966. There was a long struggle for control of the new firm at the managing director level which led to the departure of two members of the hereditary families, John Green and David D'Ambrumenil, and upset a great many others. The experience taught some sharp lessons on the necessary basis of successful mergers.

The merging of Janson Green, Hogg Robinson and Capel Cure, and Gardner Mountain D'Ambrumenil and Rennie created a conglomerate that was placed high in the league table of Lloyd's brokers, whether measured by brokerage, profits, number of employees or any other criterion. But in the experience of those who worked for the constituent firms and its successor at the management level, the more significant change was the slow and sometimes painful metamorphosis from a small family firm to a modern public company. The patriarchal tradition not only survived but remained the most significant feature until this period. Men who joined the firm as clerks but were not related to the partners or their descendants had little expectation of becoming directors, and a 'lords and serfs' situation survived in which, in a very real sense, the owners of the business were the masters and every other employee belonged to an inferior caste. Future managers were recruited by patronage and connection, but in return for this favour their fathers were expected to supplement a meagre salary for years. By way of compensation it was understood that staff were assured of the possibility of long service and security, for the family always looked after its servants and never sacked anyone. There was no management training and no career structure, and rises were negotiated only by those who had the temerity to approach the owners. The founding families were more interested in maintaining a comfortable life style, supported by their family business, than in profit figures as such, and the varying performance of the different departments was not known to the different managers of them.

Change began to creep in after the war. The pushing entrepreneurial part of the leadership, Hogg and Dove, declared an interest in open management and, in particular, giving young men a chance to prove themselves, and the response was impressive in some sectors of the business. New ideas were now generated in informal discussions between small groups of senior men, and the board considered their reports. In the middle 1950s Albert Tuggey, who had started his career as a messenger boy in 1928, took over the secretarial function and began to analyse the costs of various services and attribute them to the different departments. As chairman, Percy Smith maintained the autocratic outlook to which he had been inured by long years of service to Ernest Capel Cure; he wrote up all the minute books by hand himself and never revealed them to anyone else. It was not until E. S. Hogg took over as chairman in 1955 that the directors' minutes became an ordered record with a reference index. Internal management training did not begin until 1963, when a series of three-day 'familiarisation' courses were held, largely, it seems because the business had now grown so large that one department was not clear what the next was doing, and the easiest method of selling insurance is to encourage a client to extend his cover from one kind of risk to another. The first manager to attend an external management course was allowed to go only when he threatened to pay for his own course. When Staple Green was launched young managers were able to buy shares at a discount and so became more closely identified with the new company's interest.

The impact of the change was much more far-reaching for management style. The policy and performance of a public company in the vanguard of its industry is a matter of wide public interest, and the financial press demand to know the how and why of the year's activities, while the investment analysts challenge the directors with their shrewd commentaries on a company's strengths and weaknesses and telling comparisons with competitors. The remnants of the old easy-going family-firm outlook were swept away and mistakes had to be frankly acknowledged. The Staple Green combine did not always get an easy or sympathetic press. The disastrous error of making joint appointments to posts after the Gardner Mountain merger never leaked out, but Staple Green's failure to secure management control for their 75% interest in Hartley Cooper (1968–72) was public knowledge. The press were not slow to point out the lessons of such failures.

This was followed by a further move towards professionalism. In the late 1960s management consultants' reports were much in vogue, and the Staple Green board commissioned a report on their problems. Whilst this had little direct result, it emphasised the need for more professional management, which was satisfied by the subsequent appointment of the successful team of Francis Perkins as chairman and Morris Abbott as managing director. The Staple Green name was changed back to the better known Hogg Robinson under which most of the group's subsidiaries traded. The remnants of the old easy-going family firm outlook were steadily discarded and the new approach spread throughout the group. The result was the rapid growth of the group in the early 1970s, which has been more and more connected with young and energetic professionals. It was in this exuberant period that Hogg Robinson was identified by the financial press as one of the top dozen Lloyd's brokers. First Division status was accepted with pride, not least by those who knew the modest origins and slow development of the constituent firms in their early years, and the domination of the old families into the post-war years.

## Note

Like so many businesses, the Hogg Robinson group has retained very little in the way of historical records, and the fragments that have survived are scattered round various departments or held by the private individuals who saved them from destruction. The only major items discovered in this research were a Hogg & Robinson account book of 1845–62 and two G.F.A. letter books of 1869–70 and 1892–99.

Consequently most of the material from which this chapter is assembled comes from retired and present staff, who do not wish particular statements to be attributed to them. During the course of 1978–79 the following furnished me with useful information for the present study: Mr Morris Abbot, Mr G. N. Capel Cure, Mr R. Capel Cure, Mr D. McClure Fisher, Mr F. Crossman, Mr G. Geddes, Sir Peter Green, Mr E. S. Hogg, Mr J. G. Hogg, Mr A. V. Hopkinson, Mr C. Hood, Mr E. A. Johnson, Mr H. S. Lawrence, Mr P. Rook Ley, Mr R. W. Leggett, Mr E. Neale, Mr M. Nesbitt, Mr L. Percival, Mr F. L. Perkins, Mr G. Pirie, Mr C. Ratcliffe, Mr D. A. Risbey, Mr J. C. Robinson, Mr T. Royle, Mr A Tuggey, Mr R Walshe. Their help is acknowledged with grateful thanks.

# Index

Aachen and Munich Co., 122
Aberdeen, 106, 184
Accident insurance, 6
Accident Offices Association, 6
Adams, E., 11
Adelaide, 175
Albion Co., 17, 19
Alliance Co., 19, 76, 80, 82, 86, 90, 115–17, 170
All-Russia Co-operative Society, 184
Allied Assurance Co., 163
America Co., 124
Amicable Contributors, 3
Amicable Society for a Perpetual Assurance Office, 4
Anchor Co., 19
Argentina, 114–28, 169
Argentine Fire Insurance Association, 118, 124
Argentine fire insurance market, 115:
 agency system, 115–16, 117–18
 Argentine government policy, 120–1, 125–6
 Argentine insurance companies, 116–17
 British merchant houses' role in, 114–15, 119–20, 126
 British purchase of Argentine insurance companies, 126
 See Association of Foreign Insurance Companies in Argentina (Local Board of Agents)
Asociación de Aseguradores Argentinos, 124
Association of Foreign Insurance Companies in Argentina:
 formation, 121
 operation, 121–2
 challenge to market control, 122–4
 relations with local companies, 124–5
 See Argentine fire insurance market
Atlas Co., 19, 47, 59, 62
Austin, C. E. W., 177–8, 180–1
Australia, 175–6
Azulena Co., 126

Bailey, A. H., 170
Bain, A. W., and Sons, 143
Bank of England, 50, 117, 175, 179
Baring, Alexander, 76
Barcelona, 169
Barclay, David, 92
Basle Co., 114
Batavia Co., 115
Bates Stokes and Co., 115–16
Bath, 29
Bath Co., 19
Bath Sun Co., 19
Beacon Co., 19
Belfast, 105–6, 143, 176
Belgium, 155, 159
Benevolent Co., 19
Bentham, William, 99, 102–4, 109
Beresford, M. W., 11, 14
Berkshire, Gloucester and Provincial Co., 19
Berwick on Tweed, 15
Bignold family, 39–67 *passim*
Birmingham, 61, 109, 182
Birmingham Mutual Co., 142; *see also* Central

## Index  191

Blandford, 27
Bolton Cotton Trade Mutual Co., 142
Board of Trade, 158, 181
Bolton, 143
Boult, Swinton, 72
Bradford, 21, 23, 178, 181
Brazil, 175
Brisbane, 175
Bristol, 15–16, 61
Bristol Co., 19
Bristol Crown Co., 19
Bristol Union Co., 19
British Co., 17–19, 43
British Commercial Co., 19
British Crown Co., 147
British Dominions Marine Co., 182–3
Brokers, 173–89
    fire insurance, 136–7
    impact of tax legislation on, 185–6
    increasing scale, 186
    *See* Lloyd's, Hogg Robinson
Bubble Act, 46, 75, 85
Budapest, 160
Buenos Aires, 114–29, 169
Buenos Aires Co., 126
Butt, J., viii, 11, 45

Cairo, 169
Calcutta, 115
Caledonian Co., 150
Cambridge, 61
Canada, 163, 169, 175
Canterbury, 13, 61
Canterbury and East Kent Co., 19
Capel Cure, 178–80; *see* Hogg Robinson
Central Co., 142, 146–7
Chapman, S. D., viii, 3, 10–11, 14–15
Chartered Insurance Institute, 15
Church of England Co., 19
Clerical and Medical Co., 19, 170
Coal Exchange, 75
Cockerell, H. A. L., 15
Coffee houses, 75, 90
Colonial Life Assurance Co., 100, 110
Comité de Aseguradores Argentinos, 124
Commercial Union Co., 116, 139–40, 145, 147–8, 180
Congreve and Co., 115
Continental Co., 124
Coode, G., 31

Copenhagen, 160, 168
Cornhill Co., 153
County Co., 19, 43, 47, 57, 59
Coventry and Warwick Co., 19
Credit Insurance Association, 181, 184
Customs House fire, 28

Dana Co., 168
Darlington, 59
Deane, P. M., 10
Denmark, 168
Devizes Co., 19
Devon South Co., 19
Dewsbury, 23
Dickson, P. G. M., 9, 13, 150
District Co., 19
Donnachie, I., 45
Dove, J. T. L., 181–2, 185, 188
Dublin, 61, 103
Dundee, 176, 178
Durban, 184

Eagle Co., 19
Eagle Star Co., 166, 183
Eden, Sir F., 18, 44, 68
Edinburgh, 13, 16, 61, 95–6, 103, 105, 110–11, 158, 160
Egypt, 169
Ellis, W., 86, 88–9, 91, 93
English and Scottish Co., 19
Equitable Co., 5, 139, 163
Equitable Life Assurance Co. of America, 165
Equitativa Co., 172
Equity and Law Co., 162, 164, 170
Essex and Suffolk Equitable Co., 19, 30
Essex Economic Co., 19
Estrella Co., 116, 120, 123–4
Excess Co., 180–1
Exeter, 13, 48

Fayle, C. E., 74
Fine Art and General Co., 141
Fire Insurance, 4
    agents, 23–8, 57, 115–16, 133, 137
    business practices of companies, 22–8
    companies, 46–50
    growth and competitive development 1750–1840, 15–22, 44–50

Fire Insurance (cont.)
  London offices, 4, 9–10, 16–19, 22, 25, 39–40, 46–52, 54, 57, 63, 66, 76, 77, 115, 117, 126, 166–7, 184
  provincial offices, 23, 48
  policy valuation, 28–34
  See Fire Offices' Committee, Non-tariff companies, Argentine fire insurance market, Fire insurance records, Norwich Union
Fire Insurance Records, ix, 2
  accessibility, 14–15
  information contained in, 12–14
  interpretation, 22–34
  recent use of, 9–11
  survival, 12–15
Fire Office, 3
Fire Offices' Committee, 66, 118, 121, 124, 126, 130–49
  assessment of strength, 148–9
  attitude to fire sprinklers, 138–9
  discussions with Lloyd's, 146
  market control, 133–8
  organisation and methods, 132–3
  rationale, 131–2
  response to non-tariff entry 1898–1907, 144–8
  tariff and adjustments, 145, 148
  See Fire insurance, Non-tariff companies
Fisher Working Party, 173
Floud, R., 15
Foreign business, 6, 114–27, 168–9; see Argentine fire insurance market
Freijoo and Co., 123
Friendly Society, 3
Friends' Provident Co., 170

Gardner Mountain D'Ambrumenil and Rennie:
  origins, 182
  merger with Hawley Mountain, 182
  Edward Mountain and the Eagle Star, 183
  merger with Barber and D'Ambrumenil, 183
  marine business, 183
  merger with J. T. Rennie, 184
  merger with Hogg Robinson (see also), 185
Gargrave, 23
General Maritime Co., 76
General Shipowners' Society, 77, 92
Germany, 177
Gladbach Co., 114
Glasgow, 24, 29, 105–6, 115, 141, 144, 176
Glasgow Faculty of Procurators Widows' Fund, 164
Globe Co., 17–19, 24, 26, 28–9, 33, 43, 46, 56–7, 76
Gloucestershire Co., 20
Green, E., 15
Greenock, 106
Gresham Life, 159
Grinnell sprinkler, 138
Guardian Co., 19, 115, 170

Halifax, 23, 37
Hamburg, 75, 128, 175, 177, 179
Hampshire Sussex and Dorset Co., 20
Hand in Hand Co., 3, 16–17, 19, 46, 136
Hawley Mountain, 182
Heath, C. E., 136, 141, 146, 174, 180–1, 186
Herts Cambridge and Country Co., 20
Hogg Robinson, 174–89
  Origins, 174–5
  nineteenth-century business, 175–7
  management problems, 177–8
  merger with E. Capel Cure (see also), 179–80
  American development, 180
  credit insurance, 180–1
  provincial offices, 181–2
  life assurance, 182
  merger with Gardner Mountain D'Ambrumenil and Rennie (see also), 185
  growth in business after 1945, 185
  merger with Janson Green, 187
  problems of merger, 187
  changes in management attitudes, 187–9
Hong Kong, 115
Hope Co., 19
Hozier, H., 92
Huddersfield, 21, 23
Hull, 79
Hull clubs, viii, 74–5, 78–9, 81–2, 85
Hungary, 155, 159–60

Index  193

Industries:
  agriculture, 32-3, 39
  brewing, 12, 33, 39, 167
  building, 11
  coal, 78, 86
  cotton, 10-11, 18, 45, 57, 60, 108, 138-9, 141-3, 145, 148-9
  engineering, 142, 166-7
  furniture, 11
  grain milling, 11, 31, 56, 119, 138, 142, 145
  hosiery, 10
  leather, 142, 144-5
  metal, 142
  pottery and porcelain, 11, 15
  printing, 29, 33, 143
  shipping, 84
  sugar refining, 57, 120
  textile, 2, 10-12, 15, 18, 45-6, 48, 59-60, 167, 176, 178
  timber, 78, 86, 138, 175
  woollen and worsted, 10-11, 21, 39-40, 56-7, 60, 143
Imperial Co., 17, 19-20, 32, 43, 46, 115, 117
Indemnity Co.:
  formation, 77-81
  hull club basis, 78-9
  Staniforth's resignation, 80
  break with mutual basis, 80
  competitive methods, 85-6
  distribution of business, 86-8
  underwriting methods, 88-90
  investments, 90
Independent and West Middlesex Co., 19
India, 169
Industrial Assurance Act, 156
Insurance generally:
  business history, vi-vii, 2
  economic unity, 1-2
  function, 1
  historiography, 3, 4
  institutional basis, 2
  origins, 1
  records, 2
  significance, vi
Instituto Mixto Argentino de Reaseguros, 126
Instituto Nacional de Reaseguros, 126
Inverness, 106
Investment, 6, 90, 170
Ireland, 55, 62, 98-9, 103-5, 108, 117, 155
Isle of Man Co., 20
Italy, 3

Jamaica, 175
Janson Green, 186-8
Jenkins, D., vii
Joint-stock companies, 46-7, 75-7, 81, 84, 91
Jones, C., viii

Kent Co., 20
Keynes, J. M., 170

Lancashire Co., 114, 121
Leather Trades and General, 142, 144-5
Leeds, 11, 21, 23, 59-61, 109, 143
Leeds Fire Office, 16, 20
Leeds and Yorkshire Co., 20-1, 24, 30, 32
Legal and General Co., 166, 170
Leicester, 109, 181
Leicestershire and Midland Counties Co., 20
Liverpool Co., 20
Licensed Victuallers' Co., 19, 24, 27, 28, 33
Life assurance, viii, 4-5
  first world war, 157-61
  group pension agreement, 166
  growth and competitive development 1850-1864, 107-9; 1914-1939, 155-70
  investment, 169-70
  pensions business, 164-6
  product development, 1919-1939, 162-4
  *See* Standard Life
Lima, 128
Liverpool, 48, 60-1, 66, 76, 115, 117, 131, 178, 184
Liverpool and London Co., 20
Liverpool Co. (I and II), 20
Liverpool London and Globe Co., 114, 147
Liverpool St George Co., 20
Lloyd's, vii-viii, 2, 7, 81-2, 85, 88-91, 140-1, 146-8

## 194 *Index*

Lloyd's (*cont.*)
  growth and competitive development, generally, 173–4; 1800–1850, 75–6; 1919–1939, 179–80, 182–4; 1945–1960, 185–6
  fire underwriting, 136–7
  *See* Brokers
Lloyds Bank, 160
Local Board of Agents (Argentina), *see* Association of Foreign Insurance Companies in Argentina
London, 3, 12–16, 23, 29, 31–2, 46, 53, 55, 62–4, 75, 77–8, 99, 105, 110, 114, 117–21, 125, 131, 143, 163, 167, 175, 177, 181–2, 184–5
London and Lancashire Co., 114–15, 126–7, 178, 180
London and River Plate Bank, 169
London Assurance, 4, 28, 74–6, 80, 84–6, 91, 93, 114–16, 118
London County and Westminster Bank, 164
London Edinburgh and Dublin Co., 19
London Life Co., 164
L'Union Co., 114

Manchester, 18, 59–61, 109, 138, 141, 143, 178
Marine insurance, 3, 74–5
  chartered companies, 76
  company operation, 82
  formation of joint-stock companies, 76–7
  growth and competitive development, 1800–1850, 74–7, 81–5; twentieth century, 179–80, 182–4
  repeal of restrictions on corporate underwriting, 76
  *See* Lloyd's
Macnaghten, S., 162–3, 166
McCulloch, J. R., 76
Manchester Co. (I and II), 20, 48
Marine Co., 76, 82, 92
Mather and Platt, 138
Melbourne, 176–7
Metropolitan Life Assurance Co. of America, 166
Minerva Co., 19

Montagu, S., & Co., 186
Montefiore, Moses, 76
Montevideo, 117
Moretonhampstead, 26
Mountain family, 182–3
Mutual Co., 138
Mutual offices, vii–viii, 46–7; *See* Hull clubs

Nassau, 175
National Co., 19
National British and Irish Millers' Co., 142, 144, 145
National Mutual Co., 170
National of Great Britain Co., 141, 144
National Provident Co., 164, 170
National Provincial Bank, 160
National Union Co., 19, 64–5
Neptune Co., 76
Newcastle, 20, 23, 59, 61, 71
Newcastle and North of England Co., 20
New York, 174
Non-tariff companies:
  expansion in numbers 1898–1907, 139–44, 147
  method of operation, 135–8
  use of brokers, 137
  *See also* Fire Offices' Committee
Nord-Deutsche Co., 177
Norske Forenedi Co., 168
North and South Shields Co., 20
North British and Mercantile Co., 115–16, 118
Northern Co., 20, 116, 126
North Western Co., 142
Norwich, 39–40, 42, 54–5, 59, 61, 65
Norwich General, 20, 40–42, 50, 53–4, 61, 65–6
Norwich Union, vii, 20–1, 115, 122, 170
  formation and early growth, 50–5
  'first dispute', 53–4
  T. Bignold consolidates control, 54–5
  provincial expansion, 55–61
  competitive policies, 55–7
  underwriting losses, 57–9
  local committees, 59
  industrial risks accepted, 60
  acceptance limits, 62

Index 195

second dispute, 1818, 62–5
T. Bignold dismissed, 64
Bignold's sons' assume control, 64
amalgamation with Norwich General, 65
S. Bignold becomes secretary, 65
joins tariff, 66
Nottingham, 176, 178
Nova Scotia, 175

Oldham, 32
Orbell, J., 11
Otago, 175
Owen, E. R., 116–18, 123

Paisley, 106
Palatine Co., 150
Palladium Co. (I and II), 19
Palmer, J. H., 77, 92
Palmer, S., viii
Paris, 118, 179
Peebles, 111
Pelican Co., 5
Phoenix Co., 4, 11, 16–17, 19, 21, 27–30, 33, 43, 46, 56, 62, 126–7, 131, 163
Pollard, S., 10–11
Port Natal, 184
Portugal, 175
Price Waterhouse & Co., 169
Protector Co., 19–20, 43
Protestant Dissenters Co., 19
Providencia Co., 114
Provident Association, 170
Provincial Co., 143–4
Prudential Co., 158, 166

Queen Co., 115, 121

Ramsay, R., 115–16
Rank, J., 143
Raynes, H. E., 170
Reading Co., 20
Redstone, A., 15
Rennie, J. T., 184
Rickards, R., 77, 80, 92
Rio de Janeiro, 175
River Plate Trust Loan and Agency Co., 123
Robinson, A. O., 174–7

Robinson, J. S., 177–8, 180
Rooke Parry & Co., 114
Rostow, W. W., 10
Royal Exchange Assurance, ix, 4–5, 9–19, 23, 27, 28, 32, 42–3, 46, 59, 75–6, 85, 97, 114–15, 122–3, 126, 163–5
Royal Farmers' Co., 19
Ryan, R., vii, 22

Salamander Co., 20
Salop Fire Office, 17, 23
San Francisco, 175, 180
Schwarz, L. D., 15
Scott family, 153
Scottish Life Offices' Association, 157–8
Scottish Union Co., 150
Scottish Widows' Fund, 97, 99, 107
Sedgwick Collins & Co., 180, 186
Select Committee on Joint Stock Companies (1844), 81, 93
Select Committee on Marine Insurance (1810), 75–6, 78, 91–2
Select Committee on the Coal Trade (1837), 78, 92
Sheffield, 23, 109
Sheffield Co., 20
Shropshire and North Wales Co., 20
South Africa, 169, 184
Spain, 169, 172, 175
Sprinklers, 138–45, 148
Standard Life,
  early growth and problems, 95
  successful development 1845–1860, 95
  geographical directions of growth 1850–1864, 96–9
  original tontine basis, 100
  policy development 1850–1864, 100–1
  marketing management 1850–1864, 102–6
  declining reversionary bonus, 107
  new participating policy 1865, 110
  first world war, 157–61
  policy development 1919–1939, 162–4
  pensions business 1919–1939, 164–8
  foreign life business 1919–1939, 168–9
  investment 1919–1939, 170

Standard of India Co., 169
Staniforth J., 77, 79–80, 92
Stenhouse, A. R., 144
Stockholm, 160
Suffolk Co., 20–1, 24, 30, 59
Sun Fire Office, ix, 4, 9–28, 30–3, 43, 46, 56–8, 60, 63, 66, 114–15, 117–18, 184
Supple, B., vi–vii, ix, 9, 15, 168
Surrey Sussex and Southwark Co., 20
Sweden, 160
Sydney, 176–7

Textile Mutual Co., 141, 146
Thomson, W. T., 95, 100, 105–7, 109–11, 113
Todmorden, 59
Tooley Street fire, 149–50
Trade Indemnity Co., 180–1
Transatlantica Co., 115, 122
Treble, J. H., viii
Trowbridge, 57, 72

Union Co., 17, 19, 46, 70, 126
United States, 6, 114, 120, 138, 144, 156, 165, 180, 184

Uruguay, 114, 117, 127, 169

Valparaiso, 175
Vickers, 166
Victoria Co., 110

Wakefield, 23
War Risks Insurance Office, 183
West Middlesex Co., 101
Westerham, 40
Westminster Co., 5, 16–17, 19, 46, 70–71
West of England Co., 20, 47–8, 59, 71
Williams, H. J., 102–3
Willis Faber, 180, 184
Winchester, 13
Wooler Co., 20
Worcester Co., 20
Wright, C., 74

Yarmouth, 57
York, 13
York and London Co., 20, 96
York and North of England Co., 20
Yorkshire Co., 20–1